A WOMAN'S GUIDE TO CYCLING

Susan Weaver

A Woman's Guide to Cycling

Illustrated by SALLY ONOPA

with a Foreword by SUSAN NOTORANGELO

TEN SPEED PRESS
Berkeley, California

To the hundreds of women cyclists
who shared their experiences as inspiration for us all,
and to my husband, Joe,
who encouraged me throughout
the writing of this book.

Copyright ©1990, 1991 by Susan Weaver. All rights reserved. No part of this book may be reproduced in any form, except for the purpose of brief reviews, without the written permission of the publisher.

Foreword copyright ©1991 by Susan Notorangelo
Line drawings copyright ©1990 by Sally Onopa

"Nine Special Months of Cycling" is reprinted in condensed form from the March 1981 issue of *Bicycling* magazine, by permission of Rodale Press Inc., copyright ©1981.

Cover photo reproduced by permission of Dan Burden.

Ten Speed Press
Box 7123
Berkeley, Ca 94707

Library of Congress Cataloging in Publication Data

Weaver, Susan
A woman's guide to cycling/Susan Weaver.
p. cm.
Includes bibliographical references (p.) and index.
ISBN 0-89815-400-6:
1. Cycling for women. I. Title.
GV 1057.W33 1991
796.6—dc20 90-49555
CIP

Printed in the United States of America

3 4 5 — 95 94

Contents

List of Illustrations

FIGURES

PHOTOGRAPHS

Acknowledgements

I want to thank the many people who helped make this book possible, beginning with editors Derek Wyatt, who asked me to write it, and Margot Richardson, who conducted the first survey of British women cyclists. At Methuen, editorial director Ann Mansbridge, Sarah Hannigan and Tony Pocock had key editorial roles; Christopher Holgate designed the book.

Many individuals at Rodale Press (Emmaus, Pennsylvania) assisted me. My former editor at *Bicycling*, James C. McCullagh, as well as Barb Slider and Rita Nederostek, enabled me to survey North American women cyclists. Bill Billick and Joanne Eisenhauer helped design my survey instrument. *Bicycling* staff members Liz Fritz, Stan Green, Michael Koenig, John Kukoda, Ed Pavelka, Nelson Pena, John Pepper, Linda Weider, and Fred Zahradnik, shared expertise and resources, as did librarians Janet Glassman, Vicki Jacobs and Rebecca Theodore.

Product testing was made possible by Georgena Terry, of Terry Precision Bicycles; John Van Anden, of Full Cycle Bike Shop (bike assembly); and by clothing manufacturers – Andiamo, Bellwether, Cannondale, Descente, Moving Comfort, Pearl Izumi, Schwinn, and Vigorelli.

Research in the UK was facilitated by Nick Reardon at Cannondale, and Richard Benn, Carmel Mulvanerty and other staff at Bike UK shop in London. At *Bicycle Action* magazine Graeme Gibson and Andrew Sutcliffe shared perspectives on British cycling. Joy Potts of the British Cycling Federation assisted with racing. Butterfield & Robinson, of Toronto, hosted me on a bicycle tour of the Cotswolds.

In Canada, Bev Barton-Wagar and Dinah Kerzner, both of Toronto, assisted with contacts for interviews.

In addition to experts in a variety of fields named and quoted in this book, I thank exercise physiologist Diane Fowler, MEd who consulted on stretching exercises.

For reviewing manuscript prior to publication, thanks to John S. Allen, Curt Bond, Katherine Brubaker, MD, Edward F. Coyle, PhD, Jennifer Dodd, Ellen Dorsey, William Farrell, Ann Grandjean, EdD, Nancy Kaiser, Barbara and Mel Kornbluh, John and Lesa Kukoda, Everett L. Smith, PhD, as well as my husband Joseph C. Skrapits.

The Women's Cycling Network also helped circulate my survey. My sincere appreciation goes to all the women who completed our surveys, many of whom wrote at length of their cycling experiences. Their essays give this book its special flavour.

Foreword

In 1979, at 27, I returned to college. Being budget-minded, I thought cycling the 5 miles to and from class would save me money in addition to keeping me fit. This introduction to bicycling eventually led me across the country several times in cycling marathon events and dramatically changed my life.

The initial impetus in my development from student commuter to avid cyclist was a man named Fritz Miericke. My local bike shop owner, he rode with me my first year and taught me enough mechanics so I was unafraid to ride alone.

In 1979 I was riding 30 or 40 miles with Fritz in tennis shoes and running shorts. Though I don't remember any discomfort, I do recall Fritz wore cycling attire. I'd bought a bicycle helmet and a $25 U-lock to protect my $150 bicycle. Quite naturally Fritz introduced me to other important accessories—shorts and gloves. I thought I was set! The following spring a bike ride caught my attention, Bicycle Across Missouri (BAM), a 540-mile endurance event. I thought it was just a cross-state tour... and signed up. Its organizers nearly refused my entry because of my inexperience! This got my goat and fired me up for training to complete the 3-day ride. Fritz gave me a fitness program and helped me with bicycle improvements like a triple chainring to climb the Missouri hills. On Labor Day weekend I managed the grueling BAM with the help of Fritz and my brother Mike, who met me every 40-50 miles to feed me and Tom, a friend who rode along with me. I was very sore at the end with stiff knees, sore butt, numb hands and feet. But I was the only woman to finish, along with thirteen men. I felt tired but very proud.

I feel fortunate so early in my cycling life to have found someone like Fritz. But such mentors are few and far between. In this book Susan Weaver wisely advises every newcomer to join a club or search out a cycling companion or family member to share enthusiasm and training rides. Obviously, I believe in that too. To boost the new riding partnership and solve cycling problems, I recommend the book you now hold in your hands.

For example, several chapters address the crucial question of bike fit and the mechanics of cycling, so you can meet your specific needs. In my novice years, stem adjustment was my most difficult problem because of my limited flexibility. Susan's thorough research can eliminate many hassles in finding a bike that fits and back then could have saved me lots of time and discomfort. With women comprising an increasing market segment, American bike shops, manufacturers, and cyclists can all benefit from this book's clear discussion of equipment.

Even if a partner is a well-seasoned cyclist, there may be days when he or she is busy, or you may find differences in your interests or perspectives. Even as knowledgeable as Fritz was, he could not possibly offer the wealth of experience contained in this book. Women in this guide share and cope with many concerns he probably never thought about, such as the fears of harassment on the road, the search for saddle comfort or properly proportioned clothing. This book can fill in the gaps and prepare you for the inevitable days when you must be self-motivating and self-sufficient.

Susan Weaver's *Woman's Guide to Cycling* draws on the author's own experience, her in-depth research, and on the experiences of women from all over the United States, Canada, and the United Kingdom. In every chapter women offer advice and enthusiasm that encourage the reader to take the next step—whether that be a first time ride, a century, or putting your chain back on! Their love of the sport comes through as they expound on touring, commuting, racing, or just being out on their own —under their own power! And they provide an added perspective: just what cycling means to them *as women* in terms of freedom and confidence gained. The mental and physical strength they've developed through their miles of riding gives their stories a special appeal. The stories wrap around the book's technical knowledge, inspiring one to try, while telling how. As an introduction to cycling for a novice rider or resource material for the very experienced cyclist, *A Woman's Guide to Cycling* offers the best compilation of cycling material I've ever read.

It also addresses the relationships a woman has and how they may touch on her cycling—and vice versa. The chapter on "Cycling with the Family" particularly hit home with me. For instance, what do you do in a partnership when one person, like my cycling-marathoner husband Lon Haldeman, has a much stronger commitment to cycling than the other? There've been times I could have used the coping strategies in that chapter. After I had my first child, the conflict between my maternal instincts and his athletic ones were a great source of frustration. Lon would speed off with my newborn in the Burley trailer, leaving me trailing behind, trapped in my post-pregnancy body. A solution described in that chapter, returning to our tandem, saved the day.

This guide also shares hard-to-find research and insights on cycling during the various special times in a woman's life. I can really appreciate the chapter on riding during and after pregnancy. Even with 150,000 miles logged in my racing career and my after-pregnancy record-setting Race Across AMerica, I still benefit from motivation provided by Kristen Profitt's cycling diary during her pregnancy, as I am now expecting for a second time. In "Cycling for Two," Kristen's expression of joy in providing a healthy prenatal environment spurs me on to cycle regularly for this baby. Even I need that inspiration to put aside the daily grind to make time for myself to ride.

Susan Notorangelo, September 1990

Introduction

1

This book is about women like you, and the sport they love – cycling. It's about *why* they love it, how they got into it and how it's opened worlds to them, changing the way they feel about themselves in the process. But most important, it's about how you can be a part of all that and why you might want to.

Maybe you're a cyclist already. Here then I hope you'll find a new way to share your sport with other women, and a wealth of tips to help you improve.

But if you are just teetering on the edge of discovering cycling, as I was twelve years ago, this book can help you plunge in. If I could do it then, you can do it now. Here's my story.

I got into cycling in an oh-my-God-what-have-I-done sort of a way. I didn't know a dangling derailleur from a dangling participle. That is, I knew zilch, zero, zip about bikes. I didn't even *own* one.

I was a few years over 30, single, and a writer. And I had the audacity to land a job as an editor at *Bicycling* magazine, which was and still is America's (in fact the world's) largest circulation publication for adult cycling enthusiasts.

I was never the team sports sort in school, probably because I hated having things thrown at me. But I always liked camping, hiking, the outdoors . . . and a challenge. So I bought myself a new twelve-speed bike and promised my editor-in-chief I'd learn fast.

My beat at the magazine was fitness and racing and touring and cycling accessories – almost anything except the most technical equipment reviews and repair articles.

Was I nervous? Of course. My new officemate cycled to work over what's known locally as South Mountain. His idea of office ambience was a clutter of odd bicycle parts, beat-up cycling shoes, and a sweaty jersey drying on a chair. The way he knew bikes, he must've come out of the womb with a wrench in his hand. And many of my audience were just like him.

Bikes, too, had 'men only' written all over them. The ones everybody was buying then had been designed for men – *racers*, at that – by an industry whose decision-makers were men. A look at those 'girlie' poster ads for tyres and such told me women were viewed less as consumers and more as decoration in the business. This attitude still oozes from some of today's ads, so you know what I mean.

What could I do but prepare as best I could and just wade in, asking questions? Happily, I met many coaches, racers, everyday cyclists, and industry executives, as well as my own staffmates, who loved the sport and were willing to share it.

The excitement was catching. Since I covered racing for the magazine, I found myself at the biggest bike races in the country. A seat in the press truck for 100-mile road races in the Rocky Mountains meant the drama and strategy of team racing played out right in front of me. Speed was very real as the truck screamed down around mountain curves at 60 mph to stay ahead of the racers. Between races I interviewed America's best riders about their diet and training routines, their doubts and triumphs. I talked to coaches, mechanics, and bicycle designers from all over the world.

Perhaps most rewarding was to see women's role in the sport becoming more visible. As a *Bicycling* spokesperson at trade shows, I talked to the industry about women's needs: so many of us were making do with ill-fitting bikes and clothing that looked like big brother's hand-me-downs. After all, there was a fitness boom going on. Women were a big part of it, and we deserved to be recognised. Time passed, and finally I could buy cycling clothing off the rack, designed and sized especially for women. A few years ago, bicycles began to follow suit.

Meanwhile, women racers gained better sponsorships here in the United States (although money is still hard to come by), and women's bike racing became an Olympic sport. Imagine my excitement to be in Los Angeles in 1984 to cover the first women's Olympic bicycle road race. There I stood in the press stands at the finish line surrounded by a thundering crowd as two of my countrywomen – Connie Carpenter Phinney and Rebecca Twigg – won gold and silver.

When distance cycling (which made Eileen Sheridan's name a household word in England in the 'fifties) became popular in the US, women too became involved. In 1982 Susan Notorangelo challenged the existing coast-to-coast record of fourteen days, fourteen hours. Susan had been on the road eleven days with almost 3,000 miles behind her when a few friends and I joined her on the backroads of northeastern Pennsylvania. It was in the dark, early morning when body rhythms slow and a marathon cyclist becomes heavy-lidded and leaden-legged. But she talked gamely about the beauty of the country and the people who'd come out to cheer her along the way. She was an inspiration to me, and she went on that day to set a new record of eleven days, sixteen hours and fifteen minutes.

My own cycling has been much more modest. I started out riding to work. My route was 7 miles each way through a green, wooded park; quickly I discovered how invigorated fresh air and brisk pedalling made me feel. I admit, the first day I wasn't sure my legs would carry me up the steps to my office, but gradually I felt better and better on the bike.

Part of my vacation that fall was a four-day bike tour in Louisiana bayou country – different from anything I see at home in Pennsylvania. Veils of Spanish moss hung from the trees, romantic in the early morning mist. There were old plantation homes and riverside fishing camps with houses on stilts. Even watching the sugar cane harvest in roadside fields seemed terribly exotic.

Wherever I stopped, people were friendly – in fact, solicitous at the idea of a woman cycling alone. After riding about 25 miles each day, I'd camp at night, usually in a supervised campsite. One night when I couldn't find one, a minister kindly let me pitch a tent in his backyard.

This brief tour was four days full of little discoveries – plus the important one, that I could do it.

That was just the beginning for me. I love bicycle touring – my favourite cycling – but I also enjoy riding at home. And whether my rides are short or long, whether it's a golden-green sunny day or grey and drippy, once I'm out of the door and on my bike, I feel good. If I'm in a bad mood or depressed, a ride perks me up. I like the fresh smells, the bird sounds, the breeze against my skin. I am in charge, self-propelled, free. I win a small battle climbing every hill; I fly down the other side. The bike becomes part of me.

I've made many new friends through cycling and – just as important – increased my sense of competence, fitness, and independence as I have gradually become stronger and learned to cope in new situations. So many women have told me that because of cycling, not only are they fitter, they also feel better about their bodies and about themselves in general. I know just what they mean.

But you won't have to take my word for it. In these pages you'll hear from many women I've met and talked with through the years. You'll also be hearing what several hundred women have to say through surveys I've conducted for this book, as well as those carried out by one of the book's editors in England, Margot Richardson, a cyclist herself. These women tell me, as I've learned myself, that we're much stronger and tougher than we may give ourselves credit for.

As you know, if you're already into it, cycling can be many things to many people, from casual recreation to highly competitive sport.

And if you're thinking now of buying a bike and starting up, you're about to discover what is surely the most versatile sport. A sport you can enjoy at your own pace, alone, with a friend, or with a group; on the road or in the woods; simply to get outdoors and loosen up, to take you to work or school, to explore your own county, or to combine with your favourite form of travel – anywhere. And all the while you'll be increasing your level of fitness.

It's difficult to imagine a better time for a woman to begin cycling, to increase her involvement, or to experiment with a new aspect of the sport. Cycling opportunities and products for women continue to be on the increase, especially in America and Canada, with the effects beginning to be seen in the UK as well. No, we don't yet have all the products we'd like, or in all the sizes we need, but things are improving. (Sometimes finding what we need requires hunting around, and in this book we'll talk about products you may not have realised are available and how to make a selection to meet your needs.)

How has this change taken place? As cycling has boomed in the US and Canada, it's become possible to service a more diverse group of cyclists, says former bike shop manager Tracy Harkness, of Toronto, Ontario. There's been room for fuller lines of women's cycling clothing, proportional bikes for women, and the like.

And women themselves help make the difference. She explains:

> Women are getting to be more vocal, knowing what they want and asking for it. For years I sold bikes to women that didn't really fit them, but their

husbands were standing there saying, 'Oh, yes, that will be fine.' Now more women are coming into the shops unaccompanied by men and looking to make up their own minds for themselves.

There are more women taking part in all areas of the sport to offer inspiration and help to newcomers.

There are more women in the industry pushing for women's products or working in bike shops, and women seek us out for advice.

That's just a hint at what's been happening. And if bike shops in your area haven't begun to reflect these changes in the market, you'll find out later in this book what you can do about it. And so that you'll be on speaking terms with all the parts of the bicycle as we refer to them later in the book, a diagram follows immediately after this chapter.

In the hope you will join us, I'll pass along in these pages the things you'll need to know to make a start or to progress further in whatever aspect(s) of the sport you choose. Again, it won't be just my voice you hear, but the encouragement, advice, and rich experiences of women at every level of the sport. They welcome you, and I welcome you.

I hope you'll keep reading. I'm going out for a ride.

Fig. 1
Derailleur bicycle

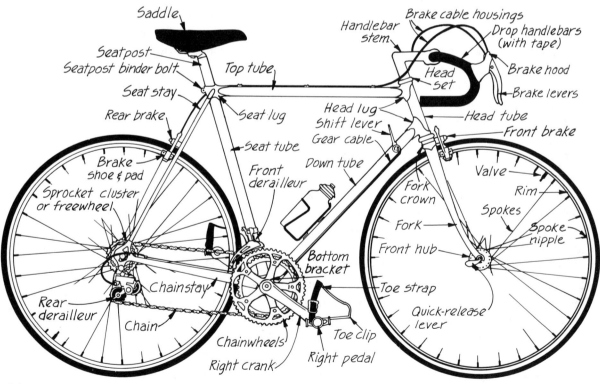

Bikes Let the Good Times Roll 2

What sort of cycling suits your style, your idea of a good time, and your way of building fitness?

No other sport could offer more variety, which is one reason why cycling continues to grow in popularity as lifelong recreation for adults. No other sport could adapt as well as cycling to the differences that make you unique. Nor could any other sport so well suit your changing interests, goals, and moods from year to year or day to day.

Perhaps today you need to be relaxed, tomorrow you want to be stimulated. One day you want to ride alone or with a friend, another you'd enjoy a group to talk and joke with. This month you appreciate the reassurance of a familiar route, next month you'd like a bit of exploring. This year you use your bike for commuting and day rides in the country, next year you take a bike tour or try time trial racing. And that's just a hint at the options!

Sound enticing? I hope so.

Bewildering? It doesn't have to be.

At this moment you don't have to map out your cycling goals far into the future. You and cycling will grow with each other. Some of us know at the outset we are eager for high adventure. Others of us will surprise ourselves: things we think we could never do will become accomplishments to remember proudly as we build confidence. And some of us may find such satisfaction in the cycling we're doing now that we feel no desire to move beyond those pleasant, familiar rides.

In any case, however, it's exciting to mull over the possibilities. And it's an important first step for getting started, especially if you're thinking of buying a new bike or of fixing up one you already own. Ask yourself:

- What sort of riding will I do immediately?
- What direction would I like to take in the near future?
- What would be pleasurable, fun, satisfying, crazy, wild, irresistible, the ultimate?
- Which cycling activities would be a natural extension of things I'm already doing now?
- Is there some part of me that's crying out to be recognised and allowed to develop through cycling? Are there inhibitions I'd like to throw off? (Dare to imagine something you'd really like to do, even if you're not sure it's possible. There'll be plenty of time later on as you keep reading, to answer practical questions and examine the obstacles.)

You may not know all the answers right now, but that's okay. Just think about it.

And keep an open mind as you hear what other women, perhaps not too unlike yourself, have to say about the cycling experiences they enjoy most. Whose cycling shoes would you like to step into?

CYCLE-TOURIST

Erica Springstead, 41, from Saratoga, California, had been cycling less than a year when she took her first bicycle holiday – in her words, 'an unbelievable experience!' The setting for her tour was Tuscany, Italy's magnificent, green hill country where umbrella pines and cypresses punctuate the undulating landscape; where olive groves and vineyards surround medieval towns and villages; and where Florence and Siena are truly worthy destinations.

It was a professionally organised tour. So the tour operator took care of all the fuss, like booking hotels, planning routes, and providing a vehicle to carry luggage, leaving the group free simply to enjoy pedalling through this rustic landscape. Erica suggests why this sort of travel is becoming more popular – not so much because it's inexpensive, in fact it isn't always – but because it gives an intimate view of the region. She writes:

> It was very challenging cycling because I opted to go with the 'goats' rather than the rest of the group. But I found my fellow cyclists to be fabulous people, the countryside beautiful, and the wines wonderful. The villas and hotels we stayed in were great. It was a very positive and memorable first tour.
>
> Cycling through the countryside gives you a far better view of things than whizzing by in a car. You get a much better sense of how people live. I loved cycling through a forest and seeing Italians emerge from the trees, carrying shopping bags full of wild porcini mushrooms they had just picked. I got a kick out of the astonishment and delight on the faces of some Italian cyclists (men, of course) when they saw the hot pink cycling shorts worn by another woman in our group as we hopped on their paceline and stuck with them for 10 miles. A great trip!

BICYCLE COMMUTER

After ten years of using her bike for commuting and other transport, Gaynor Mallinson, 28, exults in the practicality and the pleasure of it. Gaynor, who lives in Eldwick, West Yorkshire, observes that 'my bike is always there when I want it. It starts every morning! It avoids the awful queuing at bus stops; it's a cheap form of travel, and it keeps me fit as well.' That's important to Gaynor, who's an instructor in a health club. But fun counts, too.

'For me, going downhill is definitely the best thing: the thrill of going really fast, with no effort at all, and being able to sit and watch the world go by.'

There's also that wide-awake feeling from a morning bike ride to start the work day, and the chance to wind down and be alone with her thoughts on the ride home. Gaynor adds, 'I think more people should use cycles as a form of transport. We would be a lot fitter . . . plus bikes don't pollute.'

MOUNTAIN BIKER

'The most fun I've had on a bicycle has been riding my mountain bike – it's the ultimate in cycling freedom,' says Marty Carnes, 41, a teacher from St Simons Island in Georgia.

I bought my bike four years ago and tried it out on some hills. I've had some impressive bruises from falls but I don't do really dangerous stunts. I picked up the basics of off-road riding just from reading a few pointers and trying it.

What I enjoy most about this bike is I can ride it virtually anywhere. I have taken it up and down 'mountains', through streams, into the ocean (though I don't recommend it), across pastures, and in the woods. I haven't found a place I couldn't ride, especially since I discovered thorn-resistant tubes and liners and Kevlar tyres. Now that I live near the ocean, I believe this is the only bike to have! Besides, I like the more upright position. I sold my touring bike and bought a second mountain bike, to serve as a spare and lend to friends who visit.

I ride to work, 10 miles each way – 4 miles of that on a causeway littered with glass. But I've never had a flat with these tyres.

This is a wonderful way to start the day – the causeway goes through the marsh, which is home to thousands of red-wing blackbirds. The sun is just coming up, and as I climb the bridge over the intercoastal waterway I can see out to the other islands and the glittering Atlantic.

FAMILY CYCLIST

Three children don't hold Rita Menet, 38, and her husband back. Summertime is cycling time for this family from Appleton, Wisconsin.

'We ride as a family on a regular basis,' says Rita. Their sons, Luke, 10, and Peter, 8, ride ten-speed proportional bikes (described later in chapter 6). Joy, 5, who can ride a two-wheeler for a mile or two near home, gets a free ride in a Cannondale bicycle trailer often pulled by Dad on his bike.

'I like the Cannondale,' says Rita, 'because when I ride behind, Joy is facing me. I talk to her and sing songs to her, throw her candy from my bike bag. She has some toys she can play with. And we make a point of stopping about every 10 miles to do something the whole family enjoys; we take a swim, or visit the zoo or feed ducks in the park. That lets her move around, too.'

'We get the kids into bikes with gears as soon as possible,' she adds. 'We have a 22-inch wheeled five-speed bike that each of the boys rode as soon as they were big enough. When they got their ten-speeds, they really appreciated what a good bike

17

means.' No nagging, then, about taking good care of their bicycles. Rita notes that once the equipment is purchased, cycling pays for itself as a family activity. It's actually less expensive than many other things families often do together.

Cycling is family fun for this mother-daughter duo. A bicycle trailer makes it safe and simple (*Dan Burden*).

'Here in Wisconsin we are fortunate to have nine off-road bike trails (once railway beds) – they're safe and scenic. One crosses a marsh over a tramway; others traverse beautiful farmlands. Our favourite is a 30-mile trail that goes through three tunnels, where it's so cool inside. In fact, it "rains" in the tunnel from condensation.' To the children, that's sort of magic. There's a campsite along the way, so the family makes a weekend out of it.

Rita believes that cycling is more fun for her with the kids along and that their family is closer for it. 'Our kids never lack enthusiasm for it. I feel bad for other people who don't try it with their kids!' she admits.

NOVICE RACER

At 21, Susan King, from Turlock, California, is one of a growing number of licensed women bike racers, who are riding in road races, in time trials, and on the track. A college student, Susan also works as a clerk/mechanic part-time in a bike shop. Although she'd been riding for a few years, she began racing only recently. Here she describes her idea of a good time:

'My first criterium race was scary, but exciting,' says Susan, referring to those crowd-pleaser, mass-start bike races that usually consist of many laps around a course that's less than a mile long. The pace is fast. Riders try to stay in a pack or string out, one behind another, to take shelter from the wind. They whizz through the corners, a dizzying blur of bright jerseys and humming wheels.

Susan admits she was less nervous than she might have been because a friend was also racing for the first time.

> Right after the start the pack left us behind. We couldn't keep up, but that didn't bother me! The guys at the shop said I'd probably only last three or four laps . . .
>
> Once we were dropped, my friend and I and a third girl worked together, taking turns at the lead. I absolutely loved the feeling of flying around the corners super fast, especially one 'S' curve that was narrow and dangerous. I liked speeding by the crowd as my companions and I would call out to each other, 'Okay, take over!' or 'Let's go, work hard!' I felt very professional.
>
> The pack caught us after our seventh lap, and we had to drop out, but I sure felt powerful when we stopped. I couldn't stop talking about it all the way home! I was proud I'd managed to avoid a near accident early in the race when riders closed in on either side of me; somehow I missed locking wheels with both of them.

As for the guys at the bike shop, she couldn't wait to tell them: 'I lasted twice as long as those guys thought I would!'

CLUB RIDER

Hilary Brooke, 26, from Acomb, Yorkshire, is enthusiastic about club riding. Hilary, who hated sports in school, began cycling when her brother invited her to go for a ride with his cycling club. 'I went out of curiosity,' she says, 'and I've been hooked on cycling ever since.'

Why join a club? For many of us it makes cycling more sociable. Group rides and picnics are a terrific way to spend time with friends and make new ones. We learn from each other, motivate each other. The miles go by faster if we're part of a group that can laugh at the hills or hunker down in a headwind on a paceline, or 'chaingang', as you say in the UK.

Hilary particularly emphasises 'the amount of fun you can have if you join a cycling club'. Now racing herself, she says, 'Most people think cycling clubs are only for men who race every week and have legs of iron. But even if you do join a racing club, you can have a real laugh and enjoy yourself. Many clubs, however, are general cycling clubs and cater for everyone from schoolchildren up to 70-year-olds. And they organise a lot of social events.'

For a racer, a
serious moment
before the start
(*Sam Kleinman*).

RECREATIONAL RIDER

Faith West, 34, a court reporter in Plymouth, Minnesota, is an active cyclist who enjoys club outings and weekend and longer tours. She hops on her bicycle to do errands and rides a stationary bike indoors to stay fit during the snowy Minnesota winters. For her it's a big change from her former sedentary self. But aside from whatever else she looks for in cycling, she values the day-to-day pleasures of her local rides.

She's found, as many women do, that the more regularly she rides, the more she appreciates how cycling helps her feel good about herself and about life in general. The fresh air and sense of freedom on a bike ease tension and raise the spirits. This is especially true if – like Faith – we've found scenic, lightly trafficked routes easily accessible from home. They're worth searching out, even worth putting the bike in a car and driving to, if need be.

Here Faith describes the rewards.

It was late November. Bad weather had started early that year as it often does, but then there was a break; a few temperate days seemed a last blessing before the long, hard Minnesota winter set in.

I was feeling really blue (who knows what for, this time!), but I forced myself to go out since it might be the last chance before it snowed. I rode 12 miles to a natural preserve in a county park that has 7 miles of trail through beautiful country. I'd been there many times before, but this time the leaves in the woods had fallen, and the tall grass was yellow. I could see farther through the marshes and the trees than ever before. I was gawking at hundreds of white egrets, perched on the naked trees in a swampy lake. Suddenly I realised I felt nothing from the waist down. Were my legs really moving? I couldn't hear my tyres on the trail. I was floating! And I was no longer blue . . .

TRIATHLETE

Each year in her cycling, Shari Klarich, 40, of Bonner's Ferry, Idaho, sets a personal goal. During her second year of riding that goal was to complete a triathlon. To many who haven't tried it, this triple-threat event sounds far out of reach. But what Shari accomplished in just three months – one summer – shows the difference conditioning can make.

Shari says:

So far, my most pleasurable, challenging, and rewarding experience was that triathlon. Held in July, it was a 1-mile swim, 25-mile bike, and 6.2-mile run. When I started training in May I was already a year-round runner, but I could barely swim one lap of a pool or ride my bike for forty-five minutes. My goal during training was just to *finish*.

I enjoyed the training, and by race day I was a bit more ambitious: my goal was not to be last! I met my goal by placing third from last. My friend told me I smiled all the way. I loved it!

In these snippets of other women's cycling lives you can't help but notice that enjoyment is the common thread running through each. That's what encouraged each one of them to make time for riding in their busy schedules. You may be interested to know every woman here is convinced cycling helps her with weight control and/or keeping fit. Those things have followed naturally. But they aren't their only concerns in cycling. Pleasure is the reason they're still riding.

No matter what other personal goals you may set for yourself in cycling, do look for ways to have a good time with it.

In chapters that follow, you'll find all you need to know to step into the shoes of these women and to try still other aspects of the sport. I hope we've started you dreaming.

Are you ready to get on with it? (If so, you might want to skip the next chapter for now.)

Or are you feeling some hesitations?

We'll talk about surmounting the beginning obstacles in the next chapter.

3 *What's Your Road Block?*

The best advice is: if you don't cycle, you should. And if you do, then cycle more! Katrina O'Doherty, 22, Brighton, Sussex

Since you picked up this book, you've at least been thinking about pedalling toward some personal goal. If you haven't started yet, maybe something's got in the way. Or you've begun, but your progress isn't spinning along as smoothly as you'd hoped. Maybe lack of time is a problem: you're just not riding as often as you wish you would.

No matter what sort of 'road block' you're up against, you aren't the first to struggle with your particular hesitations. That doesn't make them any less real, but they can be dealt with – other women have.

Let me introduce a few of these women to you. Then perhaps you'll be saying, 'If she can do it, I can do it!'

'I'M NOT THE ATHLETIC TYPE'

Is that what you say? Take heart. Studies show that those who are least active and most out of shape stand to show the greatest improvement when they take up something like cycling, if they just stay with it. In later chapters we'll talk about conditioning to build endurance and cycling strength. Meanwhile, meet Janet Lewis.

'Hey, I have never been an athlete,' laughs Janet, 37, who lives in Huntington Beach, California. Growing up, she wasn't into sports.

But now on a sunny day she'd rather cycle 20 miles along the bike path near the ocean, wearing a bikini top, watching the waves and the surfers, than anything else. She says, 'This is the most athletic I've ever been. Compared to most of my friends, I'm a real jock!'

It took a severe shock to make Janet change. Fourteen years ago she went to the doctor for a pain in her knee and learned she had ostogenic sarcoma, a bone cancer. She required not only chemotherapy, but removal of her left leg up to the hip joint. There was nothing for a prosthesis to hold on to, so a sort of plastic bucket with straps that fitted around her hip was devised to allow use of an artificial limb, though it was uncomfortable and she had to walk with a cane.

She survived the cancer and continued to work as a teacher in Michigan, where she lived at the time.

One day a friend banged on her door at eight o'clock in the morning, waving a newspaper. In it was a photograph of a one-legged cyclist who was riding coast-to-coast. 'Janet,' her friend urged, 'if he can ride across the US, you can certainly ride around Ann Arbor!'

The cyclist's name was Bruce Jennings. When Janet eventually contacted him at his home in California, he encouraged her, told her how to compensate for the missing leg and what to buy. She followed his instructions, but then the bike sat in her living room for weeks.

'I was scared to death of crashing. Finally a neighbour said, "I'm coming over and we're going to take your bike to a parking lot and try it out."'

She was shaking, but she managed to sit on the saddle with his help. Visions of herself, bloody and bruised, made her stomach turn over. But as she coasted down a slight incline, she found the balance was in her arms. The missing leg made little difference. Then she tried pedalling, using a toeclip. She could do it, but her leg muscles tired quickly.

Eventually she mastered it. Gradually her leg strengthened and her endurance improved. Then she gave in to a long-time urge to move to California, where she could *really* be outdoors. She started a new life with her own apartment near the ocean, convenient for her favourite rides.

What does cycling mean to Janet Lewis? Off the bike she depends on crutches, since years ago she abandoned the painful prosthesis. 'The prosthesis was worse, but I still feel earthbound on crutches,' she says. 'Bicycling makes me feel free and in control. Independence is so important to me, probably most important!'

She doesn't always ride alone, however. Sometimes she partners yet another one-legged cyclist on his tandem (as cyclists term a bicycle-built-for-two). She takes the rear, 'stoker' position, and together they've completed several centuries – organised 100-mile rides – that are to cyclists what marathons are to runners. Big hills? No problem. 'On the tandem we can do anything!'

On her single bike, Lewis's longest ride is a respectable 42 miles, but she hopes to beat that. Her new, lighter bike with lighter wheels should help, but Janet will always be handicapped climbing hills alone, as she can't stand up for extra leverage.

On her single bike, she admits, she avoids big hills. 'I can do hills I couldn't do before, but they're not major ones.'

But she enjoys her own abilities and likes meeting other riders on the bike path and making friends. Sometimes they'll go for miles without noticing she has only one leg.

'Other times people will notice, and they'll say "Good luck" or "Keep up the good work." Or they'll tell their friends about me, so when their friends see me, they point and say, "There she is!"'

Many people stop and tell her she inspires them, and that always makes her feel good. To anyone who asks, her advice is 'Go for it!'

'I'M TOO OLD TO START NOW'

You may think so, but you're not. That's what Nora Young, of Toronto, Ontario, would say. So would researchers, who've demonstrated that, no matter when you start exercising, you can actually reverse the effects of aging. You can improve the functioning of heart and lungs, build muscle strength, quicken reaction times, become more flexible, and feel more energetic! While you're about it, you'll be less vulnerable to depression and may even find you're thinking more clearly.

Start gradually, as Nora Young did. Today, at 73, Nora Young lives up to her name and is in better shape than she was a dozen years ago.

Always a natural athlete and an 'all-rounder', Nora first raced bicycles in Exhibition Park in Toronto in the 'thirties. But after the Second World War she dropped out of cycling and didn't take it up again until 1978, when she was 61. As she puts it, she 'started slowly, going on a couple of tours' and bought a twelve-speed touring bike. When the First International Masters Games were scheduled for her city in 1985, Nora contacted some riders she'd known in the early days 'and in a few months got in reasonably fair shape'.

As her description of that race shows, her competitive spirit was also rekindled.

The 45-kilometre (28-mile) road race was tough – very hilly, and the temperature was over 90 degrees. I was dropped on the first hill but plugged along, and about a mile or so from the finish I looked ahead and saw a rider. I thought she was tiring, so I drew on my reserve, caught up going down the hill, raced to the finish, and she nipped me at the line. They gave us both the same time: one hour, forty-two minutes. Boy, were my legs aching, but it was a wonderful feeling!

Since then she's been competing at Masters events across North America, travelling as far away as Florida, where she won all ten events she entered in a recent Golden Age competition.

'I feel I can do things today I would have had a hard time doing twelve years ago,' she says. 'Competing just gives you a nice feeling – you are trying to better yourself, trying to stay on top when someone else is trying to beat you. I like that sense of improvement.'

The sense of purpose is important too, especially at an age when women often have more free time than they did a decade earlier. Retirement blues? Not Nora. 'I couldn't sit and watch television all day – there's too much to do,' she exclaims. In addition to cycling, she attends exercise classes three times a week, skis, lawn bowls, skates, and plays golf.

The variety of activities also helps her stay competitive on the bike, despite a short outdoor training season. 'We have a little, wee school track out here. I figure everybody is saying I'm a racer, so I'd better get out there and practise.'

When we spoke, Nora was looking forward to the Senior Games in New York State – the bike races, 'And I might also try the discus and shotput. What have I to lose, except a sore arm?'

And what have *we* to lose, except the feeling that we're getting old faster than we'd like? We don't have to race like Nora Young, but we can get into the game.

If you truly have been sedentary, that's even more reason to take up cycling – you should begin to see benefits fairly quickly. Bear in mind, you can ride at quite a leisurely pace if you choose. And cycling is easier on the joints than, say, jogging, since cycling is a non-weight-bearing activity. In fact, women who've been troubled by arthritis often remark that riding a bike helps them overcome stiffness and keep mobile.

If you've been inactive, ask your doctor whether an examination is a good idea before you begin. If you're over 35, a 'stress' test is in order, especially if you smoke, have high-blood pressure, diabetes, a family history of heart disease, or have previously experienced symptoms. The test should be given by an experienced cardiologist in a facility that has full resuscitation equipment.

A 'stress' test is a wise precaution – not meant to scare you off – and if you've had anxieties about whether it's safe for you to exercise, it will most likely put your mind at ease and encourage you to get on with it.

'MY LIFE IS TOO MIXED UP RIGHT NOW'

When something goes terribly wrong – a marriage ends, you lose your job, a parent dies, a transfer forces you to move – it's natural to feel overwhelmed. And you're likely not to want to tackle something completely new and challenging. You may feel too depressed, as if you're already walking underwater just trying to make it through the day.

Luckily, cycling isn't new to most of us. If we haven't been on a bike in years, at least we learned in childhood. Remember the wind rushing cool against your face as you coasted down a hill? Can you recall the thrill of going so very fast under your own power? Did you watch spring leaf out from the seat of your bicycle? Reliving those girlish sensations might help you cope with the stresses of your adult life.

How could this be?

'After my marriage broke up, cycling was one of the ways I not only kept a grip on my sanity, but also recovered,' says Jane Jackel, 37, of Montreal.

> The most important thing I did after my life fell apart was to go for counselling, but bicycling played a role in my recovery. I had joined a bicycling club and was able to practise some of the things I learned during my counselling sessions – for instance, being able to trust other people and learning to relax both with myself and with others.
>
> There's something about the rhythmic motion of pedalling, especially out in the country, that frees your mind to think more clearly and raises your spirits. Not only that, but the improvement in fitness makes you feel powerful and confident.

If a major disruption has taken place in your life, you might follow Jane Jackel's lead and reach out for help. At the same time you'll probably survey your own resources to discover how to make yourself feel better in a healthful way. Interestingly, recent psychological research shows that regular exercise like cycling can be a catalyst for

25

healing the spirit. And in my own survey, 85.6 per cent of all women who responded said that cycling usually lifts them out of a blue mood; another 12.9 per cent said that it sometimes does. In a later chapter we'll delve deeper into why this is so.

'I'M TOO FAT'

With the current thinness fetish it's easy for any woman with slightly more padding than a hatrack to feel self-conscious about her figure. Sadly enough, that not only makes us feel bad about ourselves, but it may keep us from going out and getting the exercise we would probably enjoy and that helps keep our metabolisms perking along and burns calories.

But not Adrienne Rifkind, 37, of McKinney, Texas, who became a triathlete at the astonishing weight of 21 stone (295 pounds). 'I figured I'd been laughed at all my life because of being large, so go ahead and laugh' – that was her attitude. But she quickly discovered other athletes didn't laugh, and the crowds who observed her tackling the 2-kilometre swim, the 40-kilometre bike ride, and the 10-kilometre run cheered her wildly through her first triathlon. Although Adrienne hobbled last across the finish, 'with blisters the size of double silver dollars on my feet', the accomplishment gave wings to her spirit. There was no doubt in her mind she would continue her training and competing.

How did she begin? A year and a half earlier she had no exercise programme of any kind when she checked into a clinic with a weight of 30 stone (425 pounds). Though she could scarcely walk comfortably, she began a conditioning programme on an exercise bike and restricted her calories. As her weight dropped and fitness improved, she sought new goals. A triathlete was born.

Getting over her self-consciousness wasn't easy, she remembers. 'You have to learn to ignore the hecklers. I also coped by riding where there wasn't a lot of car traffic.'

Of course, it's nobody else's business to assess our bodies, but too often there's the idiot who has to have something to say, regardless of what size we are. I've had people look me up and down when I'm cycling or running, and say, 'What are you doing that for? You're thin enough already!' Such people truly miss the point of what cycling is about. No wonder they make such stupid remarks.

But the attention doesn't help if we already feel critical of our bodies, a pervasive attitude among women. Several years ago *Glamour* magazine surveyed 33,000 women. Seventy-five per cent of them said they felt 'too fat', while in fact only 25 per cent of the respondents were overweight according to the fairly rigorous standards of the 1959 Metropolitan Life Insurance height/weight tables. And 45 per cent of the *underweight* women felt they were 'too fat'. We'll talk more about body image and weight loss in a later chapter. Let's say for now that we are probably our own harshest critics.

The best thing we can do is put aside those hangups and get on our bikes. If you can, find a friend to ride with – someone who will keep a compatible pace – on scenic, lightly trafficked roads, and you'll be having too good a time to worry much about what others think. And try to remember that those who yell rude remarks from car windows are jerks. Anyone who knows the least bit about fitness and exercise will admire us for our efforts.

'I'M TOO BUSY'

If you haven't muttered that to yourself, you're a rare individual. Any exercise programme takes time, and cycling is no exception.

What to do? Make cycling a priority and schedule the time as you would any other important appointment. Carol Merfield, 35, of Tucson, Arizona found the answer by scheduling her 1½-hour training rides before work – at 4.30 am! At that hour she had the streets to herself and she was riding in the coolest part of the day, a real bonus in Arizona.

The payoff for that training was completing her first century and winning one of the gold medallions awarded to any woman finishing in under seven hours. Crossing the line at 6.49.42, Merfield again demonstrated great time management.

Are the early morning hours too cruel? Try cycling to work. It may well be quicker than driving or taking public transport, or it may take a little longer, but there's much to recommend it, including that you automatically build cycling time into your regular schedule. Some top racers have told me they do much of their training on long commuting rides to and from work. Using the bike for shopping and other errands is another way to sneak in extra riding.

Time management experts tell us that the way to find time to do things we want to do is not to work harder, as a rule, but to work *smarter*. The idea: eliminate some of the unnecessary things we're doing now, by delegating them to others or simply realising they can be left undone.

For example, Susan Krueger, 23, is married, works at a pro bike shop in Augusta, Maine, and has recently taken up racing. Her biggest problem is lack of time. She says: 'Since I started riding, I haven't had time to work, ride, *and* clean house, so I gave up cleaning the house. This has been a great source of frustration.'

It is frustrating to have to relax our standards, but it may be the happiest and healthiest way to do the things we really find fulfilling. Saying 'no' more frequently to requests for our time, persuading family members to be more self-sufficient and to assume more responsibilities at home – these sorts of changes take thought on our part and cooperation from the people who share our lives.

Speaking of racers, even former world champions aren't immune to the time demands of families and, often, the world of work. In 1982 England's Mandy Jones won the World Championship road race in cycling. Four years later she gave birth to her little boy, Sam, and despite the pressures of motherhood, she raced time trials the following year and won two national championships. She had some financial support from a sponsor, but even so it wasn't easy. 'I was cycling over to my mum's with Sam on the back and dropping him off, to go training with a babyseat on the back,' she said recently.

Creating the time takes ingenuity, especially after she lost her sponsorship. But

Mandy and her husband, former cycling pro Ian Greenhalgh, vowed when she was pregnant that they wouldn't let Sam's birth stop them. They have no car, which helps to keep them on their bikes. They do have a wind trainer which simulates wind resistance and permits mounting their own bikes indoors when the weather is foul or Sam needs watching. Mandy is still racing at time trials, but fewer than before.

When we spoke, Mandy, who lives in Lancashire and now works as a secretary, was looking forward to a brief holiday during which she would cycle up to Scotland to see her grandmother – with Sam, of course, in the babyseat.

'WHAT ABOUT ALL THOSE CRAZY DRIVERS?'

If this is a concern, it's not entirely unrealistic. In my survey of women cyclists, out of a dozen things that might create problems, 'inconsiderate motorists' was ranked most troublesome by more respondents than any other item. This is the driver who makes a turn right in front of you so you have to brake to a halt (or turn quickly even though you hadn't intended to). This is the driver who passes you at 60 mph on a dirt road, his wheels spraying gravel and dust on you as he goes by. Sooner or later we all meet this driver, and we are wary.

On the other hand, I've found that this sort constitutes a tiny minority of motorists. Apparently, many women I've surveyed would agree, since 'fear of riding in moderate traffic' was mentioned much less frequently as a concern. In our experience, traffic generally operates in an orderly flow, and the cyclist can learn to become a part of that flow. Later on in this book we'll talk about:

- learning to take your rightful place on the road where you're likely to be seen and can avoid road hazards
- using hand signals before turning to communicate your intentions clearly to motorists
- choosing the best roads (usually lightly travelled)
- making yourself more visible to motorists by wearing brightly coloured clothing and, if you must ride after dark, being properly lighted.

You can also increase your protection by wearing a good helmet – always a wise practice, traffic or no traffic.

Particularly if you live in an urban area, you may decide to make your influence felt by joining an activist group to work for bike lane markings on your city streets and other cyclists' causes. Or you may choose to go off-road and escape automobiles entirely. After all, these mountain bikes, selling so popularly now, can give you the best of both worlds.

Whenever you are on the tarmac, of course, you'll follow the rules of the road yourself, knowing that doing so sends the right message to drivers about cyclists.

'I'M PUT OFF BY THE MACHINERY'

I well remember hopping on a borrowed ten-speed to join friends on a bike hike years ago. Nobody explained how the gears operated, and I twiddled the two shift levers but couldn't do anything except spin the pedals aimlessly around and go nowhere; or else suddenly I was in such a high gear it was leg-wrenching just to turn the cranks. I suppose I eventually blundered into the right combination, because I did manage to stick with the group. I was lucky we stayed on fairly level ground because I had no idea what I was doing.

Later on when I bought my own bike, I discovered how simple gearing really is *once somebody shows you.* So if you've been hesitating about buying a new bike for fear of gears, stop worrying. If you've recently begun riding a ten- (or more-) speed and it isn't going quite smoothly, I have pointers for you, too. It's all covered in chapter 7. Soon you'll be amused that you ever worried about it.

Maybe your bugaboo isn't learning to shift – you already have the hang of it, or you have a simpler, internally geared bike (a three-speed or some five-speeds) or the simplest, a single-speed. You are more concerned about keeping it in good repair, mending the inevitable puncture, and so on. If you've an older bike, you may be mostly worried about fixing it up enough to ride safely.

You aren't alone. In my own survey, handling bike repair and maintenance proved to be the second most serious concern of the women who responded. We need articles and books written in terms we can understand, they said.

In this one we'll start with the very basics. I'll assume it's all new to you, and we'll cover the things that most frequently go wrong and how to take care of them. You'll also find a bike safety checkup you can do yourself to get your bike out on the road.

A last thought about our 'road blocks': cycling does offer challenges. They may include some of these we've just talked about or others that become evident later on. Ironically, it's the very challenges that provide some of the sport's great benefits. In meeting them, we build confidence and competence that enrich not simply our cycling but our entire lives. As Connie Carpenter Phinney, Olympic gold medalist, has said, 'To accept the challenge of the road is to take a journey within yourself.'

4 To Your Health – Cycling and the Psyche

There has never been a time when I haven't felt better after a ride, even when I felt great to start with!   Cathy Nestor, 37, Honolulu, Hawaii

I certainly feel much happier in general whenever I exercise – it's the best way of diffusing aggro. I also feel stronger, fitter, and more energetic and 'firm' body-wise.   Cynthia Scott, 37, London

I was looking for a vote of confidence in cycling to promote good health, and I received it with the hundreds of survey questionnaires women cyclists returned to me from all over the US, Canada and the UK. Their enthusiastic responses confirmed the results of medical studies and findings of health professionals about the benefits of regular exercise – and in the most human and meaningful terms.

While numbers and studies are significant, there's special inspiration in real-life experiences. In instance after instance, women told how cycling enhanced already active lives or helped them to make dramatic, positive changes to create, phoenix-like, a healthy, new woman. By their own account these women are excited, uplifted, strengthened, fulfilled, contented, and energised by their riding and what it has helped them to discover and develop within themselves. They – we – have discovered a way to build fitness, better our health, and set our minds and bodies in tune with each other . . . and we don't mind at all that we have a good time while we're about it.

We'll take a look at both the research and some of these experiences.

RIDING BACK FROM DEPRESSION

Medicine has long recognised the mind's power to help heal the body. Today researchers are also proving the reverse: that the body can strongly influence our state of mind. Especially exciting is evidence that exercise can assist in safeguarding or even improving our mental health.

One woman who proved that to herself is Jane Stockwell, 30, of Ramona, California. Jane has been cycling about three years, but she was relatively new to it when she tackled her first 100-mile ride. She explains why it was a barometer for the emotional struggles in her life:

I rode alone on my first century, though I had my family to see me off and receive me at the finish. To them, I was attempting a cycling milestone, but to me it was more. It was my way of celebrating life, health, and happiness after a particularly difficult two years spent coping with serious depression. The ride was a way of convincing myself that I had done more than survive. I had rallied to new heights.

Through my riding I had found new reserves of physical and emotional strength. The miles had tallied up into a greater sense of self-respect. I had learned to relate to myself with a new, more gentle persistence. Cycling had offered me a sense of achievement and a metaphoric pathway through many of my life's obstacles by allowing me to learn a skill or tactic on the road and then apply it to the broader scheme of my life. I had so much to be thankful for when I crossed that finish line, for I sensed this was just the beginning of a new, wonderful life.

Depression is a major health concern in our society, especially for women, since it plagues twice as many women as men. According to a recent study by the National Institute of Mental Health (NIMH) in the United States, during a six-month prevalency period about 3.1 per cent of the US adult population aged 18 or over will experience major depression. Typically, feelings of gloom and worthlessness drag on for weeks or months. Other symptoms can include: lowered energy or activity levels; poor concentration and muddled thinking; disturbances in eating, sleeping, and sexual patterns; thoughts of death and suicide. Depression may mask itself in physical symptoms like chronic fatigue or headaches.

Since depression often goes undiagnosed or is improperly treated, a few years ago NIMH launched a campaign to make the treatment of depression a national priority.

One bit of good news in depression research is recent experimentation with exercise as treatment. It has meaning for all of us, whether we should ever suffer from clinical depression or not.

Here's a sample of the work being done. In a large study involving 561 university students, researchers identified 101 students as clinically depressed, and 460 as non-depressed. Each group was divided in half: into an experimental group which would participate in a ten-week, regular exercise programme and a control group which would not exercise. After ten weeks, all were re-evaluated. The exercising groups – both depressed and non-depressed students – showed real improvement in their mood state. The symptoms of those classified as depressed had lessened, and they were more cheerful and energetic at the end of the ten-week programme. Those two groups which didn't exercise did not show an improvement in mood.

I think it's especially interesting that *both* depressed and non-depressed students who exercised found their moods bettered – an indication of the broad benefits of regular exercise for combatting depression, whether it be clinical depression or simply the occasional 'blue' mood anyone experiences from time to time.

A much smaller study demonstrated that exercise could even outperform psychotherapy. Twenty-eight patients with mild or moderate depression were divided into three groups. Two groups would have psychotherapy; a third group would not. Instead it would follow a regular exercise routine at least three times a week for ten weeks. The exercise happened to be jogging, but the psychiatrist heading the study, John H. Greist, MD, of the University of Wisconsin, told me in an interview that 'cycling or any other programme of exercise that uses large muscle masses in regular rhythm should have the same effect'.

On a bike we escape our personal demons and discover unsuspected strengths. Beneath the trees, among open fields and scattered farms, we find joy and serenity on the open road (*Dan Burden*).

What did he learn? In three weeks most of the exercising patients were 'virtually well'. And the exercise treatment had a higher success rate than psychotherapy in treating the depression.

How does he explain it? Doctor Greist views depression as a person's response to loss of control. 'People who are able to stick with a regular (exercise) routine . . . get a sense of success and mastery from it,' he observes. 'When people find they're able to do something they didn't know they could do, they begin to realise they also can make other changes in their lives for the better.'

In addition to that, regular doses of exercise appear to produce chemical and physiological changes in the body and brain which affect mood. Precisely what these changes are is still undergoing study. Is it increased blood flow, more oxygen in the system, or some neurotransmitters produced by the brain?

'At the bottom of every thought we have is that there is some electrochemical process in the brain,' says Greist. At this point scientists have theories but not definite answers. Nevertheless, regular aerobic exercise is clearly one of the things we can do, along with good nutrition, to promote *homeostasis*, the body's natural propensity to balance automatically its own chemistry.

A cautionary word: the seriously depressed individual may need more than an exercise programme to resolve her problems. But more conventional therapy might well be given a boost by the addition of regular, pleasurable aerobic activity. Certainly women would benefit from further research in this area.

Other depressions to which we're vulnerable – like the depression often associated with PMS (premenstrual syndrome) – are complex and not fully understood either. Indeed, much controversy surrounds the more than seventy different treatments currently used for PMS, many of which are contradictory, untested, or expensive. But one treatment that probably can't hurt – and which many women find helpful – is exercise.

It's one of the first things Sally K. Severino, MD, recommends. She is associate professor of psychiatry at New York Hospital-Cornell Medical Center in White Plains, New York, and author of *Premenstrual Syndrome: A Clinician's Guide* (The Guilford Press, Inc., 1989). Women may be willing to put up with the bloating, breast tenderness, and constipation many experience with PMS, she notes. But when they develop emotional symptoms – irritability, anger, depression, or anxiety – they are often driven to seek help.

'And when they do,' says Doctor Severino, 'I feel it's sensible to advocate exercise for most patients. First, it may help relieve symptoms related to bloating; second, many women find that regular physical exercise improves their self-esteem, especially in our fitness-oriented culture. And third, depression and anxiety may be relieved.'

Gloria Knoll, of Appleton, Wisconsin, has found this to be true:

> A bike ride helps take the edge off PMS. I so look forward to an hour or two on my bike each day. I am a 41-year-old mother of five children and have experienced the tension and depression of PMS. I usually ride before I pick my kids up from school or after supper. It's my quiet time and a tension release. Cycling helps me keep things in perspective, and the bouts with depression aren't nearly as severe.

As for how to go about it, what Jane Stockwell has discovered for herself is good advice for others with similar needs:

> I need to remember to ride to please myself because if I ride too fast, too hard, or too far, the magic goes out of the ride and I'm ready for the bike-toss. If I'm riding to please another, I return depleted and resentful. Yet if I ride with respect for my own desires and limitations, I return exhilarated and eager to ride again. So to avoid these 'bad rides', I plan rides that are challenging and yet well within my grasp. Success breeds success.

DE-STRESSING

Job, family, home – with all those responsibilities, no wonder today's woman is often stressed. And, since women typically do for others first and themselves last, their personal time is the first thing down the drain. Unless you realise how important it is, your exercise time may be one thing you give up.

I say 'important' because one of the best antidotes for stress is exercise, stress management experts tell us. Individually, many women cyclists have commented that cycling plays an important role in helping them handle stress.

Bicycle commuter Charlotte Vasey, 32, of Meavy Lane in Devon, describes her 'time to unwind': 'Leaving work after a long, oppressive day in the office, having plenty of time to spare and heading for the cycle path . . . There are few places prettier on a hot summer evening, and the long ride home is so relaxing.'

A number of studies validate this experience. In research with both men and women, psychologist Richard Dienstbier, PhD, at the University of Nebraska, has found that people do become 'more stress-tolerant after taking up a regular programme of aerobic exercise than they were before.' His recent work has involved measuring reactions to stress such as heartbeat and skin conductance (the same sorts of things measured in a 'lie detector' test), as well as hormonal responses. These tests, given before and after a few months of training, showed striking improvement in the individual's ability to handle tension. In a telephone interview Doctor Dienstbier explained:

> I think regular exercise changes the hormonal balance of the body so that if you face psychological stressors after you've been involved in a training programme, you tend to generate more energy and less tension. Energy tends to be associated with adrenaline and noradrenaline. Adrenaline particularly is associated with blood glucose, and glucose is the fuel of the nervous system – the only fuel the nervous system can burn. Exercise increases our ability to generate those hormones.

Dienstbier calls this process 'toughening', and he suspects cycling is a particularly good way for women to achieve it. 'I have a feeling,' he reasons, 'that bicycling is one of those things women can typically do at least as well as men, and get a big amount of satisfaction from.'

OVERCOMING DRUG AND ALCOHOL DEPENDENCIES

I can't think of a health problem in which the mind and body are more connected than in substance abuse. It is popular politics today to worry about drug abuse among teenagers or among a certain lower-class subculture while ignoring the dependence on drugs and/or alcohol of middle- and upper-class adults, many of them women. This is a genuine women's health issue and, although it's largely beyond the scope of this short chapter, I'd like to comment on the role exercise has begun to play in treatment of substance abuse.

'Exercise that produces cardiopulmonary stimulation is a helpful means of reducing drug hunger and anxiety during recovery therapy,' notes David E. Smith, MD, in speaking of the treatment programme for cocaine abusers at the Haight Ashbury Free Medical Clinic in Berkeley, California. 'We regularly use the exercise alternative as part of the recovery programme, and others have used (it) successfully as well,' he writes in the *Journal of Substance Abuse Treatment* (Vol. 1, 1984).

For many women drug abuse begins, not as thrill-seeking with illegal substances, but with some medical indication for drug therapy for pain or emotional crisis. Gradually the patient becomes dependent. In the case of Linda Parker of West Bromwich in the West Midlands, for example, dependency began with a doctor's incorrect diagnosis and his failure to monitor her prescription carefully. Through her own determination she's been free for five years of a Valium addiction which lasted thirteen. 'I feel I've lost thirteen years of my life,' says Linda, 36. 'But that's in the past now, and I only look forward.' Here she tells how cycling aided her in her struggle to cure herself:

When I was 21 I had a frightening dizzy spell while shopping. I'd never experienced anything like it before. I went to a doctor, who said I was suffering from high blood pressure (I later learned this wasn't true), perhaps because of my upcoming marriage. He prescribed 5 mg Valium to be taken three times a day.

I didn't know then that Valium is a tranquillizer. The pills knocked me out; I slept nearly all day. After seven days I returned to the doctor, who told me my blood pressure was normal but gave me another prescription in case the symptoms returned.

All went well for a few days. Then I had another dizzy spell, even worse. I took a Valium and felt much better. They weren't making me so sleepy now. This carried on for a few weeks. If I had a dizzy spell, I'd reach for the pills. When I ran out, I had only to phone my doctor for a refill. It was so easy. He never asked me to come in for an examination or a blood pressure test. After a time I wouldn't go out without taking a Valium.

When I became pregnant, I asked the doctor whether it was safe to take the pills during pregnancy. He said it was, and I did. During my ante-natal checkups I asked about my blood pressure and was told it was normal. I gave birth to a healthy son, though I now realise he was probably addicted to Valium at birth and must have suffered withdrawal.

While in hospital having the baby I didn't take any Valium and realised I felt much better. Once again at home, however, I feared to go out without taking one. I resumed and was like a zombie, often irritable, but still I took them. I thought they helped.

We moved house and changed doctors, but all I had to do was phone the doctor and ask for a refill – no questions asked.

I took Valium throughout a second pregnancy and gave birth to another son.

I had now diagnosed myself as agoraphobic, but my doctor laughed at this

35

and said there was no such thing. He sent me from the surgery with another hundred pills.

Now with a toddler and a baby I was taking more Valium. I felt I couldn't cope. I suffered palpitations, faintness, dizzy spells, headaches, and insomnia. I couldn't concentrate on anything. I used to have a good memory but now was forgetting appointments, birthdays, and even what had happened the week before. I never seemed to have energy for housework or making love. The children were all I could manage.

This went on for another four years. Then I read an article saying Valium is addictive. The more you take, the more you need. I'd never considered myself an addict and was really shocked.

I went to the doctor, told him about the article, and asked him to prescribe something different. He said Valium is completely safe and that he had no doubts about prescribing it.

It was then I decided I wanted a better life. I wanted to be happy and enjoy my children. I wanted to be a normal woman, normal wife, and normal mother. If the doctor wouldn't help me, then I'd help myself before it was too late.

I went home and cut all the pills into halves and quarters. Now instead of taking a full pill, I'd take three-quarters. When I felt I needed one, I'd make myself wait at least a half-hour before taking it. The first week I went to hell and back. I felt really ill and couldn't sleep, but refused to give in. I didn't want to be a drug addict. I stayed at this dose for about nine months, then I cut down to a half.

Again I felt terrible, but I couldn't give in. I must do this for my family.

After about the same period of time I cut down to one-quarter. Once again it was agony, but I was nearly there. It was about this time my husband bought me a bicycle for Christmas. He said I needed the exercise. My sons and my husband already had bikes and rode together.

They were all surprised I could actually ride my new acquisition, and it wasn't long before I was riding with them. We cycled for miles in the evenings and on weekends. I enjoyed it and felt so well. I was still taking my quarter pill but now felt I had to find the right time to stop altogether. I felt better than I could ever remember.

I chose the family holiday as the time to stop. I packed the bottle of pills just in case. I went through the entire two weeks without taking any Valium and still felt good. I had none of the earlier withdrawal symptoms. I think that was due to the cycling.

The big crunch would come when I got home. Would I manage? I'm glad to say that I did. I haven't taken any Valium since that day. I still have the occasional panic attack, but I breathe deeply and relax and it just flows away.

Linda adds that her husband has been supportive of her throughout these years and that her sons, now 14 and 12, are 'intelligent and well adjusted . . . in spite of the start they had'.

She herself feels 'a hundred per cent' now. She's enjoyed taking night school courses over the past few years, and her memory and concentration have returned. Not long ago she was busy with yet another move, 'getting our new house and garden into shape. But now I'm ready to start cycling again, and I have the long summer days to look forward to.'

Evidence indicates there are many more 'Lindas' still dependent on Valium. In the United States, for example, it's by far the most widely used tranquillizer.

Alcohol is even easier to abuse. No prescription needed, it's readily, legally available. Drinking is socially acceptable and, in some lifestyles, almost unavoidable. So it was for Elaine Fisher, 33, of Stockport, Cheshire, who was a cocktail waitress and a student at the time:

> When I started participating in sports, I came to know once again what it was like to be healthy. Three years previous to my cycling, I had fallen into the habit of drinking every night. It was almost normal to be hung over.
>
> I gradually began drinking less when I started riding. One of the problems of tapering off is that on the nights when you don't drink, you can't sleep. But I found that the tired feeling from cycling was far more effective than a drink-induced sleep, especially the next morning, as you don't wake up depressed and hung over . . .

Certainly I don't mean to imply that an individual should always expect to beat a dependency by herself, as Elaine and Linda have done. What each of them happened to discover by accident, however, is worthy of more study by the medical community than it's received to date.

PUTTING THE PIECES BACK TOGETHER

One Christmas, Jennifer Shea's life began falling apart. She was 25. Her vivid account expresses the kind of healing we've been talking about.

> December 1985 was the year my cohabiting boyfriend gave me a Trek eighteen-speed touring bike. I cried when I saw that shiny, new Trek. Now, most people would be glad to replace an old bicycle with a new one, but this bike symbolised the end of our relationship. I had given my boyfriend an option that Christmas: all I wanted for Christmas was a commitment from him; if not, my only request was a Trek, just like his.
>
> I kept the bike; I left him.
>
> The following month my bicycle and I returned home to care for my ailing grandmother. She was not just another grandmother, but much, much more. When I was 5 years old, my father had abandoned my mother, older brother, sister and myself. My grandmother raised us from then on, while my mother watched in an alcoholic state.
>
> On Fourth of July 1986, I became a holiday statistic. A drunk driver ran a red

light and totalled me and my car. With a fractured sternum, ribs, and right ankle I was laid up the rest of the summer. When I returned to my job, I found I'd been demoted. I then quit.

That October my grandmother had to be put into a convalescent home, and that was when she gave up the will to live. On 23 May 1987, I sat with my grandmother and watched her die. I never felt such pain in my life. I cannot even express it on paper.

I moved in with a girlfriend for the summer, out in the country. I had reached the bottom, and I did not have the inner strength to climb back up. What little self-worth and security I had built up through the years was gone, as was any sense of control over my life. All life to me was pain, and I did not want to go on.

But one Saturday in June I woke with the sun and felt my survival strength returning, something I learned about as a child. I took out my Trek and hit the country back roads. On this ride I felt every emotion possible, except perhaps joy.

I cried as I rode, I felt anger inside as I pumped up the hills, I felt inner strength, I felt drive. 'I've got to make it up this hill!' I competed with the hill, I competed with my Trek, but most of all, I competed with myself and I made it to the top.

I flew down the hill, pedalling faster and faster. I couldn't stop my legs, but just kept going. I passed some horses and smiled at them. I waved to an old farmer on a plough and talked to his cows as I flew by them. I looked up to the sun and the crisp blue sky. I talked to my grandmother and started to cry some more. I talked to my inner self, and I yelled out loud on that deserted country road.

I stood on the pedals and pumped up another hill. My legs felt tight, my body felt strong. Sweat ran down my face, mixed with my tears. I splashed my face and drank water from my water bottle as I kept going and could not stop. I felt 'the sweet spot' – the perfect rhythm and flow of energy athletes feel at their best moments. I felt at one with nature, with my bike, with myself. I was in control of my life and destiny. I had the inner strength and drive to do anything. I wanted to fight again . . . and to live again.

The rest of that summer I did not trust people or life, but I did trust myself and my Trek. My bike could not hurt me. My Trek and I got through the hardest time in my life. We got through it together: I did belong here and I was not alone.

A year later I live in my own home in the country where I was cycling. Recently I've been riding those roads, but it isn't the same now. I feel contentment and inner peace. I'm learning how to love myself for the first time in my life, and I'm thankful my bike guided me down the right road and gave me strength to go on. Now I feel there is so much to live for.

A Long and Healthy Life 5

Cycling can put you on the road to better physical health and, possibly, longer life.

'I'm a walking health story,' chuckles Sherry Denny, 36, of Winnemucca, Nevada. Sherry doesn't know what her blood pressure and cholesterol levels were nine years ago before she started cycling for real, but she knows they had to be high.

Back then Sherry had a cheap, heavy bike that rarely left the garage ('it wasn't much fun to ride'), and there were no other sports or fitness activities she liked. There never had been. At 27 she was 'sedentary', as the researchers say.

But she became involved with a bike club when somebody asked Sherry and her husband to drive sag wagon (to pick up stragglers) on a club ride. 'I saw how much fun everybody was having and how fit they were,' she says.

She wanted that for herself. She and her husband ordered good bikes and, while she waited for hers to arrive, she began chugging around on the old one. She knew the club rode in hilly terrain and she wanted to be prepared.

When the new bike came, shiny and full of promise, Sherry was ready for a challenge. Eight miles from her front door (she lived in Texas at the time) was the top of a mountain. The 5-mile stretch of road going up gained 1,350 feet in elevation. Torn between hope and self-doubt, she set out to ride up the mountain. And she did it.

'Here I was 40 pounds [3 stone] overweight and I was able to bicycle up this mountain. Looking back, that was as much a psychological mountain as a physical one. It inspired me to stick with it.'

She has. 'I've lost about 30 pounds [2 stone]. I eat better, my blood pressure is down to normal (from 150/95 five years ago, to 120/80 when we spoke), and her total cholesterol level has dropped by 46 points.

'I've discovered cycling, as a life-sport, and it has changed the course of my life.'

If we're looking for a long and healthy life, coronary heart disease (CHD) and other diseases of the heart including high blood pressure are a woman's number one enemy. These killed more women in the United States in 1985, for example, than any other single cause, according to *Statistical Abstracts of the US*. Cancer was a fairly close second.

What can we do? We can sit back and be vulnerable, or we can fight back by becoming active. By getting out on our bikes we can put a great deal of distance between ourselves and many of the medical problems that plague our deskbound, convenience-food car-culture. If we're already suffering from some of these ailments, we can help to work for our own cure. We can add quality to our years – and years to our lives.

39

That's a fact, confirmed by a recently reported study by the Institute for Aerobics Research and the Cooper Clinic, in Dallas, Texas. The study, which followed more than 13,000 men and women for an average of eight years, correlated fitness (measured by performance in treadmill tests) to death rates. Participants were divided into five groups, from the least fit (sedentary) to most fit.

The good news for anyone just starting to exercise: the greatest drop in the death rates from one group to the next occurred among the group that was just one step above the sedentary group. Women and men who'd taken up regular, moderate exercise showed the most dramatic gain in health benefits, especially in lower rates of heart disease and cancer – proof that just breaking out of those old sit-on-your-bum habits can make a big difference.

Death rates continued to drop among the fitter groups (although less dramatically), indicating that the fit and the fittest do have something further to gain for their efforts.

Now here's a look at some of the ways aerobic exercise like cycling works in favour of your body.

FOR A HEALTHIER HEART

It's never too soon to start doing your heart a favour.

Because men are so much more frequently the victims of heart attack in their middle-aged years, women may be lulled into thinking we have nothing to worry about.

That's how it seems in our early adult years when estrogen works in our defence to keep blood cholesterol levels low. But time starts to catch up with us, warns Elaine Eaker, ScD, of the National Heart, Lung and Blood Institute in Bethesda, Maryland. 'From the age of 35 to 50 there's a very steady, dramatic increase in cholesterol level prior to menopause,' says Doctor Eaker. 'At about the age of 50 a woman's cholesterol level typically *surpasses* the level in men and averages about 260 (in the United States). That is well into the high-risk category.

'Women should start exercising prior to menopause in order to beat that high-risk curve, to keep down that steep rise in cholesterol as they age,' urges Doctor Eaker. They should consider their intake of saturated fats and dietary cholesterol. *Saturated fats* (found mainly in animal products like fatty meats, as well as many dairy items) raise one's cholesterol level more than anything else in the diet.

And women should have their total cholesterol level checked. A level below 200 (mg/dl) is desirable; 200–239 is considered borderline-high; and 240 and above is considered high. If your level is in the desirable range, you want to know how to keep it there. If you test above 200, you can do something about it, as you'll see here. (You should also talk to your doctor, who may recommend a more complete cholesterol test showing the ratio of total and HDL cholesterol.)

You've heard plenty about that disagreeable sludge called cholesterol and how it can build up in the main arteries of the heart and its network of lesser, connecting arteries – a condition called *arteriosclerosis*. Eventually it may cause clogging. That's why people with high levels of cholesterol in the blood have a greater chance of

40

developing coronary disease than those whose cholesterol levels are lower. You may have been trying to cut down on cholesterol and saturated fat in your diet, which is all to the good.

What you ought to know is that the body fights its own 'street war' against cholesterol. Here's how exercise can help in that fight.

What happens to fat from the food we eat – say, an ice cream cone or some chips? After being broken down into its component *lipids* by the small intestine, the fat from food is absorbed into *lymph*, the watery fluid flowing between the cells of the intestine. The fat-laden lymph moves through tiny lymph vessels and is finally discharged into the bloodstream. The insoluble fat can travel in the watery lymph and blood because the lipids have been combined with protein into *lipoprotein* particles, which form a suspension in water.

At their destinations, these lipoprotein particles are broken down by enzymes. Some of the lipids are stored in body cells as fat. The leftover lipids are recombined into smaller lipoprotein particles containing cholesterol and other lipids.

These smaller lipoprotein particles vary in size and weight, and scientists classify them accordingly. There are lightweight ones, called *LDL cholesterol*, which tend to stick to the walls of the arteries like snow on a city street. A few snowflakes don't make much difference, but if they continue to accumulate, the street (artery) eventually could become impassable. If a clogged artery impedes the flow of blood, that may cause a heart attack.

In the healthy body, before that can happen, heavier lipoprotein particles, called *HDL cholesterol*, plough their way through, taking some of the LDL 'flakes' with them. If there are enough HDL particles, they can make the 'streets' more passable, maybe even clear them.

The more HDL you have, compared to LDL, the better.

Here's where exercise comes in. While all this is going on, regular exercise does two things: it cuts down the amount of total cholesterol and increases the percentage of the beneficial HDL. Just how exercise does this is still debated. Some studies indicate a relationship to weight loss, which often occurs when sedentary people become more active.

How much exercise is required? And how strenuous should it be? Researchers come into conflict here, and there is much still to be learned. If you're not already fit from other sports, it's safe to say riding three times a week for a half-hour to an hour at a time can prove beneficial. The important thing is to increase your level of activity over what you were doing before. With a moderate pace you are more likely to enjoy cycling and stick with it than if you try to become Wonder Woman overnight. (If you have been sedentary, remember to get your doctor's okay.)

If you are already athletic, or as you gradually get into shape, you may want to do more. We'll cover more ambitious approaches to training in later chapters.

Meanwhile, as Doctor Eaker notes, give your eating habits a quick review. Could you improve them by:

- Cutting down on butter fat?

- Making unsaturated oils your choice for cooking and salad oil? These include the *polyunsaturated* oils like safflower, sunflower, corn, soyabean, and sesame oils; and *monounsaturated* oils like olive, peanut, and canola (rapeseed) oil. For years nutritionists have urged us to replace saturated fats in our diets with polyunsaturates. Now health experts are telling us that olive oil and other monounsaturates are even more beneficial because they actually increase your level of 'good' HDL cholesterol.
- Watching out for 'tropical' oils in commercial baked goods? Coconut oil, palm kernel oil, and palm oil are highly saturated. Learn to read the labels and avoid foods with these ingredients.
- Avoiding *hydrogenated* oils when you have a choice? Some of the unsaturated fats in (normally beneficial) vegetable oils are made more saturated by the process of hydrogenation to give a firmer texture and lengthen the product's shelf life. (Stick margarines are more hydrogenated than tub margarines, for example.) Labelling on commercial food products will tell you if they contain hydrogenated vegetable oils.
- Cutting back on red meat and eating more fish and poultry? The latter is best eaten skinless, since most of the fat in chicken, turkey and other fowl is in the skin.
- Using low-fat preparation methods? Thumbs down to deep-fat frying. Thumbs up to roasting, baking, broiling, and simmering meat, poultry or fish. Stir frying uses very little fat and lets you play up the vegetables. De-fatting meat and poultry juices and liquids left from stewing is easy if you chill them in the freezer until fat becomes solid, then spoon it off.
- Adding more whole grains, rice, and dried peas and beans to your menus? These can replace meat as a source of protein in some meals and at lower cost. These foods can be made quite tasty and give variety to your menus. If you've little experience, treat yourself to a good vegetarian cookbook.
- Eating more fresh fruits and green and yellow vegetables?
- Upping fibre intake with bran? Soluble fibre appears to be the cholesterol-lowering agent in oat bran. (A good-for-you, inexpensive source: oatmeal.) New studies say rice bran has similar benefits.

The accompanying chart shows examples of substitutions one could make gradually and stick with, not only for a healthier heart but for all-round better health. There's no calorie-counting involved here, and these changes could easily be incorporated into meals for an entire family, as they are recommended for anyone over age two. If, like many families, yours has certain favourite menus you serve again and again, take a particularly close look at modifying them to increase nutrition without sacrificing taste; or select several new good-for-you meals to make standards. Remember, if you don't want to give up something – like your favourite cheeses – you could choose to cut down on portion size.

Further measures beyond increasing activity levels and making sensible modifications in diet are beyond the scope of this book. Currently controversy is on the rise

What to Eat?
Tips for lowering dietary cholesterol and saturated fat

If you need to make changes in eating habits, do so gradually. Try one or two of the following tips at a time and get used to them. And talk it over with your health care provider or a nutritionist before you start. You may already be eating a fairly wholesome diet. Radical and unnecessary dieting can be harmful.

Eat this	instead of this
Olive, safflower or sunflower oil or other unsaturated oils	Hard shortening, lard or bacon grease
Tub margarine	Butter or stick margarine
Two egg whites or egg substitute	A whole egg
Fish, shellfish, skinless poultry, or lean cuts of meat; tofu (soyabean curd) and dried beans for vegetable protein	Fatty cuts of beef, lamb, pork
Turkey breast, tuna packed in water, natural unhydrogenated peanut butter	Luncheon meats
Low-fat and semi-skimmed cheeses	Cheeses containing more than 2–6 grammes of fat per ounce
Skimmed or 1 per cent milk	2 per cent or whole milk, non-dairy creamers
Fruit ices, sorbets, low-fat frozen yoghurt	Ice cream, especially the richest speciality ice creams
Mock sour cream made from blenderised low-fat cottage cheese and lemon juice	Sour cream or imitation sour cream
Raisin, whole wheat, or pumpernickle bagels	Doughnuts or pastries
Gingersnaps, wheatmeal biscuits or fig bars (made with corn, sunflower or safflower oil)	Chocolate chip and other high-fat biscuits
Low-fat whole grain crackers, soda crackers or bread sticks	High-fat crackers (including unsalted versions)
Unbuttered popcorn or pretzels	Commercial crisps and cheese puffs

regarding cholesterol-lowering medications and their long-term effects. And medical experts point out that, to date, women and the elderly have received little study regarding the role of blood cholesterol in causing heart attack. As researchers turn their attention to these population groups, we'll be able to know more. In the meantime, heart-healthy exercise and good nutrition are wise prevention.

More information should be available from your local heart association.

TAKING THE PRESSURE OFF

Another bonus of regular exercise is the role it appears to play in helping to prevent high blood pressure (*hypertension*) and even to lower blood pressure that is above normal healthy levels. Often undiagnosed and so called 'the silent killer', high blood pressure can contribute to heart disease or cause stroke or kidney failure.

The average blood pressure of a healthy adult is about 120/80 mm Hg. Here's what those numbers mean and a simple trick for remembering. When your heart beats, blood *surges* from the heart, and pressure in the arteries rises. This is the *systolic* pressure, the first number in the fraction (remember, 'surge' and 'systolic'). Between beats the heart rests, no blood is pumped, and pressure *decreases*. This is the second number, the *diastolic* pressure. Both pressures are measured in millimetres (mm) of mercury (Hg). Keep in mind, 120/80 is the average for a range of healthy blood pressures, so if you have a question about yours, talk it over with your doctor.

Considerably more study is required for scientists to completely understand hypertension, as there are various types and varying degrees. Research on the effect of regular exercise on high blood pressure remains controversial, although a number of studies have shown beneficial effects. Other research indicates that non-exercisers have a markedly greater risk of developing high blood pressure than women and men who are active.

If your blood pressure has begun to creep up, discuss the options with your doctor. If you've been inactive, cutting down on salt in your diet and beginning a regular programme of exercise might be enough therapy to avoid taking medication. If medication is recommended immediately, discuss also the advisability of exercise. There is considerable evidence that forty minutes to one hour of gentle to moderate cycling, three times a week could be helpful.

Just what brings about improvement is still under debate. It may be the effect of exercise *per se*, or again it may partly be due to weight loss which accompanies the exercise.

PROTECTION AGAINST CANCER?

In 1985 the American Cancer Society began recommending exercise to protect against cancer. Again, much more medical sleuthing needs to be done before anyone can explain the apparent relationship in numerous studies between lower cancer rates and higher levels of exercise.

Particularly pertinent to women is one study, first reported in 1985, that surveyed over 5,000 female college alumnae, graduated between the years 1921–1981; ages ranged from 21 to 80. Women who were active in sports or other regular athletic pursuits in college had markedly lower incidence of breast or reproductive-organ cancer than the alumnae who had not been athletic in college. Although family histories of cancer for the two groups were statistically similar, the former non-athletes had nearly twice the risk of breast cancer and 2½ times the risk of cancer of the reproductive system, compared to the former athletes.

What could explain it? Of the former college athletes, 73.5 per cent were still exercising regularly at the time of the survey, compared to 57 per cent of the former non-athletes. And 82.4 per cent of the college athletes had taken part in sports in high school or earlier, compared to only 24.9 per cent of the non-athletes.

How does long-term participation in athletics affect a woman's body? The researchers suggest a number of possible effects. At all ages in the study, the athlete group had a lower percentage of body fat and a higher percentage of lean muscle mass, compared to the non-athlete group. Possibly related was a later onset of menstruation and earlier onset of menopause in the athlete group; both phenomena would suggest lower levels of estrogen, which may in turn be related to the lower cancer rate. Or might it be due, the researchers query, to better eating habits or otherwise healthier lifestyle of the athletes?

Obviously this pioneer study, probably the first to examine the risk of cancer in relationship to physical activity in women, raises many questions for further research. Its authors, Rose Frisch, PhD and colleagues (at Harvard), sum up, 'Long-term athletic training establishes a lifestyle that somehow lowers the risk of breast cancer and cancers of the reproductive system.'

This work deserves follow-up, as do the even more recent findings of the Institute for Aerobics Research/Cooper Clinic study (described above) which demonstrated a relationship between better fitness and a lower death rate from cancer.

It would be foolish to imply that athletic people don't get cancer. Sometimes they do. In those cases, is cycling or other regular exercise good therapy during recovery? Can cycling help to keep cancer in remission? Does it somehow help the body to marshall its own defences? Or aid the spirit to rally a greater will to live? Certainly I don't know the answer to that.

In Carlyn Hove Roedell's life, however, cycling has made a difference. Carlyn, 37, a teacher in Seahurst, Washington, writes:

'My husband had cancer in 1985, a year after our 1,000-mile bike tour in France. His ability to ride was greatly diminished, as was his entire being.

Although I wasn't sure whether I could do it, I completed a ride for the American Cancer Society, a 90-mile day up a mountain pass by Mount St Helens. It happened I won a prize on the ride (not for finishing first!) which was a Klein custom bicycle frame.

I gave it to my husband as a get-well present. It worked! He's back riding, stronger than ever. He went to the Hel'en Back tour last year with me for the American Cancer Society. We had a great time. It makes one love biking and life all the more!'

DODGING DIABETES

That same pioneer study by Harvard researchers which discovered lower cancer rates among college-athlete alumnae also found startling news about diabetes. They discovered the incidence of diabetes among former college athletes was much lower than that of their non-athletic classmates.

To take into account the effect of college athletics, the researchers included all cases of diabetes beginning at the age of 20 and older. They found that '0.5 per cent of the former college athletes had diabetes compared to 1.2 per cent of the non-athletes.' This marked difference occurred despite minimal differences in family histories of the disease.

As these researchers remind us, the benefits of regular exercise (along with proper diet) in managing non-insulin-dependent diabetes have already been well demonstrated. Mild or moderate exercise assists in burning excess calories which would otherwise cause blood sugars to rise above normal levels. And some data indicate that exercise may help the insulin-dependent diabetic.

As one enthusiastic cyclist/diabetic, Charlotte Versagi, notes,

> With diabetes it is extremely important to maintain an even, consistent level of exercise. Cycling allows for the sustained kind of exertion that is best for the disorder. And I can do it nine months out of the year! It is easy to monitor by my physical responses the food intake I need, and people are usually nearby in case I should get into blood-sugar trouble. But that hasn't happened yet.

Charlotte, 41, is an adult-onset, non-insulin-dependent diabetic who believes that 'there really isn't a better way to see the country, meet people, and be kind to your body while having a wonderful workout'.

She did just that on a solo tour across her state, Michigan, cycling about 60 to 70 miles a day and camping at night. She'd start each day with a good breakfast – bread, fruit, muesli and juice – and then ride most of the day except for snack breaks. About 3.00 or 4.00 pm, just before arriving at her campsite, she'd stop for a big meal. 'I'd be in camp by five or six, shower, set up camp, and read or talk to folks until around nine or ten and then just *die*!'

She adds,

> People were, without exception, kind and curious and helpful. Once during a horrible rain storm in the middle of a country road, a big bearded guy (whom I called St Joseph) stopped in his pickup truck and lifted my bike and all its packs into the back of the truck and invited me, dripping wet, to get into the cab. There he turned on the heat to try to dry me off. He drove me the last 10 miles to my campsite.

Obviously, Charlotte cycles a great deal more than absolutely required to control her diabetes. So others shouldn't let that put them off. Six miles a day, as well as sixty, could make a difference.

FREEDOM FROM SMOKING

Studies like that of Frisch and her colleagues may raise as many questions as they answer. But there's little doubt about another issue – the link between smoking and, one, heart disease; two, lung cancer (now the biggest cancer killer among American women); three, emphysema; four, complications during pregnancy (such as premature delivery and a higher percentage of miscarriages and stillborn babies); five, high blood pressure; and six, circulatory problems that complicate diabetes. If you smoke now, you already know that you could do your health the greatest favour by quitting.

Smoking is a physical, psychological, and even social dependency. Not recognising these three faces of the dependency often makes quitting more difficult. It's crucial to find coping behaviours to address these three types of needs.

One such behaviour could be taking up cycling or getting back into it. '[On the *physical* level] exercise is one of your greatest allies in fighting off cravings,' says the American Lung Association (ALA) in its self-help programme manual, *Freedom From Smoking in 20 Days*. Give yourself a *psychological* boost: look on cycling as a positive habit to replace a bad one and as a reward you will have earned by quitting. If you share cycling with friends or find new ones who enjoy it, it becomes a *social* coping technique – something to do besides sitting together over coffee and a cigarette. And there's never a worry about what to do with your hands.

John Williams, speaking for the ALA, suggests:

Giving up cigarettes is plenty stressful. Regular exercise like cycling can help reduce overall tension. When really bad jitters strike, perhaps you can escape for a short ride.

People often smoke from boredom. Find something to do if you have time on your hands. Go for a bike ride, or call up a friend and plan one for later. Read another chapter in this book. Lube your chain. Do something to interrupt that smoking urge.

Weight gain is often a worry after kicking the habit, and cycling can help to prevent it.

Once you're caught up in the pleasure of it, cycling does become a reward in itself. After quitting smoking, one couple took off for a two-week holiday on their new bikes to ride in the hills and along the coast in California. Despite 'sore back ends' they discovered 'how much fun cycling can be'. Another former smoker remarks, 'As I've become fitter, the urge to smoke has vanished. Besides, I need all my vital capacity!'

It's almost never too late to quit and benefit from it. Clarissa Gerhardt and her husband began their retirement years by giving up smoking. She was 43; he was 64. They bought new touring bikes and spent four months in Florida, riding every day. Back home in Ohio with the warm weather, they set off to see their state . . . on their bikes. Enjoyable in itself, the tour was especially wonderful 'because of our pleasure in knowing we'd recaptured our health,' she exults. 'We built up our tired bodies so we could cycle those back roads that most people our age would see only from their camper vehicles.'

You can quit smoking, and you don't have to do it alone. The Health Educational Council offers three very helpful booklets: *Women's Health and Smoking, How to Stop Smoking for You and Your Baby* and on the dangers of passive smoking, *Breathing*

47

Other People's Smoke. In the US, your local ALA chapter offers copies of *Freedom From Smoking in 20 Days* as well as a ten-day programme book for pregnant women entitled, *Freedom From Smoking for You and Your Baby.*

If you've tried before and failed, don't be afraid to try again. Often it takes a third or fourth attempt to quit and *stay* quit.

EASING ARTHRITIS

If you don't use it, you lose it, says the Arthritis Foundation. Accordingly, the big movement in treatment of arthritis is a comprehensive approach including joint protection, taking medication as prescribed, and exercise or physical therapy.

'We recommend that everyone get involved in recreational exercise,' says Annette Gomez of Philadelphia, speaking for the Foundation, 'though we don't mean to suggest that it should replace prescribed physical therapy. But exercise is a good supplement to therapy.'

The Arthritis Foundation recommends exercise that promotes stretching (to increase range of motion), muscle strengthening, and endurance. In fact, if you have arthritis and your own doctor discourages exercise as treatment, the Foundation suggests you seek a second opinion. As their booklet *Exercise and Your Arthritis* notes, 'If you have already lost the function of some joints, a regular exercise programme can help prevent further loss. It may also help you to regain function.'

Cycling, as Iva Oshawnesy of Albuquerque, New Mexico, has discovered, can work wonders.

Life begins at 50!

In August 1983 at age 47, I developed arthritis from a rubella vaccination. Anger and depression were consuming my energy the following June, when I met a man who told me his arthritis decreased after he started cycling regularly.

The very next week I bought a heavy six-speed bike and started learning to ride. No one can imagine how little I knew about cycling, but I blundered along and by August of that year I was able to backpack!

The following summer after reading up and asking advice from a cycling female co-worker, I bought a Bridgestone 700. I had a lot to learn about handling this new bike, but I wasn't going to let that stop me. Six weeks later, without any idea what I was doing, I signed up to ride 200 miles in three days. It was really too much, but pride kept me going through those 200 miles.

A year later, in 1986, I celebrated being 50 by going on the same 200-mile ride and enjoying it. A year of cycling regularly had strengthened my legs, built up my endurance, and let me surround myself with healthy, happy, active friends.

In 1987 I rode the Bridgestone more than 5,000 miles. Now I have a new custom bike and am more healthy mentally and physically than at any other time in my life.

So You Want to Buy a Bike?

6

If you're planning to start out fresh with a new bike, you have the opportunity to buy just the one to meet your needs – to suit your style of riding and to fit your particular proportions which, since you are a woman, may be different from those of a man.

But you need to be a canny consumer. Many women tell me they were quite naïve when they bought their first adult bike. So was I. In this chapter you'll learn how to avoid the mistakes we made and buy the bike you really want – the first time around. After all, bicycles can be as different from one another as a jeep is from a Jaguar. And you wouldn't flip a coin over *that* decision. Nor would you take somebody else's advice without lots of thought. Even if you buy a used bicycle, it pays to be well-informed.

In this chapter you'll find the essential information in terms easy to understand. Bike parts you might be unfamiliar with are identified in figures 1, 2, 3 and 10. (More advanced riders, if you skim over what you already know, you'll also glean tips helpful to you.) Furthermore, though we'll look at what's available in the marketplace, the market continues to change. So we'll also talk about fundamental needs and how to meet them. That basic understanding will never go out of style.

Here are the questions I encourage everyone to think about before buying.

1 WHAT KIND OF A BIKE SHOULD I BUY?

There's a huge range of bicycle types available in today's marketplace. To make the best choice, first decide what kind of riding you want to do:

- Which of the cycling goals in chapter 2 most appeals to you?
- Where's the best riding in your area? Have you miles of paved country lanes or other scenic roads with little traffic? Is there a network of off-road paths or wilderness trails beckoning to be explored?

With your answers in mind, find the bike that best fits them among the categories that follow. You'll see that some bikes are highly versatile. Others are exactly right for one particular purpose, which is why many avid cyclists own more than one bicycle.

Here's a look at six types of bikes and what each can do. By the way, note they all have one thing in common: all are *multigeared derailleur* bicycles. (For all practical purposes this means a bike which has ten speeds or more. Shifting is accomplished by a *derailleur*; if you watch you can see it pick up the chain and drop it on a different cog to change gears.) Unless you live in Flatsbury with no hills to climb, you're better off with a derailleur bike than with a three-speed or single-speed.

Sport Touring Bike

This Jill-of-all-trades is the most popular drop handlebar/derailleur bike, primarily because it's so versatile. It's frequently called a ten-speed, although it often has twelve or fourteen speeds these days, thanks to a freewheel with six or seven sprockets instead of five.

What distinguishes a sport touring bike? This is a road bike which handles corners adequately and can be used for pleasure and fitness riding or, if you add a rack, light touring (carrying clothes etc., but not camping gear). This bike could be very serviceable for a beginning triathlete or time trialist, since neither type of racing usually involves much cornering.

You'll see an almost limitless range of prices with quality varying accordingly.

Expect to find a head angle of about 73 to 74 degrees on a sport tourer with standard size (27-inch or 700C) wheels.

Loaded Touring Bike

Are you looking for a beast of burden for a long bicycle camping trip? This is the bike designed for stability when carrying over 20 to 25 pounds of your gear. You may not see much difference between this bike and its cousin, the sport tourer, but you'll feel it on a test ride. The loaded touring bike has a longer *wheelbase* (distance between the centre of the front axle and the rear axle), assuring a smoother, more comfortable ride for long days in the saddle. The shallower head angle (about 71 to 72 degrees on a bike with standard size wheels), also contributes to the comfort.

Desirable features on a loaded touring bike include *cantilever* brakes for extra stopping power and a triple *chainwheel*, or *chainring*. That third, small chainring adds extra-low gears for climbing hills when loaded down with heavy bike bags. This extra-low gearing would be appreciated by many women on hills, even if you're not carrying a load.

On these bikes you'll find eyelets for mounting racks and possibly the racks themselves. These bikes will probably have mountings (called *braze-ons*) for water bottle cages and may also be sensibly equipped with *mudguards*, or fenders. (Or you can add mudguards yourself so on a rainy day you don't get soaked and muddied by wet spray from the wheels.)

(For more on bikes for touring, see chapter 23, Planning Your Own Tour.)

Racing Bike

These bikes are not for beginners but for experienced cyclists who want a little more speed in their lives. Some of the best bikes in this category sell for well over £600 ($1,000) but for considerably less you can get a bike that lets you graduate from recreational riding to competition if you should ever want to.

Typically, these bikes offer great manoeuvrability and tighter cornering than touring or sport touring bikes, and narrower-range gearing. In other words, a racing bike will be geared higher (for speed) and won't have the lower range of gears needed for hills by the average rider.

Expect to find a head tube angle of about 74 to 75 degrees on a racing bike with standard size wheels.

The less expensive racers are usually equipped with conventional tyres, known as *clinchers* because they have a wire bead that 'clinches' the tyre to the rim. These tyres are narrow to minimise rolling resistance. They're called *high-pressure clinchers*, as they take more air pressure (usually between 100 to 130 psi, or pounds per square inch) than most clinchers, again reducing rolling resistance. If you do buy a racer with clinchers, keep your options open by selecting 700C rims (instead of 27-inch rims). Then, if later you want to buy an extra set of rims with lightweight, *tubular* racing tyres (which always come in 700C), they'll be interchangeable.

Mountain/All-Terrain Bike (MTB or ATB)

In recent years these have been hot news in bikeland. Want to get away from it all? This fat-tyred, off-road bike with flat or upswept handlebars was originally designed for rock-studded mountain descents and trail climbing. Is there a stream in your path? A log? You ride through it or over it. Okay, there's some technique involved, but you can learn it. (Chapter 22, Mountain Biking, will help you.) If you're the go-for-it type who likes the woods, this could be for you.

You can also use MTBs in a flatter, less spine-tingling environment – on dirt or gravel roads, country lanes or in town. You can take one anywhere you'd take a road bike. In fact, if you have to thread your way through broken glass and rough pavement, these knobby tyres may be just what you're looking for. Ditto the handlebars: many women who don't like drop bars on a road bike prefer this more upright position for seeing traffic and greater back comfort. For this reason, more and more mountain bikes are coming on the market in 16-inch or smaller frame sizes.

A true mountain bike will have a triple chainring, wide-range gearing, and a quick-release seatpost (to raise the saddle for off-road climbs and lower it for descents). This bike will have a chrome-molybdenum, manganese-molybdenum, or aluminium frame; aluminium-alloy ballooner rims and other alloy components; and of course fat (1.5-inch or wider) tyres. Wheels are usually 26 inches in diameter. Heavier than a road bike because it's built to take abuse, a mountain bike will weigh 28 to 30 pounds; some higher priced models are a few pounds shy of that.

Tell the salesperson what sort of off-road riding you intend to do (mild and mellow, or wild and wacky) and ask for a bike with appropriate handling characteristics.

If you plan to ride your MTB on road, be aware that the more upright seating position and the wide, relatively low-pressure tyres will make for a slower pace than you'd have with a road bike. If you plan to ride mostly on the road, you should look not just at MTBs, but at city bikes and hybrids.

City Bike

These bikes were born as cyclists discovered how great an MTB can be for city riding – for cruising through potholes without damaging the wheel rims and, with that upright position, keeping an eye on traffic. So mountain bikes were modified for urban use and, *voila!* – city bikes. Generally they have two chainrings instead of three (thus they lack that low, low gearing); and they may have overall higher gearing than mountain bikes since you can handle a higher gear on the road. You'll find street treads on the ballooner tyres, which may be a little skinnier than on an MTB. Handlebars are likely to rise higher for greater comfort.

Despite its monicker, you don't have to limit your city bike to pavement. How nimble it is off-road depends on the type of tyres and whether you go with a double or triple chainwheel. If you intend to keep your city bike on the road, mudguards and a *chainguard* (to keep chain grease off clothing) are good features to have, especially if you commute on it in work attire.

For city use you might also consider folding bikes, which (naturally) fold up for carrying on a bus or the underground. Some can even be slid under an airline seat.

Hybrid Bike

Ever wish you could cross a road bike with a mountain bike to get the best of both? Meet the hybrid bike. This bike is so new it had barely been invented when I started writing this book. It still eludes definition and defies illustration: it could have flat or dropped handlebars; 26-inch wheels or 700C.

But you can count on lighter tubing and higher pressure tyres than those on a mountain bike; and the frame resembles a road bike's, to allow for an aerodynamic position and livelier, faster performance on the road than with a mountain bike.

This is a real do-anything bike. A hybrid that has flat bars and positions the rider fairly upright would be an excellent beginner's bike. With its triple chainring and wide-range gearing – plus its eyelets for mounting racks – a hybrid could be the ideal vehicle for bicycle touring.

Off-road, some hybrids are more aggressive than others. All can handle packed dirt trails, gravel roads, and modest climbs to let you keep going where the pavement stops. Some are made for wilder antics. Discuss your intentions with the sales-person.

Expect sizing to run more like that of a mountain bike since a hybrid will have a higher bottom bracket than a road bike.

Even this minor treatise on bike types doesn't cover everything on the market. I haven't talked about bikes for track racing or about tandems, for example, as these more specialised bicycles are not usually a first-bike purchase. Tandems are discussed in chapter 18, Cycling with the Family.

2 HOW MUCH SHOULD I SPEND?

There is no single 'right price' to pay for a bike. As you mull over the possibilities, keep an open mind about cost and look for quality. In this chapter you'll learn how. Just how far adult bikes have come since the toys we rode as kids may come as a shock. I mean, we're talking aircraft technology and space age materials. The very best bikes (costing thousands of dollars) are on the cutting edge with this sort of thing, but there's a trickle-down effect that benefits the low end of the good-quality bicycle market. Even these will be an investment for most of us. But a good bike will be more pleasurable to ride, lighter in weight, and in the long run will be easier to keep in good repair than a bargain-basement cheapie.

3 WHERE SHOULD I BUY MY BIKE?

At a bike shop. There you are more likely to find knowledgeable salespeople to answer your questions, and the kind of personalised service to help you keep your bike in good repair and get the most out of riding it. Prices are usually lower at a department store or (in the UK) at a large auto chain store, but you won't find the service there. Furthermore, bike shops generally offer bikes of superior quality and a far wider range of quality levels. You also have a better chance of being able to test-ride a bicycle from a bike shop.

First-time buyers are often intimidated by bike dealers and their technical jargon. This guide should ease you over some of that self-consciousness. Take it with you if you like. You might also invite along a well-informed friend, but make sure *you're* convinced your selection is right for you in fit and features before you buy.

And don't feel embarrassed if you don't know everything – many men don't either! If a dealer is impatient or unhelpful, go elsewhere. You should be able to ask questions and get answers you can understand. Bike shopping is a learning process. Don't let anybody rush you.

Should you find little selection locally, it could be worthwhile to go to a city with a number of shops. In the UK, for example, it's not unusual for cyclists to travel some distance to London if they have special requirements.

In any case, it's wise to shop around. There are many good bicycle brands, but some may offer a greater variety of models in your frame size or the bike type you prefer. You may find the same bike at a lower price in another shop or a dealer willing to throw in a woman's saddle or other accessories to make the sale. Likewise, once you find a frame that fits, don't be shy about asking to change the saddle, toeclips, tyres, or even gearing. Do bear in mind that the profit margin on bike sales is often quite low, even in bike shops. Some changes may justify a nominal charge.

By the way, many US and some Canadian bike shops have a fitting aid called a Fit Kit, designed by American cycling coach Bill Farrell. Where the service is offered, you'd probably benefit from it, right down to placement of shoe cleats, if you use them.

Anatomy of a smart buy: Derailleur bicycle
Fig. 2

You're entering a new world of brand names, not just in bicycles, but in tubing and components that are added to the frame. Here you'll find some of the more important names plus guidelines to choosing a sport touring bike. Much of this will be helpful in any bike purchase.

Weight. With bicycles the more you pay, the less weight you get. Strong, lightweight metal alloys and other materials may cost more than steel and require more time-consuming manufacturing processes. A lighter bike is the object if you have hills to climb. For quick acceleration lighter wheels are important; if you ride with a group, you don't want to always be playing catch-up.

How light a bike you need will depend on your goals and the type of bike. Maximum weight should be 28 pounds or less.

Tubing. Tubing is so important it has recognisable brand names which you'll see on the decals on some better bikes. High carbon steel tubing is the minimum to settle for. Don't be confused by 'high tensile', a buzz-word for less desirable low carbon steel. Better than high

carbon steel is alloy steel, with its higher strength-to-weight ratio. The lightest and strongest of these alloys are manganese-molybdenum (such as Reynolds 531) and chrome-molybdenum (or chrome-moly, found in seamless tubing bearing names like Columbus, Tange Prestige, True Temper, and Ishiwata.)

The term 'butted' refers to tubing with thinner walls in the centre of the tube than at the ends where tubes are joined; this puts strength where it's most needed, saves weight, and absorbs more road shock. The term has been abused in advertising so ask for details when considering a frame that is 'butted', 'double-butted', 'quadruple-butted', etc.

Other frame materials in high performance bicycles include aluminium and carbon fibre; the former is more popularly priced.

Wheels. Aluminium alloy wheels are a must for lightness and far better braking in rainy conditions. A bike of acceptable quality will have a quick-release on the front wheel (permitting wheel change without tools). Quick-release on both wheels is a step up. If you can afford it, buy a bicycle with this feature.

Tyres. Clinchers are standard. 'High pressure' tyres (rated at 90 psi or higher) have less rolling resistance and so are preferable to tyres with lower ratings.

Gearing. A range of figures, measured in inches, will tell you how well the bike will handle different types of terrain. Most recreational riders need wide-range gearing. Indexed, or 'click', shifting makes for smoother, easier shifting of derailleur gears. Brand name systems with click shifting include: Shimano SIS Hyperglide, SunTour AccuShift Plus, Campagnolo Syncro, and Sachs/Huret ARIS. Mavic is expected to be coming out with one.

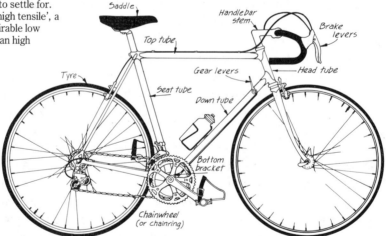

Saddle — Handlebar stem — Brake levers — Top tube — Head tube — Gear levers — Tyre — Seat tube — Down tube — Bottom bracket — Chainwheel (or chainring)

Shifters or gear levers. Many new riders fear reaching to operate levers mounted on the downtube. So the least expensive bikes come with levers on the stem. More experienced cyclists generally prefer downtube or bar-end shifters; these are a sign of a better bicycle. If considering stem shifters, do test-ride standing up to make sure your knees don't knock the levers when you get out of the saddle.

Brakes. Brake extension levers (so-called 'safety levers' located just under the top part of dropped bars) signify the least expensive sport touring bike. Their failing is that they come out of adjustment easily and are unreliable. Ask to have them removed if you buy one of these bikes – and use the regular brakes shown here.

Crankset. Transmits power to the rear wheel. The cranks and bottom bracket spindle assembly should be aluminium alloy for light weight and durability. Alloy chainwheels will be lighter than steel, but steel chainwheels aren't a great sin.

Saddle. Women's sit-bones are about 1 inch farther apart than men's. Ask about an anatomic saddle.

Anatomy of a smart buy: Mountain bike
Fig. 3

Here's what to look for in an all-purpose, or 'sport' mountain bike, to give you both on- and off-road capabilities. Generally, these bikes will scramble up a hilly trail much more nimbly than popularly priced mountain bikes of a few years ago. You could even enter races on one of these, and maybe you will.

Frame size. Corresponds with seat tube length. An MTB frame should be *at least* 2 inches smaller than your proper road bike size. Why? The bottom bracket is an inch or 2 higher to clear obstacles when riding. Ideally, for off-road use, the frame should be 3 or 4 inches smaller than your road bike so that you don't hit the top tube if you hop off the pedals quickly to steady yourself. If you can't find this sort of stand-over height in a diamond frame MTB, consider a step-through frame. For good fit don't forget a comfortable reach to the handlebars.

Weight. A mountain bike will outweigh a road bike of comparable quality because of larger diameter tubing, more durable components, and wider, bigger tyres. Look for one weighing 30 pounds or less.

Tubing. For a relatively light but strong frame, select an aluminium frame or look for steel tubing of chrome-molybdenum or manganese-molybdenum.

Reinforcing collar. Without this, sliding the saddle up and down repeatedly could fatigue the seat tube. A reinforcing collar strengthens the seat tube and is a sign of quality.

Brakes. A recent development for MTBs is the U-shaped brake for the rear wheel, mounted near the chainstays. But if you're going to play in the mud, don't buy a U-brake; it's vulnerable to mud buildup and thus damage. Cantilever and roller cam brakes are options instead.

Handlebars. For riding off-road, buy flat bars. For street-use, upright bars are fine and they allow some adjustment in the reach. Bike shop personnel can advise.

Seatpost quick-release. Lets you lower the saddle for challenging descents, raise it to normal height for other riding. Since the frame is smaller than a comparable road bike's, the extra-long seatpost gives you optimum seat height. Some mountain bikes come with a Hite-Rite quick adjust seat locator, handy because it lets you change seat height without dismounting.

Thumb shifters. Let you keep hands on the bars when shifting.

Pedals. Ask whether pedals will accept toeclips and straps, desirable for off-road riding. Some cheaper pedals may not take them.

Chainstays. Other things being equal, bikes with shorter chainstays (17 inches or less) make climbing easier, especially when standing.

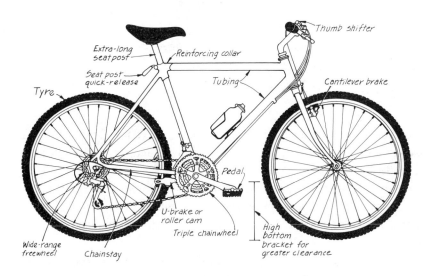

Wheels. Rims should be light-but-strong aluminium alloy. Quick-release hubs are convenient and considered safe for off-road use, assuming you know how to close them properly. (See chapter 17.)

Tyres. For all-purpose use, a combination tread is practical: it combines a continuous centre section with a surrounding knobby pattern for a smooth, quiet ride on tarmac and traction on the trail. For the maximum in off-road performance, get full knobbies. Compared to narrower ones, standard fat tyres (1.9- to 2-inch width) give a more sure-footed, forgiving ride on wet or soft surfaces.

Gearing. Indexed shifting is almost universal on rear derailleurs and available on some front derailleur systems. This latter is a nice feature, but if it's hard to come by, you can do without it. It does simplify shifting, especially with triple chainwheels. For any trail climbing you'll want the wide-range gearing of a triple.

55

4 DO I NEED A 'WOMAN'S BIKE'?

Just what a 'woman's bike' might be has changed radically in the last few years.

In the UK a 'gent's frame' still refers to a bicycle with a top tube running parallel to the ground, and a 'lady's frame' or a 'girl's bike' still means a bike with a lowered top tube to accommodate a skirt. There are two frame geometries which meet this need (see figures 4 and 5). Of these, the *mixte* (pronounced MIX-tee) frame is stronger and thus preferable.

Fig. 4
Step-through or 'ladies' frame

Fig. 5
Mixte frame: twin lateral tubes attached at the seat tube and running back to connect with the seatstays and chainstays make the mixte stronger than a step-through frame.

If you wish to cycle in a skirt, such a bicycle obviously serves a purpose for you. (And here's one instance where being tall can be a disadvantage, since these frames typically aren't made in large sizes.)

Otherwise, however, this sort of frame is no more suitable for a woman than it is for a man. Someone with stiff joints – male or female – might prefer mounting this type of frame, for example. So let's leave behind the gender association and call it a *step-through* frame.

For similar reasons let's kiss the term 'gent's frame' or 'man's frame' goodbye. It's commonly called a *diamond* frame because its main tubes, including the chainstays, make almost a diamond shape. In the US and Canada women have taken enthusiastically to the diamond frame, as it's structurally stronger than even the mixte. So it's more efficient, more responsive and fun to ride. Besides, it comes in a much greater range of quality levels than does a step-through frame. For top performance from a bicycle a diamond is a girl's best friend.

In the UK short and even average height women may have to search a bit to find a diamond frame in the small size they require, especially in a good quality bicycle. But the market is expanding in this area, and there are also custom builders whose services may be reasonably affordable.

Now, to speak the unspeakable: some women are afraid to try riding a diamond frame. Truth is, there's no reason to worry, if the bike fits you. This aspect of fit is called *stand-over height*. With your feet on the ground, if you can straddle the bicycle with an inch or two to spare between the top tube and your crotch, you aren't going to land on that top tube and see stars. Think about it: if that really was a danger, men with their extremely tender genitals would have stopped buying diamond frames long ago. Mountain bikes are a special case, however, since 3 to 4 inches of clearance are recommended. Some diamond frames in small, high quality MTBs are designed to allow that much clearance; otherwise, it may be necessary to settle for a step-through frame.

If you aren't as limber as you'd like, here's how to mount a diamond frame: before swinging your leg over the rear wheel and saddle, tilt the bike toward you. I mean *really* tilt it. This lowers the bike's effective height.

5 HOW CAN I FIND A BICYCLE TO FIT MY PROPORTIONS?

Ann Counts, 36, of Euless, Texas, found a bike that fits . . . the hard way:

> When I bought my first one, I knew nothing about bikes and depended on the salesperson. Thus I wound up with a bike that was never comfortable because it didn't fit. I had no clearance over the bar. Too-big brake levers made it tough for me to stop. My arms ached as the handlebars were much too wide, and I always hurt from having to reach too far.
>
> I had too much money in the bike to start over, so I slowly changed items, trying to make the bike more comfortable. I replaced the brake levers and handlebars, shortened the stem, and switched saddles three times. Even so, the bicycle wasn't as comfortable for my build, at five-one, as a bike can and should be.
>
> Ultimately I found a different, local bike shop. I made an effort to know the personnel. This shop gives fabulous service and honest answers to their customers. Following their advice, I went through a complete Fit Kit (see page 62) before buying a new bike this month which I am truly pleased with.

Although a bike shop is your best bet for well-informed sales help in buying a bike, as Jean Welch, 42, of Van Nuys, California, points out, you cannot simply throw yourself at the shop's mercy. 'I had to research bike fit for myself,' she says. 'Bike shops usually wanted to sell me whichever bicycle they had that came the closest.' Having done that research, adds Mary Davies, 27, of Vancouver, British Columbia, 'Ninety-nine percent of the time I found I knew more about fitting a bicycle than they did.'

What's the problem? Stand a woman and a man of the same height side by side, and the woman will usually have shorter arms and a shorter torso, longer legs, smaller hands and feet, narrower shoulders, and a wider pelvis. We certainly aren't built like men, but for a long time the bicycle industry ignored these differences.

Take women's often-shorter arms and torsos, for instance. This anatomical difference didn't matter so much with old-style 'sit-up-and-beg' bicycles—the kind with upright handlebars you still see ridden to market in Britain. But today's drop handlebar bicycles are another story. They come to recreational cycling from the traditionally male world of racing, where bending low over the bike minimises wind resistance and permits maximum speed.

A Bike That Fits: Some Solutions and Opinions

"Six years ago with the knee-pain I had from an ill-fitting bike, I never thought I could cycle cross-country. But after getting a custom bicycle, long rides on a comfortable, forgiving frame proved fun, relaxing, and didn't leave my body aching. So I joined a sea-to-sea trek for the American Lung Association—the most pleasurable, challenging, and rewarding thing I've ever done. I cycled 3397 miles without ever riding in the sag vehicle. At the thrilling conclusion, 197 of us rode in a double paceline with motorcycle police escort to the Atlantic City boardwalk. With this bike I had the trip of a lifetime!"

Flo Hendry, 36, Moraga, California

"I thought, at five-eleven, it was just my weird body that wouldn't reach those far-away handlebars. When I bought my bike, they measured nothing but crotch-clearance. Luckily a stem with a shorter extension fixed my problem."

Clarissa Gerhardt, 48, Ashtabula, Ohio

"A five-footer, I was riding a much-too-big 21-inch frame. No wonder my peak cycling experience was shopping for my new Terry bike. At first I found nothing smaller than a regular 18-inch until I hit a shop run by women. One, a statuesque five-two, let me try her custom Terry. She told me I'd say, "So this is what it's like!" And I did. I never knew it was like that for normal height people. That day I bought my bike, a production Terry they ordered."

Linda Fetter, 38, Atlanta, Georgia

"I have 3000 miles on my Terry. It has a proportional top tube, a full-size front wheel, and a 21-inch frame. It's a perfect fit for me at five-six."

Willa Friedman, Springfield, Virginia

"I think Terry bikes are ugly and over-priced. Besides, though five-two, I have a proportioned torso."

E.J. Winkler, 35, Bakersfield, California

Proper fit is more critical with these bikes, most of which even now are designed for male proportions. A bike that stretches a man out just far enough will often have too long a reach for a woman, although the frame is the right height for her. Even today some salespeople don't check upper body fit. So a customer unaware of her needs can end up with a bike that's too long in the top tube. The painful result is shoulder, neck and back strain, plus a bicycle that doesn't feel as much a part of you or handle as well as one that fits properly. (In extreme cases of poor fit, a bicycle can be really crash-prone.) Even step-through frames that are easy for a short woman to straddle are built for men's torso and leg proportions! Often the reach to the bars is to-o-o long.

Until recently the solutions were: one, retrofitting a different stem with a shorter extension to move the handlebars back toward the rider, but that means compromises in bikehandling. (Moving the saddle forward might seem a solution, but that puts our knees too far forward of the pedals as a rule, inviting knee pain.) Or, solution two, having a bicycle custom-made to fit.

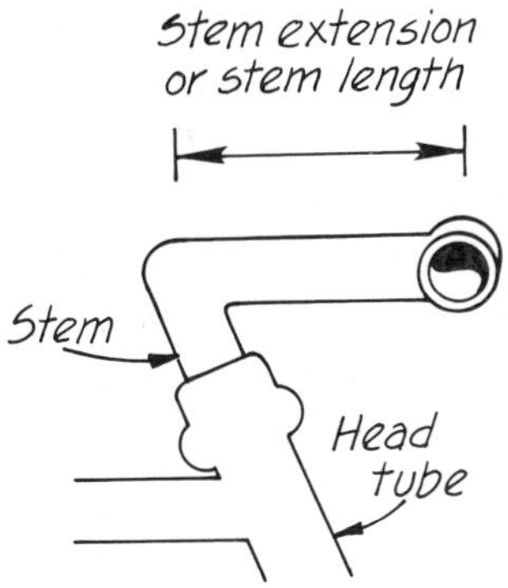

That's still an option and not always so pricey as you might think. Many racers, certainly the elite ones, have their bicycles custom-made. So do other cyclists who simply relish the idea of a well-made cycle uniquely their own. And custom builders have always gotten a fair amount of business from the very tall and the very short.

Now there's a third choice: you can buy a proportional bike, the best known of which is the Terry bike. Several years ago one (very) independent framebuilder in the United States named Georgena Terry was gutsy enough to take things a step further. After building a number of custom bikes on request for her smaller women friends, she decided to create production line bicycles for the short-torsoed. In 1985 she introduced Terry Precision Bicycles for Women – high-quality bikes in a range of models and sizes, all with shorter top tubes than standard bicycles in the same frame size. She was the first to do so.

Stem extension or stem length

Stem

Head tube

Fig. 6
The extension of the stem, or *stem length*, is measured as shown. A longer stem puts the handlebars farther away from a rider than a shorter one would. The portion of the stem which inserts into the head tube is called the *shank* of the stem. Sometimes a stem with an extra long shank (called a swan stem) is desirable to bring handlebars up higher and thus closer to the cyclist.

Her design wasn't new. She consulted another custom builder, Bill Boston, of Wilmington, Delaware, who'd urged manufacturers for years to adopt his solution for making small frames more proportional: a smaller, 24-inch front wheel paired with the standard 27-inch on the rear. The configuration permits shortening of the top tube. Terry used it. Larger frame sizes in the Terry bikes utilised two standard-sized wheels.

Immediately there was a great scurrying among the major manufacturers to imitate the small-front-wheeled Terry bike. But as imitators often do, they missed the mark. Or at least their sales target. Virtually all of the Teriyakis (as she called them) have disappeared from the market.

Meanwhile, having begun with a small production, Terry's sales increase steadily through a network of over 200 dealers in the US and Canada. To find your nearest dealer in the US contact: Terry Precision Bikes for Women, 1704 Wayneport Road, Macedon, New York 14502; Tel: (800) 289-8379. In Canada contact: Coast Leisure Activities, 3346 99th Street, Edmonton, Alberta T6N 1B5; Tel: (403) 450-4584. (Falcon Cycles Ltd, of Brigg in South Humberside, England, has a licensing agreement with Terry to manufacture her design in England, but to date they have not put Terry bikes into production.)

Do you need a proportional bike? Consider these factors: you should be able to ride with your elbows slightly bent in order to keep your upper body relaxed. That doesn't mean you should expect to sit on a bike like a pro if you're a fairly new rider. It takes time. However, you should examine your bike fit if you're shorter than five foot nine, if you're suffering neck and shoulder pain despite stretching exercises, if you're always sliding too far forward on the saddle (even though it's level), or if you're a competent rider but can't take a hand off the bar to shift gears when on the drops.

When you have the opportunity, test-ride a proportional bicycle. Of the women I surveyed, 23 per cent said they were riding bikes of questionable or poor fit. Many more must be riding bikes they only *think* fit. I was. Two years ago I test-rode a Terry 'Despatch' for most of the summer and liked it so much I eventually bought it. I didn't mind the small front wheel at all. Recently, I took a spin on the bike I'd used previously and it felt big, awkward, and unruly. Until you ride a bike that really fits, it's impossible to know how good it can feel.

We've been talking about road bikes here, but I should add that the Terry line includes a mountain bike (the 'Mount Marcy'), also proportional. Worth knowing about if you're thinking of a mountain bike.

6 HOW DO I CHECK FOR BIKE FIT?

The following tips will help you ask the right questions, starting with the frame and then moving on to components. Speaking of components, short or average height women should be aware that a bicycle in your size may or may not have smaller brake levers, a shorter stem and cranks, narrower handlebars, and smaller toeclips. It may have a woman's saddle. Then again it might not. Don't take these things for granted – ask.

Frame size: A bike's frame size equals the seat tube height, usually measured from the centre of the bottom bracket up to the top of the seat tube. As a rule of thumb, your correct frame size is about 10 inches less than your inseam (the distance between your crotch and the ground as you stand in stockinged feet). To check frame fit in the shop, remove your shoes and straddle the bike's top tube. Ideally, as you stand flat-footed, you want one or two inches of clearance between your crotch and the top tube.

Some companies measure frames in inches, while others use centimetres. Refer to the Frame Sizing Conversion Chart if unsure how the two measuring systems compare. To make your own conversions, 1 inch = 2.54 centimetres (cm).

FRAME SIZING CONVERSION CHART

inches	17	18	19	20	21	22	23	24	25	26	27
centimetres	44	46	48	50	52	54	56	58	60	62	64	66	68

Saddle height: Still in stockinged feet, sit on the saddle with heels on the pedals and backpedal without rocking from side to side. The salesperson should adjust the saddle so that with the pedal at the bottom of the stroke, your knee is just slightly bent. (This is an approximation. Some riders, especially those who use cleated shoes, prefer their saddles about 1 centimetre higher.)

Saddle tilt: While you're at it, make sure the saddle is comfortable. It should be level, since tilting the saddle nose downward makes you lean too much weight on your hands. (Men usually prefer their saddles tilted up, but this can be painful for women.)

Reach: This is the other key measurement for finding your frame size.

Just what is a comfortable upper body position on a drop handlebar bike varies somewhat with the individual. Take the bike for a test ride. As you ride with your hands on the brake hoods, there should be a slight bend in your elbows. Georgena Terry observes that experienced riders are usually comfortable when they ride with their backs at a 45-degree angle to the top tube. Some tourists and new riders are more happy at a 50-degree angle. (And some riders want to sit bolt upright and would be better served with upright rather than drop handlebars.)

If you're considering a drop handlebar bike and it seems comfortable as you ride, you can verify your impressions with a little test that works pretty well most of the time: butt your elbow up next to the nose of the saddle with your fingers straight and reaching for the handlebar. If your fingers touch or come close, the reach shouldn't be too long. Make allowances if the saddle is unusually long or short.

If you suspect the reach is too long for you, you might be interested in comparing the top tube length of any bike you're considering with the top tube lengths on Terry's production line bicycles. (If you're considering a step-through frame with dropped bars, measure the distance of the span where a top tube would be.) Here are the measurements:

Frame size	Top tube length
16 inches	18.9 inches
17 inches	19 inches
18.5 inches	19.3 inches
19 inches	19.5 inches
20 inches	19.5 inches
20 inches	21 inches
21.5 inches	21 inches
23 inches	21.5 inches

While I don't claim that these or any other numbers are the last word on proportionate sizing, they're a point of comparison to more traditional configurations. You'll notice with the above ratios that the smaller frame sizes even here have proportionately longer top tubes. Even this frame geometry has its limitations.

A reminder: the reach is determined by top tube length and the stem extension. A bike with the right length top tube can still feel too long if the stem is disproportionately long. Of course, the latter can be changed. But radical changes in stem length can affect bikehandling, so talk it over with the salesperson. If you do want to change it, strike a bargain before buying the bike.

Handlebar size: For drop handlebars, lines drawn from your shoulders to your wrists should be parallel to the bike frame when your hands are resting on the brake hoods. Racers, however, may want a slightly wider position for easier breathing.

Crank length: In bare feet, measure your inseam from crotch to floor. If your inseam is between 29½ inches and 33 inches, 170-mm cranks will be fine, although

165s might be better if you're at the short end of that scale. Anyone with an inseam above this range will probably benefit from longer cranks; someone with an inseam below that range should have shorter cranks.

Brakes: With hands smaller than men's, some women have difficulty gripping standard-sized brake levers. In your road-test check for braking efficiency and comfort. Try braking while riding with your hands on the brake hoods, as well as braking with hands on the dropped portion of the bars. And ask about proportioned levers on small sized bikes. Don't be offended if they're called *junior levers*, as they were originally created for schoolboy racers.

By the way, on inexpensive drop handlebar bikes you'll see a second set of levers (called *auxiliary levers* or '*safety levers*', a misleading term). These are operated from the tops of the bars and look very convenient. Sorry to say, these auxiliary levers come easily out of adjustment and can't be depended on when you need to come to a quick, full stop. It's better not to use auxiliary levers at all and to have them removed from the bike if possible. Or, I recommend you take a step up in quality and buy a bicycle without auxiliary levers.

Saddle: This is such an important component it merits discussion in chapter 13, Ouch-less Riding; refer to that chapter. And if you're interested in a new bike but its saddle doesn't suit you, ask to trade it for one of your choice (at reduced or no cost) when you buy.

Toeclips: These come in sizes. The right size for you places the ball of your foot directly over the pedal spindle.

Overall fit: Many US and Canadian bike shops now have a fitting aid, called Fit Kit, developed by American cycling coach Bill Farrell. Take advantage of it if you have the opportunity. It will at least help you to approximate good fit, and you can fine-tune the measurements from there.

7 HOW CAN I PREDICT HOW A BIKE WILL HANDLE?

Some bicycles are designed to be highly stable, which means they tend to travel straight down the road and take corners wide, like a truck. Other bicycles are designed to be extremely manoeuvrable, which means they take corners easily and with a shorter turning radius, but they require a little more effort to keep in a straight line. And many bicycles fall somewhere in between. We call these performance differences a bicycle's *handling characteristics.*

No one way of handling is 'best' – unless it happens to be appropriate for the way you intend to use the bicycle. A good rule of thumb to remember: don't buy more manoeuvrability than you really need.

The more technically savvy may have noticed I've avoided saying that head angle affects a bike's manoeuvrability. Head angle does play a part, but it's not the whole story. In researching the matter (particularly in regard to proportional bikes with smaller front wheels, covered in this chapter), I consulted engineer/framebuilder Bill Boston, of Wilmington, Delaware. As a pioneer designer of proportional bicycles, Boston experimented with bicycle frame geometry and gleaned new insights about how a bicycle steers.

Since cycling magazines rarely provide road-test results on bicycles in small sizes (which may handle differently from identical models in larger sizes), I believed some guideline would be useful and turned to Bill for help.

Drawing on his own computer data bank, he's created a unique chart relating frame geometry to bicycle handling characteristics. It covers bicycles with standard size wheels as well as two proportional wheel sizes. These are bicycles for road use: racing, sport touring, and touring bicycles. The touring bikes are broken into two categories: touring and loaded touring. The former is for riders who travel with a light load, the latter for expedition cyclists who need the ultimate in stability. (There's more on loaded touring in chapter 23, Planning Your Own Tour.)

How can you use this chart? Suppose, for instance, you already have a good quality bicycle, but its steering is not stable enough to take touring and that's what you want to do. You measure the fork rake on your bicycle and go to your local shop. You look for a set of forks with a more appropriate rake for your purpose. You'd probably want to talk over the change with the shop mechanic (who can also do the installation). When you've finished, you have the bike you want simply for the price of the forks. Save the old forks in case you want to restore the bike to its previous state later.

You can also use the chart in buying a new bike. After you road-test a bicycle, use the chart to validate or supplement your experience of how the bike handles. For example, you'll find a range of performance within sport touring bicycles. Some are closer to the racing end of the continuum, while others are closer to the more stable handling of a touring bike. Now you can not only test-ride a bicycle to see how it handles: you can also look at its geometry to see why it handles as it does. To do that, find out the rake and head tube angle for the bike and see where it appears on the chart. Use the chart as another tool to help you make the discriminations necessary to find what you want.

Another example: some manufacturers offer bikes supposedly designed for loaded touring but their frame geometry is really that of a sport touring bike. How could you tell? You probably wouldn't put a set of heavily-packed panniers on one for a test ride. Using the chart, you can estimate how a bike would handle with a load.

One last instance: racing bikes differ in their handling according to the type of race each is intended for. Our chart shows frame geometry for a road racing bike, which should be fairly manoeuvrable but still not require constant correction just to keep it riding in a straight line. By contrast, a criterium bike is likely to have an even shorter fork rake for quick cornering in the many turns in such races. An opposite extreme, a time trial bike's main mission is usually to ride a straight course, and that's where a rider's energy should be directed. Its geometry might be more like that of a sport touring or even a touring bike. If you're thinking about a racing bike, consider these differences.

Here's what you need to know to interpret the chart:

Fork rake The amount of bend in the fork blades. This is measured as the distance between two parallel lines, one coming through the centreline of the head tube, the other intersecting the wheel axle. You can measure rake with a right angle, aligning one side of the right angle with the head tube. Or ask the salesperson to look up the rake in the manufacturer's literature. The effect of rake is that a bike with a short rake is more manoeuvrable; a bike with a long rake is less so.

Head angle In a sense, this is an imaginary angle: if the head tube extended above the top tube, this is the angle you'd have between the two. (See figure 7.) Head tube angle is not easily measured in a shop. Ask the salesperson to look up this angle in the manufacturer's literature.

Front wheel size Standard front wheels are 27 inches or 700C. Proportional bikes are spoken of as having 24-inch diameter front wheels, but actually the size may vary. On Georgena Terry's bikes, for example, the front wheels are actually 22⅜ inches in diameter. To use the chart correctly, ask about actual wheel diameter if considering a proportional bicycle with a small front wheel.

Fig. 7
Frameset
geometry

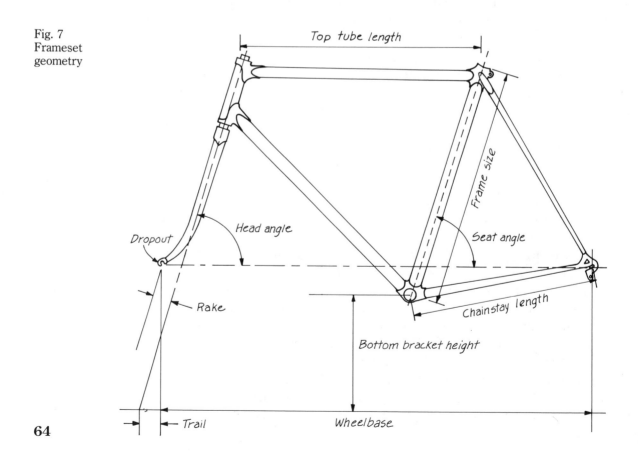

	Road Racing	Sport Touring	Touring	Loaded Touring
Rake	1.5 in	1.75 in	2.0 in	2.25 in
Front Wheel Size		*Head Tube Angle in degrees*		
27 in	74–75	73–74	72–73	71–72
24 in	73–74	72–73	71–72	70–71
22.3 in	72.5–73.5	71.5–72.5	70.5–71.5	69.5–70.5

Computer design analysis provided by MICROBIKE DESIGN SYSTEMS, copyright © 1984 by Bill Boston Cycles.

It is possible that for a given fork rake, you may find a bike with a steeper (higher number) head angle than you see on the chart. According to Boston, this will increase the stability but probably would not create a problem. On the other hand, if you find a bike with a head tube angle below the recommended range for a given fork rake, it may have dangerous instability.

8 WHAT ABOUT GEARING?

Selecting a bike that's geared too high is one of the commonest mistakes made by newcomers to the sport. The same hills that put variety and exhilaration into a ride on a bicycle with the right gearing are drudgery on a bike not geared low enough.

One reason mountain bikes are making such a hit is their low gearing. But if you never intend to ride off-road, a mountain bike may not be your best choice if speed is important to you. For road-worthiness *plus* gearing that is plenty low enough, consider instead a touring or sport touring bike with triple chainwheels, or one of the new hybrids. A bicycle with a triple crankset should have about the same low gear (about a 26-inch low) as a mountain bike.

If you're fairly athletic, even if you're a new rider, you may not need a triple. In fact, you might be perfectly happy with well-chosen wide-range gearing on a sport tourer with a double crankset. On the other hand, many women choosing this sort of bicycle would benefit from having the gearing modified.

You can make this decision intelligently for yourself, but only if you understand gearing. Why? Because one sport touring bike will not necessarily have the same gearing as another, nor will two different mountain bikes, and so on. When it comes to buying a new bike, too many women buy 'blind' because they don't really understand the meaning of *gear ratios* and *gear numbers* or *gear inches*. *If* the salesperson even brings up the subject of gearing, '42 × 14' might as well be hieroglyphics.

Actually, you'll find the whole business is not difficult. It's especially easy if you have a small pocket calculator you can use to follow me through the figuring I'll ask you to do. So bear with it and you'll quickly learn how to compare the gearing on different bikes you're thinking about buying. Or let's say you have a bike at home but you've always had to walk a lot of hills with it; you'll know how to make sure you'll get a bike with better gearing.

When you understand a bit of cycling history, the measuring system makes more sense. It goes back a century to the time when chain-driven bikes were first starting to compete with the highwheelers then in use. The huge front wheel on those 'penny-farthing' bicycles was often about 54 inches in diameter, and it would go around once with one turn of the pedals. The chain on the newer bikes turned their rear wheels more than once for each pedal revolution. To let customers know how the newer bikes would compare in efficiency to the old 'penny-farthings', a system of gearing inches was created to show how far these new bicycles would travel with one turn of the pedals. Today we still talk about gearing in terms of those gear inches or gear numbers.

The higher the gear number, the further a bicycle will travel when you turn the pedals once . . . and the more effort it takes. The lower the number, the easier the gear will be to pedal because of the shorter distance travelled.

Let's say you have a three-speed bike and you wonder whether a new twelve-speed would flatten out the hills for you. So you try out a friend's new bike. It's lovely and light, but you still can't make it up hills in the lowest gear. You begin to wonder whether the problem is you or the bicycle.

What is the low on that bike, which we'll call Twelve-Speed No. 1? You shift the chain on to the big chainwheel and sit down and count the number of teeth on the small chainwheel. You count 42 teeth. Similarly you count the number of teeth on the largest of the sprockets on the rear wheel. You count 24.

You were riding in a 42 × 24 gear. To figure the gear inches, use this formula (having a calculator at hand makes it easy):

$$\frac{\text{teeth in front chainwheel}}{\text{teeth in rear sprocket}} \times \text{wheel diameter} = \text{gear inches}$$

Here it's:

$$\frac{42}{24} \times 27 \text{ inches} = 47.25 \text{ inches}$$

Can you find a twelve-speed with a lower low? Yes. Just quickly glancing through a few bicycle catalogues, I find a sport tourer which we'll call Twelve-Speed No. 2. Its crankset has 52T and 40T chainwheels; its freewheel sprockets are 14-15-17-20-24-28T. ('T,' of course, stands for 'teeth'.) The lowest gear, then, is 40 × 28.

$$\frac{40}{28} \times 27 \text{ inches} = 38.57 \text{ inches}$$

At 38.57 gear inches, that's a considerable difference. Most women who have some hills to ride would be better off with this low gear. When you are comparing one new bike with another, the salesperson should be able to quote to you the gear ratios of any bicycle for sale. If you note them down and use this formula, you can compute the gear inches. Don't forget to check wheel size.

I'll mention in passing that while we call a bicycle a twelve-speed, for example, it doesn't really have twelve different, usable gears. First off, two gearing positions are unusable because the chain will rub. With Twelve-Speed No. 2, the 40 × 14 and 52 × 28 are not used. In the parlance, we say 'avoid the small/small and big/big combinations', meaning the small chainwheel with the smallest rear sprocket, etc. This is generally true with multigeared derailleur bicycles.

Now, what about that three-speed you have at home? What is its low gear? Three-speeds are figured somewhat differently. Use the gear number chart in the Appendix to find *normal* gear on the bicycle. Wheel size, if you're unsure, will be marked on the tyre. (If it is 700C, as some new three-speeds are, use 27 inches.) Once you have the gear inches for normal gear, multiply that figure by .75 to get low gear. Incidentally, to figure high gear, multiply the number for normal gear by 1.33.

What did you find out? That low gear on your three-speed isn't much different from low on Twelve-Speed No. 1? That's why it pays to plot out the gearing! Now that you have the idea, you can plot and compare gearing on mountain bikes (don't forget about wheel size) and tourers with triple-chainwheels, as well as various ten-, twelve-, and fourteen-speed bicycles. Test-ride bikes with different gearing on hills if you can, to see what's best for you. If you do find yourself looking at proportional bikes with small front wheels, remember it's the back wheel that should be measured.

There is more to plotting gearing than we've talked about here. If you want to know more now, so that you can determine the shifting pattern of a derailleur bicycle, see chapter 14, Tuning Up Your Technique.

So, there you have it – the end of my short course in buying a bike. I've probably told you more than you ever thought you'd need to know. But now you have the specifics on what to look for and can shop with confidence.

Whether you make a purchase now or continue riding a bicycle you already own, continue on with chapter 7, Out of the Garage and on the Road, if you haven't read it. Here you'll find a refresher on the basics of road safety and cycling technique.

You Can Modify That Three-Speed

If you have a three-speed bicycle you are generally happy with except for the gearing, you can have the gearing modified. The simplest thing would be to replace the rear sprocket with one that has more teeth. For example, if your present bike has 26-inch wheels, a 46T chainwheel and an 18T rear sprocket, it has a low gear of 49.8 inches, right? If you have the rear sprocket changed to, say, 22T (which ought to be available; ask at your bike shop), you would have a more reasonable low of 40.7 inches, a normal of 54.3 inches, and high of 72.2 inches. Yes, this high is lower than the high you had before, but if you're a leisurely rider who generally coasts down hills, you won't mind the difference.

A cooperative bike mechanic, especially one at a shop that has a supply of old three-speed parts, can make other suggestions. You have no need to buy an entire new bike unless you want to!

7 *Out of the Garage and on the Road*

Okay, let's get rolling.

For many of us, taking up cycling may not require a new bike. It simply means going out to the garage or into the cellar and moving aside the lawn-mower, the butterfly net, the old wellies, and the spare car tyres that are stacked in front of a bike you already own. Maybe you haven't been on it since your teens. Or maybe it's one you bought more recently, but somehow it never felt quite right – the saddle gave you a pain in the backside, literally, or the reach to the handlebars was too long.

Whatever its history, underneath those festoons of cobwebs is a bicycle you may be able to resurrect, so drag it out and dust it off.

Now I'd love to tell you just to hop on and ride down the street, glorying in the fresh spring air, but one, the tyres are bound to be flat and two, you want to make sure the bike is safe to ride and as comfortable as possible.

You have two choices. Either you can take it to a local cycle shop and ask them to inspect it and put air in the tyres, or you can start right now on the road to independence by giving the bike a safety checkup yourself. Take your pick – and take action!

Option 1: Turn It Over to Your Bike Shop Mechanic

If you like, you can simply ask the shop mechanic to go over the bike and make sure it's safe to ride, properly lubricated, and that the tires are fully pumped up. You'd be wise also to ask the mechanic to check the saddle height for you, adjust it if necessary, and make sure the saddle is level.

By the way, if that saddle has been uncomfortable for you in the past, consider replacing it. (To keep the price competitive, a lot of bikes have been sold over the years with cheap, hard, narrow saddles that would have made great medieval torture devices if they had been invented back then.) Ask to be shown an 'anatomic' or 'woman's' saddle; if there's a bike in the shop with one on it, sit on it and see how it feels. If that doesn't seem right for you, a good leather saddle in a woman's model (like a Brooks) might suit you. Talk it over with the salesperson at the shop. (You'll find more on saddles in Chapter 13, Ouch-less Riding.)

As with any request for work at a shop, ask before you leave your bike what the inspection will cost. And ask to be called and given an estimate in advance of any unanticipated repairs. You may like surprises, but probably not when it comes to bills you have to pay.

One of these trips to the shop is also a good time to buy a cycling helmet. It won't do great things for your hairstyle, but if you ever have an accident, your brain will thank you for wearing it. (Three-quarters of all bicycle accident deaths are caused by head injury.) Look for a helmet bearing a sticker or tag certifying that it's approved by one of two institutes licenced to test bicycle helmets: ANSI and Snell.

If the bicycle has rusted parts or is quite old, you may be told that it's impossible or impractical to try to put it back into working condition.

Should You Consider a New Bike?

If it doesn't cost much to put your present bike on the road, then I would do it. After you develop a measure of confidence in your riding, you could start familiarising yourself with what's available in new bicycles. Start visiting shops in your area and test-riding some bikes. Then you'll know whether you're missing something just because you have, shall we say, a vintage model.

But if your old bike would be expensive to rehabilitate, a new bicycle, though more costly, would pay off in much more fun for you.

Compared to derailleur bikes on the market twelve years ago when I bought my first adult bicycle, today's are much improved. The same investment today in a road bike will net you a lighter machine thanks to lighter (and non-rusting) aluminium alloy components as well as tubing with a better strength-to-weight ratio. Wheels and tyres are lighter. All this means a bicycle that has less weight to take up hills and a faster pickup when you accelerate. (Is this starting to sound like a sports car?) Not only that, but gears are easier to shift; gear ratios are more intelligently selected; and twelve or fourteen speeds rather than ten are now standard.

And there are whole new categories to choose from – the mountain bike and its cousins, the city bike and (newest of all) the hybrid.

You'll find this whole subject covered in chapter 6.

Option 2: Your Own Safety Checkup

There's no reason why you can't do your own inspection if you're willing to take a little time to do it. In many ways a bike is quite a simple machine. As Sheila Wight jokes in her bike maintenance classes for women, 'You can tell it's wrong if there are parts left over on the floor!' Sheila teaches a hands-on repair course as part of her contribution to the Women's Committee of the Ontario Cycling Association in Canada.

For this checkup, you scarcely have to take anything apart, so it's really simple. All you need is the patience to read the steps and follow them. If you find something that seems worn or broken, then you can take the bike to the shop. You'll have the advantage of knowing more about the bike than if you hadn't inspected it yourself.

You'll find the checkup at the start of chapter 17, Nothing Flat. The 'bike anatomy' chart following chapter 1 will help you with names of any bike parts you're unfamiliar with.

As suggested above, when you do take your bike in for any service, ask before you leave it for a cost estimate. And don't forget the cycling helmet.

What sort of bicycle do you have? It might be one of these:

Fig. 8
The single-speed is the draft horse of cycling – heavy but sturdy, with wide balloon tyres and coaster brakes. You have to walk it up hills, but it's fine on level ground. In the US these bikes are making a comeback as beach bikes. In the UK a similar bike but with more upright bars, called a 'sit-up-and-beg', is still widely used for errands.

Fig. 9
The internally geared bicycle, which includes all three-speed bikes and some five-speeds, was called an 'English racer' in the States when it was the rage during the 'fifties. Gear changes are made inside the hub of the rear wheel, activated by a single lever on the handlebar. Hand brakes provide the stopping power; tyres are narrow. These bikes are geared for moderately hilly terrain at best.

Fig. 10
The derailleur bicycle, commonly called the ten-speed, has gear changers which lift (or 'derail') the chain from one toothed sprocket to another. To determine how many speeds this bike has, look at the drivetrain (shown here) and multiply. A ten-speed has a cluster of five sprockets on the rear wheel and two chainwheels at the cranks; 2 chainwheels $\times$ 5 sprockets = 10 speeds. A twelve-speed has six sprockets on the rear wheel and two chainwheels; $2 \times 6 = 12$ speeds. These multi-speed bicycles have the capability of lower gearing than the internally geared bike and so are a better choice for hilly country.

Some five-speed bikes are also derailleur bikes; having a rear derailleur only and just one chainwheel at the cranks. At the opposite extreme, derailleur bicycles with three chainwheels (a triple crankset) permit the creation of a fifteen-speed (3 chainwheels $\times$ 5 sprockets), an eighteen-speed (3×6), or a twenty-one-speed (3×7). In addition to regular gearing, these will have some extra-low gears for steep hills and for riding with loaded bike bags.

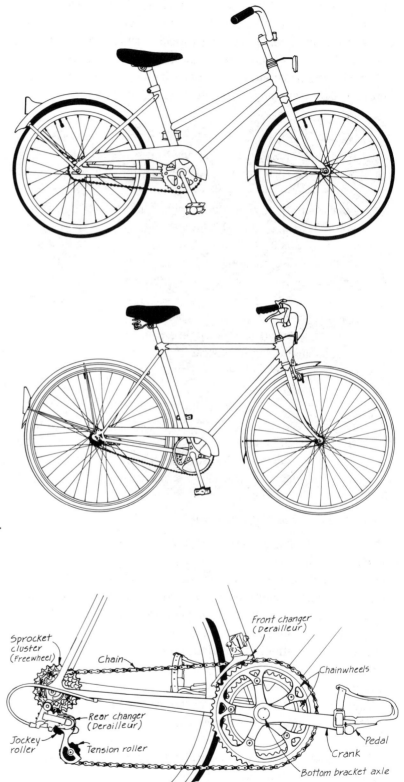

Sprocket cluster (Freewheel)

Chain

Front changer (Derailleur)

Chainwheels

Rear changer (Derailleur)

Jockey roller

Tension roller

Pedal

Crank

Bottom bracket axle

ON THE ROAD

Once you know your bike is ready to ride, what's to stop you?

You already have a healthy respect for traffic, but let me suggest a few things to sharpen up your street sense. Bear in mind that a bicycle is regarded in the eyes of the law and for practical purposes as a vehicle. As a general rule, when cycling you should be thinking as a vehicle operator rather than as a pedestrian.

- For example, you cycle *with* the flow of traffic, not against it. In the US and Canada, of course, that means on the right, and in the UK on the left. This is the safest place for a cyclist because it is the most predictable. A US study of bicycle/motor vehicle accidents indicates that riding against traffic is a contributing factor in more accidents than any other cyclist error.

  You may be worried about rear-end collisions and believe, therefore, that you should ride *facing* the flow of traffic. It's human nature to distrust what we don't know or can't see, and many riders, at least beginners, fear this type of accident. Actually, it makes up only about four per cent of all car–bike collisions. And half of these are caused by the error of the cyclist.
- Obey 'one-way' street signs just as a motorist does. (Often a motorist won't think to look both ways crossing a one-way street, so a wrong-way bicyclist could easily be hit.)
- Obey traffic signals. Maybe you could get away with doing otherwise, but in traffic following the rules of the road is the safest thing. It's also doing your bit for better relations with motorists.
- In the absence of traffic signals, yield to cross traffic at intersections with larger roads.
- Be predictable. (A key word, you notice.) Ride in a fairly straight, predictable line on the road. This makes it easier for cars to pass you safely. And leave enough space between yourself and parked cars so that a door can't be opened in your path. Don't weave in and out among parked cars.
- Be aware. Look behind you before changing lanes or pulling out into traffic. Don't rely on your ears to tell you whether there's a car behind you.

That doesn't mean sound cues aren't important. They can alert you to approaching traffic. And if you have a riding partner, you want to be able to communicate. So leave your headphones at home for entertainment when riding your stationary bike; they're a danger on the road. That's what Maxine Killasch, 32, of Northville, Michigan, tried to tell a friend who almost had more scent than sense. Maxine says:

My friend Jane and I were out for a leisurely ride along the orchards in rural Canon City, Colorado, where we both lived. Jane, wearing headphones despite my protests, was ahead of me. It was near dusk, usually a peaceful time there. But this was the Fourth of July, and the booms and crackles of fireworks made the road seem like a war zone.

71

Then a sudden blur of movement caught my eye. A near-hog-size skunk had darted through the ditch and was charging down the road in fast pursuit.

'Skunk!' I yelled to Jane, who didn't hear, and I shot past her at a speed I'd never attained before. I looked back. The skunk had closed the gap to about twenty-five feet. Jane looked back and was soon sprinting down the road with me. We reached home in record time, unnerved and, fortunately, unscented.

As a matter of fact, in some states in the US cycling with personal headphones is now against the law. In California, Florida, Maryland, Oregon, Pennsylvania, and Washington this is a misdemeanour offence. (And if you use a personal stereo while exercising indoors, keep the volume down. As you pedal away, blood goes to working muscles in legs and elsewhere, lessening the blood supply to the ears. Adrenaline, triggered by the music, increases that effect – so ears are vulnerable to damage from sound levels that normally would be safe. The audiologist who discovered this effect recommends turning the sound no higher than one-third volume and limiting use to one hour a day.)

- Signal. Remember those right and left hand signals for turning, and use them to let motorists or other cyclists know your intentions. You'll find yourself being treated with greater respect.
- Choose lightly travelled streets rather than busier, arterial routes while you're still developing your cycling-in-traffic skills and practising bikehandling.
- Be seen. Being conspicuous may not usually be your style, but on a bike you want to be seen by motorists. A bright coloured shirt is a good choice, and helmets come in vibrant colours too. Recent tests show that in broad daylight hot pink is spotted easily at a distance, whereas dark blue is not. On a grey, rainy day, bright yellow is highly visible. If you ride at night, light colours and lots of reflectors and proper front and rear lights are in order; you want to be a humanoid Christmas tree on wheels.
- Be wary of bike theft. Now that you have that bike all fixed up, don't 'give it away' to a bike thief. If you must leave it where you can't keep an eye on it, lock it up to be sure. Most reliable is a U-shaped lock large enough to let you enclose the bike's seat tube and rear wheel. If you have a quick-release on the front wheel, remove that wheel to lock it up as well. Of course, you'll secure the bike to a strong, stationary object, like a parking meter or wrought-iron fence.

BEGINNING BASICS

Riding with a more experienced friend or partner is a great way to improve riding technique quickly. That's one reason for joining a cycling club. However, there are some things experienced cyclists often don't tell beginners because we're so used to doing them, we don't even think about it. A few years ago I was helping a friend, and I couldn't figure out why she was losing her balance when stopping and dismounting from her new ten-speed. Finally she noticed I was getting up off my saddle before putting my foot on the ground. I hadn't thought to mention it. No wonder she was toppling over!

If you haven't been on a bike in a few years or if you aren't thoroughly used to the particular bike you have now, these tips will help you avoid some typical beginners' mistakes:

Clothing. Don't ride in jeans; those thick seams can mean agony. If you don't have cycling clothing yet, you can manage for a few miles in running shorts or sweatpants if the seams don't irritate your crotch. Sneakers or running shoes will do for those same short rides. And remember that helmet.

Check your shoelaces. Make sure they aren't so long that the loops could catch in your chainwheel and then in the chain. Believe me, that grinds you to a shockingly quick halt! (If necessary, double-knot the laces or tuck in the loops.)

Braking. Before mounting up for the first time, mentally review how the brakes are activated. If they are hand caliper brakes, you can practice a few times before even getting on the bike. Look over the system to see how it works, notice how the brake pads grab the wheel rim when you squeeze the lever. If you've just graduated to a bike *without* coaster brakes, you don't want to be spinning your feet wildly backwards, unable to stop as you're heading toward an intersection.

Usually there's plenty of time to stop, and you'll get the feel of just how much pressure you need on the levers to come to a gentle stop. At the beginning use equal pressure on both brake levers. As you are stopping, if you feel the back wheel begin to skid, ease up slightly on the brake levers.

Mounting and dismounting. Make a habit of always mounting and dismounting from the left side of the bike, just as if you were getting on to a horse. Also, always walk your bike from the left side. Why? The bike doesn't know the difference, but you will if you get chain grease on your legs and clothing . . . which is easy to do on the right side of the bike if you don't have a chainguard.

If your saddle is set at the proper height, you'll have to step on one pedal before sitting on the saddle. To improve your balance as you mount, raise the pedal you plan to step on, to the two o'clock position. When you step down, that will move the bike forward, and the momentum will make balancing easier as you sit on the saddle and begin to pedal.

To dismount, as you brake and the bike slows, position the pedals so one is high and the other low. Slide forward off the saddle and put your weight on the low pedal. Then remove your foot from the high pedal and extend it toward the ground. As you slow to a stop, let the bike tip a little toward your free foot and you'll touch down.

Anyone needing to practise these things can do so in a big, empty parking lot.

GEAR SHIFTING AND CADENCE

To shift gears on a three-speed or other internally geared bicycle, slow your pedalling as you move the 'trigger' to the new position. Then resume pedalling speed. Practise riding and shifting in that level parking lot, so you have the hang of it before riding in traffic or hills.

We'll get to derailleur bike technique in a minute, but first let's make sure we're all speaking the same language. Assume for a moment you have a three-speed bike. 'Low' refers to the gear that's easiest to pedal. You use it going up hills or when you start from a standstill. 'High' is the gear that offers the most resistance and is hardest to pedal. This is a good gear to shift into after reaching the top of a hill, so that if you want to pedal on the way down or as you level off, you can take the most advantage of your momentum. You'd use 'normal' or 'high', whichever feels better, on fairly level terrain.

By 'feels better', I mean that you don't want to be struggling too hard turning the pedals. You want to hit a happy medium between using too much muscle power to make each pedal revolution, and spinning too rapidly and wasting a lot of energy just moving your legs. What we're talking about is *cadence,* or the number of revolutions per minute (rpm) one foot makes going around on the pedal. A mistake many novices make is thinking they aren't getting a workout if they aren't pushing hard on the pedals.

Pick the gear that lets you keep up a brisk cadence, at least 80 or 90 rpm on level terrain and as close to that as possible when going up hills. Maintaining a sprightly cadence in a moderate gear will elevate your heart rate more than will grinding along in high gear. And raising your heart rate is important in improving aerobic conditioning.

You don't have to be obsessive about cadence at the beginning, although the current generation of bicycle computers is fairly inexpensive and you can have fun using one to see just what rpm you are doing. (They are a great training aid; just be sure to get one with a cadence function on it.) If you don't want to buy one of these just now, then count out loud as you ride, 'One potato, two potato, three potato, four potato; one potato . . .' During the time it takes to say 'one potato', your right foot should make a complete pedal revolution at about 80 or 90 rpm. You'll quickly get the feel for this cadence. A fairly level, straight road with minimal traffic signals (so you don't have to make too many stops) is a good place to practise. Keep your cadence up. If the effort becomes difficult, shift to an easier gear.

Now, you derailleur bike owners, the same meaning for 'high' and 'low' gearing applies. So does the idea of shifting to suit the rpm you want to maintain. You simply have more gears to choose among in each range. And it's even more important that you understand how to shift according to feel, since there are no markings on the gear levers.

Again, the basics: first, with a derailleur bike (unlike an internally geared bicycle), the pedals must be turning when you shift. Second, if you're unsure which levers do what, and which direction to move them in, do this: ask someone to help you by lifting the bike by the saddle so the rear wheel is off the ground; now you can turn a pedal with one hand while you move the gear levers with the other and observe what happens.

Start with the lever that would be on the right if you were sitting in the saddle (a five-speed derailleur bike just has this one, of course). This lever operates the rear derailleur. As you turn the pedal smoothly, move the lever. Notice the chain moving from one rear sprocket to another. Listen to the sound; you can hear it as the chain settles into the new gear. (With many good quality, new bikes the gear clicks into place and is thus called 'click' shifting or 'indexed' shifting.) But even without that you can tell when you're searching for the gear and when you've dropped into it.

After you've played a bit with some random shifting, move the lever through the various stops until you have the chain resting on the rear sprocket which is biggest in diameter. Notice and remember which way you move the lever to do this (as not all bikes are the same). Whichever way you moved it is the direction to shift that righthand lever to *lower* the gear. Remember, the larger the sprocket the chain rests on at the back, the lower the gear.

Now move the lever through its stops in the other direction, remembering to turn the pedal. You are shifting into higher and higher gears. The smallest rear sprocket makes for the highest gearing.

Fig. 11 (*left*)
Chain on the largest sprocket
= low gear

Fig. 12 (*right*)
Chain on the smallest sprocket
= high gear

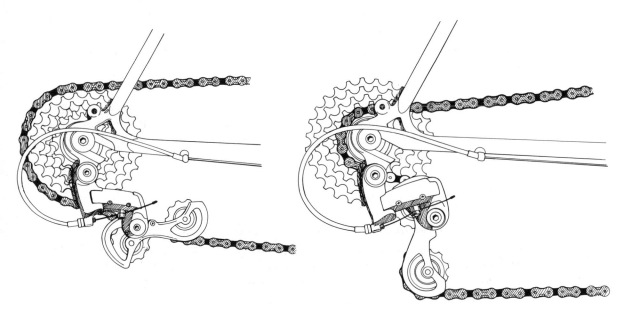

Once you've established this, you can ride and practise. Start out on level ground. Build up some speed and keep pedalling as you move the righthand lever. Don't try to watch the chain. You'll hear the chain action and know you've shifted into a different gear as you feel your feet change speed. If the chain continues to rattle, move the

75

lever slightly in one direction or the other until the chain quiets and settles into that gear. Practise shifting from one gear to the next, using these sound and feeling cues. Your shifting may be noisy at first, but you'll get better. By the way, if you really have trouble remembering which direction to move the lever, you could put a piece of masking tape on your handlebar and mark it to remind you which way is up and which is down.

Once you are used to shifting, you can give attention to which gears allow you to maintain that brisk cadence we spoke of.

If you have a five-speed bicycle, that's all there is to it.

If you have a ten- or twelve-speed, give your attention now to the lefthand lever, which operates the front derailleur. As before, experiment to see which way you move the lever to shift the chain on to the smaller of the two chainwheels. That direction lowers the gearing. Shifting the chain to the bigger chainwheel raises the gearing. Frankly, I think novices are best off at first if they simply leave the chain on the smaller chainwheel. In effect, you're using your bike like a five- or six-speed as you practise shifting the right derailleur. After getting used to it on level roads, ride in some rolling hills, remembering to shift gears to keep your pedalling cadence up.

If you do practise this way, avoid shifting on to the very smallest rear sprocket, since that will make the chain rub with the front derailleur in low.

Later we'll work on more advanced shifting techniques. Right now just ride using the rear derailleur until it becomes second nature.

If you have a new mountain bike with, say, eighteen speeds, you can do the same as above, if you need to practise getting used to multiple gearing. But shift the left lever so that the chain rests on the middle-size chainwheel. This way you can practise in a medium gear range.

A few tips for better balance: remember, you'll feel more stable as you ride and shift if you keep your cadence and your speed up. Also, if you have a drop handlebar bike with down tube-mounted shift levers, you'll find if you first move both hands in towards the centre of the handlebars, you'll stay balanced better when taking one hand off the bars to shift.

MORE SKILLS EXERCISES

The backward scan. Perhaps if human beings keep cycling for a few millenia, we'll evolve with eyes in the back of our heads. Until then, we must learn to look back while still travelling straight ahead. Most frequently we need to do that to check for motor vehicle or bicycle traffic behind us before changing lanes or moving farther out into the lane we're in. There is no substitute for a backward scan: you shouldn't depend on a cycling mirror (if you wear one), as mirrors have a blind spot. Nor (with the exception of tandemists) should you depend on a cycling partner to do the looking for you.

The exercise simply involves cycling in a straight line and looking back over your shoulder. You must practise turning your head without turning the handlebars – a natural tendency but one that makes the bike wobble or causes you to drift in the direction you're looking.

If you're pretty steady on the bike now, you can practise this on a quiet street. Ride parallel to the curb but well enough away so that you have room to pass any parked cars. Pedal along at a normal speed in a straight line. At a point where there are no parked cars, moving vehicles, or intersections, turn your head to look behind you. (In the UK this is to the right, in North America, to the left.) Then turn your head back. Are you still on course and parallel to the curb? Did the bicycle feel steady as you did the exercise? Continue on and practise again at the next opportunity. Work towards being able to look directly behind you, long enough to see a car one block back.

Make a point of also practising this exercise in situations where you would look to the opposite side – on a one-way street, for example, where you might ride on the other side of the road.

Practise the backward scan on your next several rides. It will soon be easy for you and you won't have to think about practising it; you'll be using it quite naturally each time you ride.

Riding one-handed. This is an important skill to develop quickly, so you can signal for turns, shift gears, or reach for a water bottle while riding. The trick for doing this without taking a spill is keeping body weight centred. This is especially important with drop handlebar bikes since about 40 per cent of your body weight is leaning on the handlebars; leaning heavily on one off-centre hand can throw you off-balance.

But it's easy to stabilise yourself. For example, you're riding with both hands on the tops of the bars, several inches apart, and you want to signal a turn. Slide both hands in towards the stem to centre your weight. Then remove one hand to signal, while you keep your weight centred over the other hand.

Another example: you're riding with both hands resting on the rubber brake hoods – a good position for riding because you have immediate access to the brakes, and a very steady one because of the wider hand 'stance', as long as both hands are on the bars. Until you develop really good balance, though, when you want to take a hand off the bars, do as above: move both in towards the centre first.

The same thing applies to riding the drops. Sit up a little, slip your hands onto the tops of the bars and toward the centre before taking one hand off the bars.

As noted earlier, balancing is easier when you are moving. Signal well before you reach your corner, for example, and keep your arm extended as long as you can. But if you feel wobbly as you slow for a light or to make the turn, return your hand to the bars.

Cornering. Good cornering technique makes riding more fun, helps us negotiate roads in traffic, and is one of the differences between a novice racer and an experienced one. Everybody needs cornering skills.

Leaning, not turning the handlebars, is the key to cornering. Here are the steps. Your hands should be on the brake hoods or, like racers, on the drops, to keep the centre of gravity low and hold the bike steady. If you need to slow for the corner, brake *before* you start the turn. Stop pedalling and raise the inside pedal so it can't scrape. Then lean in the direction of your turn as the bike pilots itself around the corner. To right yourself, you momentarily steer more sharply into the turn, which puts the bike underneath you again.

Proper cornering helps to make race winners. This rider leans correctly into the turn, inside pedal up (*Sam Kleinman*).

An empty road and a turn of less than 90 degrees are ideal for practice. Before entering the turn, visualise the arc you want to follow and try to stick to it by leaning into the turn. As you gain skill, you can make faster and sharper turns.

Of course, in traffic you must moderate your turns so that you don't veer into the path of another vehicle.

Dodging. There are times on a bike when it pays to be an artful dodger – around potholes, rocks, or a pile of glass. Imagine yourself pedalling along. There's a car beside you, so you haven't much room to manoeuvre, and immediately ahead you see a pothole. You can avoid it with the dodge: you turn the handlebars quickly but without leaning, and your front wheel travels around the rock. As the rear wheels follow, your bicycle starts to tip in the direction you steered, so you must steer rather sharply back in the opposite direction. You and your bike have avoided the pothole while scarcely moving from your position in the lane.

78

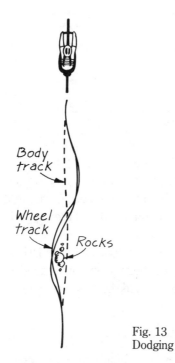

Fig. 13
Dodging

The only way to feel confident with this manoeuvre is to practise it. As John Forester advises in *Effective Cycling* (MIT Press, 1984), you can try it with a sponge in that empty parking lot. Throw the sponge on the ground and try dodging around it. Begin cautiously with slight turns of the handlebars to grow accustomed to oversteering and correcting. Gradually exaggerate the movements as you learn.

You should definitely be rolling by now. But don't worry if you don't pick up everything with the first few tries. Cycling takes skill, and you'll develop it over time. Just stick with it, and have fun.

8 *Accessories*

One cyclist I know calls them 'the necessories' – those things you need to buy, in addition to a bicycle, that are necessary for riding comfortably, safely, and efficiently. So important are they that you ought to budget at least £60 ($100) for them at the start. You could spend more, and you could find more goodies that would be nice to have, but let's start with the essentials.

You'll find, by the way, that cycling magazines regularly review products of many types, including some mentioned here. Reviews based on actual-use evaluation and/or laboratory tests can help you find the best value for your money.

DON'T LEAVE HOME WITHOUT A . . .

Helmet. You never know when a cycling helmet is going to come in handy. Anne Barnes, 25, of Cincinnati, Ohio, says that in three years of riding, her funniest experience was being hit on the head with a golfball while pedalling past a golf course. But she wouldn't have been laughing, she adds, if she hadn't been wearing a helmet.

Mountain bikers discover on their first trail ride that a helmet protects them from low-hanging branches that clunk them on the head as they duck under.

But of course our most common expectation is that a helmet will protect us in case of a crash. With a helmet 'you can reduce the risk of head injury by 85 per cent and brain injury by 88 per cent,' says William Boyle, MD, speaking for the American Academy of Paediatrics as they launch a campaign urging cyclists to wear helmets. That's 37,000 doctors who back me up on this point, so excuse me for repeating myself: along with possibly a bicycle, a helmet is the first thing I encourage you to buy. Make a habit of wearing it on every ride. I do, even when cycling just a few blocks. It's not that I don't feel confident riding in traffic, because I do. But I feel much better-protected in a helmet.

In fact, I'll admit that each of the several times I've crashed it's been my own fault, and a car was not involved. Accident statistics indicate my experience is typical: only about 18 per cent of adult bicyclists' accidents involve motor vehicles!

Many riders who are in the helmet habit believe, however, that motorists treat them with more respect because they're wearing a helmet. And I suspect it's true, since a helmet makes us *look* like vehicle users who follow the rules of the road. (If we do follow them, that makes our riding even safer.)

Are you worried a helmet will be too heavy or too hot? Until recently we referred to these helmets as 'hardshell' helmets because they had a hard plastic outer shell over an expanded polystyrene foam lining. These are still on the market, along with newer, lighter helmets *without* the hardshell; they also meet the standards. I think these new helmets are terrific, eliminating the neck strain I used to feel with my hardshell.

As for helmets making us hot-heads, temperatures under a helmet might be anywhere from 2 to 8 degrees warmer than if one were cycling bare-headed, according to tests conducted by an engineering student at the University of Southampton. Look for a helmet with vents; size and positioning of vents make a difference in the airflow. Another study, funded by the US Cycling Federation and the US Olympic Committee, determined that donning a helmet causes no significant rise in internal body temperature, skin temperature, sweat production, heart rate, or general discomfort.

Quite a lot of scientific research has gone into today's cycling helmets, and there's plenty of selection in design and colours. Some manufacturers offer separate nylon/Lycra helmet covers for riders who like to coordinate with the colour of their bike and clothing.

But most importantly, look for a helmet with a sticker certifying it's met the safety requirements of the American National Standards Institute (ANSI) or the more rigorous ones of the Snell Foundation. Both laboratories conduct a series of tests in which a headform with sensitive instrumentation has been placed inside a helmet which is dropped on a metal anvil; the impact delivered to the headform is measured and, if the impact has been sufficiently dampened, the helmet is passed. Testing is voluntary, so don't assume that just any helmet on the market has been certified.

Water bottle and cage. 'Drink before you are thirsty' is the rule in cycling. Anyone riding more than a couple of miles ought to have a water bottle, as cycling makes you perspire in any weather. Especially in the heat, dehydration not only hampers performance but can be dangerous.

A few bicycles come equipped with a water bottle and cage to hold it. Many other good quality bikes have braze-on fittings (called 'bosses'), where you can attach a cage. If your bike lacks the braze-ons, there are cages which attach with clips and others which slip over the handlebars. My preference is to mount the cage on the down-tube, well below the down-tube shift levers, where it's out of the way but easy to reach.

You'll quickly get the knack of using a water bottle. The ideal time to reach for a drink is when you're spinning smoothly along, not when approaching an intersection or other situation that might require both hands on the bars, as Chris Drillsam, 28, of Grafton, Wisconsin, observes:

> One time I was riding in a large pack, and the guy next to me pulled out his water bottle just as the light ahead of us turned red. He grabbed his brake to stop, with water bottle in hand. Trying to balance, he proceeded to spray everyone around him, yelling, 'Oh, sorry, sorry, excuse me, sorry!'

Spare tube, tyre levers, patch kit, and frame pump. For the inevitable (though I hope infrequent) puncture, it's smart to have a spare tube. Buy one when you pick

81

up your bike and the salesperson can help make sure you've selected the right size and valve type. Plastic tyre levers (you'll need two) are lightweight and won't drive you crazy by jingling in your bike bag. The patch kit may see more at-home use for tube repairs, but it's handy to have along on a ride in case bad karma strikes and you have a second puncture. All of the preceding will do you no good without a frame-mounted pump; bear in mind the valve type when you buy.

Bike bag. I suppose I've done the occasional ride carrying a bag of takeaway hamburgers in my teeth, but I quickly learned that a bike bag or day pack is a much better solution. Once you have it, you're no longer tempted to try riding one-handed while you carry something in the other – a dangerous trick. Personally I prefer a bike bag, since riding with a day pack always makes my back hot and sweaty underneath.

Bike bags come in many types, from insulated rack packs that let you carry a sixpack of your favourite cold beverage, to canvas briefcases that mount on a rear rack. In my commuting days I was partial to a pair of front pannier bags I mounted on a rear carrier to hold a change of clothing and sometimes groceries when I shopped on the way home from work. But for a first bike bag purchase I'd pass all of those by and select instead a seat bag or handlebar bag. Either will carry your spare tube, levers and patch kit, as well as other items like house keys, money, ID, or whatever.

The seat bag has been redesigned in recent years for secure mounting under the saddle; it's typically wedge-shaped and attaches both to the seat post and to the saddle rails, to minimise sway. You'll find a choice of sizes. A small one carries your spare, your repair kit, and a few other little items. Larger seat bags will do that and give you room for a lunch, your jacket, or the like. Some seat bags even expand with a zip, opening a pleat to carry big loads when you want to.

Handlebar bags are especially convenient for touring and day rides, as they usually have a transparent map case on top to keep a route map within easy view. If you like to carry a camera, I believe a handlebar-mounted bag offers more protection in case of a crash. (And you can buy bar bags specially fitted for camera gear if you choose, though they do cost.) Handlebar bags which come with a support frame (usually metal) are much superior to ones which simply strap on to the handlebars and can droop on to your wheel.

A detachable shoulder strap for carrying the bag when you have it off the bike is a desirable feature. Some handlebar bags today are engineering marvels, with multiple pockets and zips, and are priced accordingly. One with a single large compartment is much less labour-intensive to produce and will cost considerably less.

Mountain bike owners may have other preferences. A frame bag that attaches to the top, head, seat, or down-tube is easier to get at than a saddle bag. It won't be in the way when lowering the saddle, and it's less vulnerable to mud and water in this position. Do check that it doesn't interfere with water bottle cage mounts.

Reflectors or reflective striping on a bag is a plus if you do any after-dark riding, to complement (not replace) a lighting system. By the way, don't expect any bike bags to be waterproof, as zips can leak even if fabric is water-resistant. If rain threatens, I tuck a plastic bag inside to hold any items that need protecting.

NICE TO HAVE . . .

Some of the following are a bit of a splurge, and it's possible to start without these items. On the other hand, you may quickly find use for them. When you're ready to go shopping, keep these tips in mind. Watch, too, for opportunities to pick up these things used from other cyclists. Club newsletters often carry notices. I recently bought a roof rack from a fellow club member for a fraction of the cost new.

Panniers and carrier rack. What a suitcase is to the ordinary traveller, bicycle panniers are to the cycle-tourist. If you have both mountain bike and road bike, you can now buy panniers that will fit on either machine. This new generation of bags, designed for off-road riding's tougher demands, should meet any cycle-tourist's needs. They typically feature heavy nylon fabric to withstand abrasion, and extra-secure fastening systems to keep them on your rack when you're bouncing along. A few of these panniers convert to backpacks, a versatile feature.

For on-road use only, conventional pannier mounting systems work very well. Usually these consist of hooks to fasten to the rack, and a spring, strap or elastic cord to fasten the bottom of the bag to the eyelet near the rear dropout.

For carrying off the bike, panniers that have handles and either snap or strap together are convenient. An attachable shoulder strap is also handy.

It's tempting to try to save money by selecting a gargantuan pair of rear panniers and carrying all your gear in them, plus a handlebar bag. The bike will handle far better, though, if the load is distributed with 35 per cent in front panniers, 60 per cent in rear panniers, and 5 per cent in the handlebar bag.

The best type of front rack is a low-riding rack that centres these front bags over the wheel axle for optimum steering. Select racks on which members are welded together for rigidity. Racks that are bolted together (so they can be folded for cheaper shipping) are vulnerable to fatigue and sway; they're okay for kids carrying a few books home from school, but they're unacceptable for touring.

Bicycle computer. There are less expensive cadence meters and odometers available, but today's cycle-computers – especially those with heart monitors – are very useful and just plain fun to use. I've mentioned their value in monitoring cadence (rpm), and you'll read later about training according to heart rate.

Typically, a cycle-computer mounts on the handlebars and combines the capabilities of a sports watch, a cadence meter, a speedometer, and an odometer. At the push of a button the computer's LCD numerals will display in turn such things as current speed, average speed, cadence, elapsed time, trip distance, and total distance. Make certain to buy a computer that includes a cadence (rpm) monitor.

Some cycle-computers will also include a heart monitor. When you shop, look for a unit which uses a chest belt with electrode pads for detecting heart beat. These work by picking up the mild electrical activity of the heart muscle. They are more reliable than monitors which depend on fingertip or earlobe sensors to measure pulse; the latter tend to lose accuracy at higher heart rates.

83

'Having been riding for only a little over a year, I had my best moment when I saw 1,000 miles pop up on my cyclo-computer. We were riding through hilly southern Indiana on a September day, and I was watching the miles go by. At last, 1,000! It was exhilarating to believe that I did all those miles! We celebrated that night with a delicious dinner and a wonderful bottle of wine that I still have the cork from.'

Linda Chandler, 34, Toledo, Ohio

Bike rack. If you want to take your bicycle on an auto vacation or to a bike race, or if you find the best rides in your area don't start at your door, you'll need to transport by car. But a couple of bikes loaded into a car may take too much cargo space and make travelling uncomfortable; and it's an easy way to nick the paint on your bike or knock the derailleur out of line. A bike rack could be the answer. Racks come in three types according to where they mount on the car: roof, boot/hatchback, or bumper.

My preference is the roof-mounted rack. As a rule it provides the most stability for the bike. Mounted bikes don't obstruct your rear view when driving, nor your indicators or brake lights. This is the most expensive rack type. Of the various designs in this type, one which mounts bikes upright, attaching them by the front forks and rear wheels, offers the most stability. This usually requires rails to be mounted about 38 to 42 inches apart. For smaller cars, a roof rack which mounts bicycles upside down (secured by handlebar and seat) is an alternative. Units which have separate rails for mounting are easily installed by one person; where rails are joined into a one-piece unit, the rack will be heavier and require two to install. Check for compatibility of the mounting clamps with your car. And when carrying bikes, don't forget and dart into a carwash.

Less expensive are rear/boot racks, which mount on boot or hatchback, and bumper racks. Damage to bikes from backing over a curb or into a dip is less likely with a rear/boot rack than with a bumper rack. With either type, a car's rear signals and the driver's rear view can be partially obscured by mounted bicycles. In selecting, make sure any straps on the rack are sewn securely, not stapled. When using, check that mounted bikes aren't rattling against each other; padding can alleviate that.

With any rack, stop periodically to check that neither bikes nor the rack itself has worked loose, especially when travelling long distances.

'I drove into my garage, completely forgetting my brand new mountain bike was on the roof rack. Fortunately the garage door made contact with the strongest point of the handlebars, and the fork mount on the rack exploded before the bike did, so the bike was thrown off the back of the car. Aside from a few scratches to the roof of the car, a kink in the bike's brake cable, and my extreme embarrassment, we all survived to share the story with others who have done the same thing!'

Susie Short, 37, Vista, California

Indoor trainers or rollers. Here's the perfect solution to staying in shape despite daunting monsoons, winter's early darkness, or children that can't be left alone while you go out to ride. Resistance trainers (to which you affix your bicycle) are not exactly new, and rollers (on which you balance your bike) have long preceded them. Both let you bring the road indoors. I won't kid you into thinking they're as much fun as riding out in the real world, but they help you keep the form you've built up *en plein air*.

The resistance trainers simulate the feel of the road and the effects of wind resistance. They let you do power as well as aerobic workouts. In newer designs a magnetic device rubs against your tyre to increase the workload. These mag trainers are usually quieter than the wind-load trainers of a few years ago, which used a fan to create a similar load. If your storage space is limited, you'll be happy to find there are new models that fold or are otherwise more portable or compact than in the past. By the way, today's trainers are designed to fit your mountain bike's fat tyres as well as skinny road bike wheels.

Conventional rollers don't offer the resistance of these trainers and so don't give muscles the same power workout. But you can get an aerobic workout if you spin fast enough. And rollers do offer one advantage: having to balance on them helps you toward a smoother, faster cadence. The downside (pardon the pun) is that riding rollers takes concentration or you can fall off. If you want the technique training of rollers and a tough workout, some rollers are now available with wind-load fans to increase resistance. And some of these even have a support for the front forks if you really want to hammer in a power workout. Riders who've never tried rollers, you do have to develop a skill for it. I learned in one session, though, with a set of 'dished' rollers; towards the centre the rollers gradually narrowed in diameter so that they had a self-centring effect.

Is none of the above high-tech enough for you? The Computer Age has spawned sophisticated training units you might think of as pedal-powered computer games in which you race against yourself or some imaginary competitor. The visual display lets you observe your performance instantaneously. With some units you can pre-programme varying resistances for your workouts. At the high end of the market some stationary bicycles incorporate these electronics. Other set-ups are to be used with a home computer or Nintendo.

Although the electronic wizardry can be pretty pricey, standard trainers and rollers are quite affordable.

9 *Dressing the Part*

Half the joy of cycling is dressing for it. At least, that's what cycling apparel manufacturers would have you believe with those sleek, chic jerseys, those shimmering shorts and sporty gloves you see on racy-looking models in the cycling magazine ads. But most of us aren't racers, so why do we need their clothing? Regardless of appearance, what counts in cycling wear is something the ads really can't show: comfort and ease of movement.

Think about how much sensitivity you have in each of your body parts that make contact with your bicycle – hands, feet, and your seat. Putting thick-seamed shorts or blue jeans between you and the saddle, for example, will literally rub you the wrong way.

Freedom of motion to turn and look behind you and to move your legs with every pedal revolution can be hampered by clothing that doesn't move with you. If your goal is to enjoy riding and increase fitness, you don't want your clothing holding you back. With an understanding of what fosters cycling comfort and what's available on the market, you can make your own decision about what to wear.

WHERE DID IT COME FROM?

Balloon-bright colours, billboard lettering, and stretchy nylon/Lycra that follows every curve of the body – that's the look of a bicycle racer. Racers dress for aerodynamics, comfort, and flash.

Like bicycles, clothing for competition is no longer just designed, it's *engineered*. Wind tunnel tests in recent years have proved that clothing which billows, wrinkles, or even has rough textured fabric disrupts smooth air flow and increases wind resistance, slowing a racer down. And I don't need to explain that racers and teams have sponsors – hence the eye-grabbing colours and names emblazoned everywhere. As for comfort, the many hours racers spend competing and training not only require it, they also make racers potential testers for new fabrics and designs in cycling apparel. So, as it has for decades, racing clothing continues to influence designs for recreational cyclists as well.

When nylon/Lycra came into popular use, it seemed to me a real improvement over the then-standard wool shorts: the clingy Lycra shorts didn't ride up in the legs, and it was easier to find a fit in the men's and unisex sizes that were more available then (and in some places even now). Not long after that, mass-produced cyclewear became available in sizes cut specifically to fit women. I was thrilled to be able to buy cycling jerseys and jackets that didn't hang down below my bum. And the sleeves actually started at my shoulder line. There was recognition that someone with my anatomy actually exists!

Since then I've watched the selection in cycling clothing for women grow as the market attempts to meet our needs. We'll take a look at how well these new women's products actually serve us.

TWO-WHEELING WARDROBE

First, consider the various items of cyclewear and their function. What do you really need, and what's nice to complete the outfit?

Cycling shorts. Possibly the only can't-do-without piece of cycling clothing (along with sunglasses and helmet), cycling shorts should have long enough legs to prevent thighs from chafing against your saddle. Shorts should be lined so that no seams can irritate your crotch. (Those unlined Lycra shorts you may see on runners and for fashion wear are not as functional.)

For most riders I recommend the traditional, close-fitting shorts we'll call *racing shorts*, for lack of a better term. They offer superior comfort because their cling keeps the shorts from shifting on you. Today they usually come in nylon/Lycra, but some shops may still carry them in wool or wool/acrylic blends. Until recent years these shorts always had a leather chamois lining. This meant shorts required handwashing, took forever to line-dry, and afterwards the chamois needed softening with chamois fat or a non-irritating skin cream. This was a bit of a ritual, but many cycling enthusiasts took a sort of pleasure in babying the shorts that in turn babied their tender skin. They have always been meant to be worn without underwear, by the way.

Genuine chamois linings are still available in some brands of shorts. Some cyclists prefer them. However, the wash-and-wear ease of the artificial chamois lining or other substitute has won many converts. These shorts can be machine washed; line drying is recommended. They're still meant to be worn *sans* underwear, and I've worn them that way ever since the 25-mile point on my first century when I ripped off some annoying panties in a porta-loo.

During 1988 and 1989 I tested most brands of women's racing shorts available in the United States. That is, I rode in the shorts to see which ones were most comfortable for cycling. Lining fabric and construction were the critical point, and during the first testing season ('88) I was disappointed in lining design. Most models had a seam right down the centre of the lining which I found bothersome to sit on. There was one exception: because of the choice of materials and their very smooth seam, Descente's shorts proved comfortable despite the centre seam. By the following year ('89) a number of makers had done away with the centre seam in the lining, replacing it with two curved seams which fall on either side of centre, like stitching on a baseball. Two seams mean extra expense for the manufacturer, but I find this method of construction a real improvement. Women's shorts from Alitta, Cannondale, Lady Tommaso, Paramount, Pearl Izumi, and Sunbuster were among those with that feature.

Another recent improvement is a change in lining fabrics – a response to some women's concerns that slow-drying chamois linings were causing yeast infections. Most of the above brands feature new lining materials which are quick drying or wick moisture to the outer fabric layer to evaporate. Manufacturers recommend that women not use chamois fat or other lubricant on these shorts linings, as it would interfere with wicking action.

So when you shop, examine the lining. Feel to see if the seam is likely to annoy you. Also I suspect that some shorts have too much padding in them, which makes a seam more noticeable. (With a comfortable saddle you don't need a lot of padding in shorts.) Don't shop just for the lowest price; to some extent, you get what you pay for. And if selection is limited in women's sizes, consider the men's or unisex shorts.

Wearing a clean pair for each ride is good insurance against developing skin irritations. However, to cut down on laundry, some women do get away with wearing light underwear with minimal seams. Even better, there are bike shorts linings on the market; I know of one brand called Skins by an American company, Andiamo. Skins, made of a cotton/Lycra blend, come in two styles – unpadded for wearing inside crotch-lined cycling shorts and a padded version for use with other shorts. The padded ones also can be worn comfortably under unlined cycling tights in lieu of shorts. 'Skins' should be washed after every ride.

The alternative to racing shorts is *touring/recreational shorts*, for riders who prefer the hiking short look. These resemble either the traditional tailored short or the newer baggy version. If you choose touring shorts, check before buying for a crotch lining to cover seams; not all brands are lined. With these shorts expect to make a compromise on comfort for their more versatile appearance. Frankly, I can't ride 5 miles in some of these without wishing I were in my racing shorts. In some cases the shorts aren't long enough or close-fitting enough to protect legs from chafing against the saddle, especially after a few miles, when you start to perspire.

Sunglasses. These are a must to protect eyes from ultra-violet rays and glare. Equally important, they keep flying bugs out of your eyes. I've had some healthy-sized bugs bounce off my sunglass lenses, and they were going fast enough to have done damage. You may not need to buy special glasses just for cycling if you have a pair with enough lens extending above the eye to shield you as you bend over the handlebars; check that earpieces don't obscure peripheral vision.

Sunglasses especially for cycling are available in a range of prices; they often have a wraparound lens design, helpful for cutting wind that can cause tearing. Contact lens wearers tell me they have less problem with getting dirt particles in their eyes with these special glasses. When shopping, try glasses on to ensure they're the right size for you and won't slip. Some one-size-fits-all glasses fit (you guessed it) men better.

Shoes. If you're just starting out and you already own a pair of running shoes, they may be comfortable enough for riding short distances. Since I was a runner, I owned a number of pairs of running shoes and found that some – the ones with fairly smooth soles and a narrow profile – sufficed for cycling, even with toeclips.

But eventually you'll need to buy shoes, so you might as well select ones designed for the sport. That means a shoe with a sole stiff enough to protect the thick ligament under the sole of your foot (the *plantar fascia*) from the constant pressure of your foot on the pedal. A shoe that flexes in the middle of the sole puts too much stress on this ligament. That's why trainers just don't make it for cycling.

When you shop, you'll find touring/fitness shoes and cleated shoes. I suggest touring/fitness shoes for beginners.

Touring or fitness shoes were designed to have soles stiff enough to give good support on the pedals, yet flexible enough to walk in. They slip easily into your toe clips and usually have ridges or other sole modification to help grip the pedal. With a few innovative exceptions, touring shoes do not have cleats.

Cleated shoes have extremely stiff soles and allow the foot to be attached to the pedal more securely than with a touring shoe. This is done by means of a cleat or other fixture on the sole. Racers wear cleated shoes for most efficient transfer of energy to the pedals. Recreational riders also wear them for training rides or even day tours or touring. If they plan to walk about much, they take along something else to slip into . . . because the cleats on the soles make you tiptoe like Tinkerbell or walk on the heels like a duck. That's hard on the cleats. (Plus it's not very firm footing and it looks silly. I once cycled to the supermarket in cleats, tiptoed around, and almost landed on my tail in the fruit and veg section.)

Cleated shoes are used with toeclips and straps. Many are also compatible with the newer strapless pedal binding systems. Some of these newer shoes have 'base-plates' on the soles that, like cleats, aren't really meant to be walked on. Others have the advantages of a cleat without actually having one that sticks out from the sole. By the way, cleated shoes presently on the market are also pre-drilled so they can be converted for later use with pedal systems.

Any racing shoe in this group is better than a touring shoe for transferring your pedalling effort into propelling you down the road. You feel, and you are, more at one with your bike. Hills and sprints are easier, as is a smooth cadence. These shoes require a bit of getting used to, but it won't take long for any competent cyclist.

Since some of today's shoes come with cleats or base-plates already affixed to the sole, you may be tempted simply to step into your new cleated shoes and ride off. Don't do it! These devices must be positioned so they permit your knees and hips to rotate naturally. Some cyclists' natural rotation is with toes pointing inward or outward rather than straight ahead. Sometimes the position of the left foot is not even symmetrical with that of the right. Forcing knees and hips out of their natural alignment during the repeated motion of pedalling can lead to overuse injuries.

A knowledgeable coach should be able to adjust cleats correctly. Or buy your shoes from a shop which offers the services of a Fit Kit. This is particularly helpful with the new pedal binding systems, since traditional ways of aligning cleats on shoes are more difficult with these new systems. The last time I talked with the coach who invented this fitting device, there were about 1,400 bike shops in the US which had Fit Kits; and probably over 100 Canadian shops. To find the closest shop with a Fit Kit, contact the distributor.

- *In the US:*
  The New England Cycling Academy
  12 Commerce Avenue
  West Lebanon, New Hampshire 03784
  (603) 298-7784

- *In Canada:*
  Scott-Canada Inc.
  40 Laurier Avenue
  Ottawa, Ontario K1R SC4

The Fit Kit is not currently used in British cycling shops, although a few shops in Germany and France now have them.

To adjust bolted-on cleats without a Fit Kit: make sure first that your toeclips position the balls of your feet directly over the pedal spindles with shoes fully inserted in the clips. You can check that easily by painting a dot of white paint on the ball of one foot, then carefully aligning and pressing your foot to the sole of the opposite shoe while the paint's still wet. After it dries, you'll need a helper to check from below to see if the dot lines up with the spindle. If it doesn't, buy new toeclips to fit.

Then prepare to take a ride in your shoes. Cleats should be mounted slightly tight but loose enough to be twisted by a child's hand. Tighten toe straps gently, and off you go for a fifteen-minute ride on flat terrain during which you remain seated. During the ride your shoes should rotate naturally into their preferred position. Don't move out of it on your return. Stop beside a wall where you can stay on the saddle and support yourself. Your helper should be waiting there to tighten carefully the bolts on your cleats. This must be done with your feet still strapped in. Your helper should also double-check that the dots, indicating the balls of your feet, are still above the pedal spindles. If a shoe has slipped, grin and bear it, and repeat the procedure.

Because a number of women responding to my survey complained about difficulty in finding shoes to fit narrow feet, particularly in the heel, I focused on fit in looking at 1989's marketplace. Since I need a narrow width in a street shoe, I figured my foot is a pretty good test case. I was pleasantly surprised to find a perfect fit and riding comfort in several brands of shoes sized for women. Just as they should, the shoes hugged my heel, fitted snugly around the mid-foot (so my foot didn't slide forward), and the toe box was high enough and wide enough so my toes weren't cramped.

The following brands offer women's shoes in half sizes from about 4½ to 10 (UK 3½ to 9), or the European equivalent: Avia, Avocet, Brancale, Diadora, Nike, and Specialised. Cycle Binding's shoes came in a limited size range (only from 7½, UK 6½), but a wider range was expected for this year. If you're having problems with unisex or men's shoes, try these women's models.

That's not to say you might not find a good fit in a man's shoe. Avia, for example, sent a sample of its cleated model in a men's 5½ (UK 6), and it fitted fine.

The conversion chart below should help you make sense of the sizing systems.

Shoe size conversion chart – European Metric to US											
Metric	**36**	**37**	**38**	**39**	**40**	**41**	**42**	**43**	**44**	**45**	**46**	**47**
Women	5	5½–6	6½–7	7½–8	8–8½	9	9½–10					
Men			5–5½	6–6½	7–7½	8–8½	8½–9	9½	10	10½	11	11½–12

Gloves. Not just a fashion item, cycling gloves prevent blisters and protect hands in case of a fall. They give a more secure grip on the bars when sweaty hands might be slippery and help dampen road vibration that might otherwise cause numbness. And they let you brush debris off tyres that could cause a flat.

Gloves designed for warm weather riding are fingerless and may or may not have that opening on the back of the hand that gives you a 'funny' tan. They come in a variety of materials, from leather to nylon/Lycra and synthetic suede. Should you have small hands, your biggest challenge is finding a pair that fits. If your bike shop doesn't sell ladies' sizes (from Saranac or Lady Tommaso, for example), try a men's or unisex X-small. Express Line's run small, I discovered. Or you may have luck with mail order.

When trying for fit, grip a handlebar in various positions to see how the gloves feel. If they do fit snugly, remove them by peeling them off inside out. They'll last longer.

Cycling jersey. You can do without a jersey at first – perhaps forever. I find the rear pockets handy, though, for little things like my door key and a handkerchief. On one tour I carried a small 35mm camera in a pocket for quick photo stops. Racers and tourists both stuff fruit and other food in the pockets.

I like the look of a jersey. It's long enough not to expose bare skin to the sun as you bend over the bars. (As you're standing, a jersey should come down about midway on your hips.) Like many other recreational riders, I wear jerseys looser than racers do. And there are many styles to choose from besides team jerseys branded all over with advertisers' names. Bright colours are a good idea so motorists can see you more easily on the road. And keep your jersey zipped up so a bug or bee can't fly in as you're flying along.

Shiny nylon/Lycra is not the only choice in jersey fabrics these days. Since many women don't want *that* much cling, the industry (at least in North America) offers jerseys in cotton/Lycra, Cool Max, and cotton/poly blends; 100 per cent cotton cycling T-shirts and sleeveless T-shirts. And many jerseys are cut looser now.

If you prefer, though, you can wear an ordinary T-shirt, polo shirt, or anything else you find comfortable.

Raingear. The above should outfit you for cycling on warm, fair days when everyone loves to ride. In rainy weather, you'll need raingear even in marginal temperatures, because body heat escapes quickly from wet clothing. Yellow is the best colour for rainwear, as it's most easily seen on grey days. My preference is a lightweight rain jacket and rain pants (or tights in a light rain). Rain capes and ponchos can blow about annoyingly, but there's less heat buildup underneath. So take your pick.

Cool weather gear. For riding in cooler seasons there's now a range of clothing, including jackets and nylon/Lycra tights made in women's sizes, as well as thermal underwear to help keep you warm. If tights don't have a crotch lining (brands I've tested did not), then they're intended to be worn over racing shorts or thermal underwear.

Racers and other experienced cyclists generally slip on tights when temperatures drop below 65 degrees Fahrenheit, mainly to keep knees warm and lessen any chance of injury from cold, tight muscles. Nylon/Lycra tights are ideal for those days when it's just a little too cool for shorts. If the weather warms during your ride, you can easily slip them off, roll them up, and put them in a jersey pocket or your bike bag.

You'll be able to tell when it's time to add the thermal underwear. Wool tights will be warmer than nylon/Lycra. Some of these are available with front panels of waterproof fabric. You may have to turn to unisex or men's sizes for both of these. There are also new synthetic fabrics engineered to be warmer than nylon/Lycra and waterproof. Descente, for one, offers sizing for women in jacket and tights in 'alumi-taffeta', intended for riding when the mercury drops below 40 degrees Fahrenheit. Descente's Sandy Pogue suggests adding thermals if you brave temperatures down around 0 degrees Fahrenheit. Thermals are really for absorbing perspiration – 'That's actually what chills you,' he adds.

Jackets generally come in dark colours, practical for not showing dirt. But jackets should have a large, bright patch or band of colour on the front and back to make you more conspicuous to motorists. Unfortunately, they often don't.

What gets coldest, though, are hands and feet, so look into shoe covers and warm, full-finger gloves. Ask club members and experienced cycling friends what's available in local shops to keep the cold from nipping fingers and toes.

MEETING WOMEN'S NEEDS

I overheard the following comment in a bike shop as a customer was looking for clothing for a female companion. The (male) sales clerk said, 'Women's clothing is really for looks. It's not designed to be functional. You'll have to look for unisex clothes.' I found that appalling, albeit true. Look at those white touring shoes, cycling shorts that require body by Fonda to get into, and nylon/Lycra crop-tops which, if you don't burn to a crisp on a day tour, will provide a lower back tan line which matches no known swimsuit today!

Not that any of these keep me from cycling. A large T-shirt over men's shorts, and I'm gone! Ann Crepin, 34, St Louis, Missouri

Styles and fabrics. While the cycling apparel industry is booming in the US, that doesn't mean every female cyclist here wears the 'uniform'. I know at least one woman who does all her riding in street clothes. Nor does every female in hip-hugging, shiny Lycra shorts ride a bicycle. At the disco, in the schoolroom, and of course in aerobics classes, Lycra-clad young bodies are legion. In a way I see that as an advantage: cyclists in their gear no longer look like they're from outer space or something.

But not every woman loves Lycra and the racing look in shorts and jerseys. Women variously commented on their surveys that they are not model thin, or they're over 35, or they're full-busted. Some feel this clothing turns them into sex objects – a relevant point because over one-fifth (22.7 per cent) of respondents indicated they were concerned about or had experienced harassment from men while riding.

What to do? Actually the North American industry offers a fantastic variety of styles, fabrics, and colours in cyclewear for women. But I suspect that the selection available in any one shop doesn't demonstrate it. Look for these alternatives by reading labels and trying garments for size. If you see something in a magazine you like that's not on the rack in your shop (often the case), contact the company to find the nearest retailer. Some brands available in North America have also begun to penetrate the UK market, including Cannondale, Nike, and Giordana. Look for them if you don't find what you want in domestic goods. Let your dealer know you want a good quality women's product and are willing to pay for it.

Some women turn outside the cycling apparel market to other makers of outdoor wear. An alternative available in the UK though not in the US is Rohan activewear. I learned of it from Chris Mawer, of Countesthorpe, Leicestershire. Chris, 34, and her husband bought it for mountain biking in Kenya. As they rode from 5,000 feet elevation to the Kinangop Plateau at 9,000 feet, they gave the clothing (and themselves) a workout. Chris terms it 'extremely durable and great for roughing it. For touring, the lightness and small pack size are superb, as is its ability to be rinsed out in a stream and put back on five minutes later'. She also wears it to cycle-commute 15 miles a day back and forth to work, year-round.

Colour preferences. Some things have a reason for being. As Sandy von Allmen, 42, of Norfolk, New York, observes, 'Black shorts are great. You never have to worry about colour coordination or about where to wipe your hands after putting a chain back on.' Black doesn't show grass stains or dark smudges from your saddle, as pale pastels will. 'Besides,' Sandy adds, 'when I'm out cycling alone, I prefer to dress in a way that's functional to the sport but unrevealing as to gender.'

But fashion always looks for a change, so shorts now come in combinations of colours and in every imaginable hue. This makes mixing and matching trickier, especially if only a small selection of women's clothing is available in any one shop. Almost half (47.9 per cent) of women surveyed said they were dissatisfied with the range of colours available in cyclewear in shops they visit. Of course, there are mail order sources which broaden the selection, and most women indicated their awareness of them.

My preference is to buy a few pairs of the best quality plain black shorts available, and then any jersey that fits will look great with them.

In shoes, most manufacturers chose soft grey in '89, often with pink or blue detailing. That's neither as neutral nor as scuff-resistant as the traditional black leather cleated shoe of ten years ago. But it's better than white.

Fad items. In cycling apparel as in fashion in general, we have trendy clothing which may not stay in style long or be particularly functional. On the current market, this is the crop-top, which is cool and comfortable in very hot weather and probably great if you live in California, where everyone is used to seeing yards of tanned skin. On the other hand, if you took a spill you'd be likely to lose more of that skin than if wearing a sleeved jersey.

Many of these show plenty of midriff and you might not like the message they send out. I have to agree, though I did wear one a few times to see what sort of heckling I might get. It and the matching shorts have zebra stripes. I must be over the hill: nobody whistled. But somebody called, 'Look, a zebra on wheels!'

Fit. I was surprised that fit in such basics as shorts and jerseys is as much of a problem for women as apparently it is. Among survey respondents who knew or thought they had women's cyclewear available in bike shops, just over half of them (53.5 per cent) said they'd found sizes that fit. Generally, the problem, where women described it, centred around garments sized for an unrealistically thin stereotype. I shared this feedback with the industry, and one manufacturer was honest enough to admit that testing of garments on racers led them to size things too small. I think it's also a result of targeting for a young adult market and forgetting that there are many women riders in their forties, fifties, sixties and older. I hope we'll see improvement in this area.

Appropriateness. Even when cyclewear fits and flatters, you may find it doesn't suit your purpose. One of Britain's best-known cycling authors, Bettina Selby, 54, has cycled alone to such exotic places as the source of the Nile. (Her account of that journey is *Riding the Desert Trail*, Chatto and Windus, London, 1988.) Bettina knows the importance of fitting in with the local dress customs. Even in her own country, she says, 'there are very few places where I would show my shorts. I usually wear them as knickers under something else. If I went to knock on a farmer's door and asked to camp in his field, I'd want him to be forthcoming. He'd be too embarrassed [to say yes],' she explains, 'if I were in shorts.'

Women's clothing options will continue to improve as manufacturers and retailers recognise the purchasing power of women cyclists. So don't be a stranger at your bike shop. Make your wishes known, and look for shops that try to meet them. Of course, that doesn't just go for clothing, but bikes and other accessories.

As Jean Welch, 41, of Van Nuys, California, writes: 'I first started riding twenty years ago. My bike was always too big, and cleated shoes were impossible! Forget about proper riding pants and jerseys, gloves, helmet, etc. So I really shouldn't complain. The problem is we've been given a taste, and now we want more choices and better!'

Sources:

Alitta, 75 Spring Street, Sixth Floor; New York, New York 10012.
    Tel: (212) 334-1390.
Andiamo, 424 A Montana Avenue, Santa Monica, California 90403.
    Tel: (213) 394-0971.
Avia, PO Box 23309, 16160 SW. Upper Boones Ferry Road, Portland,

Oregon 97224. Tel: (800) 547-3213. UK distributor: Speedo (Europe), Peter Lawson, Ascot Road, Nottingham NG8 5AJ. Tel: (0602) 296 131.

Avocet, PO Box 7615, Menlo Park, California 94026. Tel: (800) 227-8346. UK Distributor: Madison Cycles, Unit 14, Horseshoe Close, London NW2 7JJ. Tel: 081-208 2106.

Brancale (see Ten Speed Drive Imports)

Cannondale Corporation, 9 Brookside Place, Georgetown, Connecticut 06829. Tel: (800) 245-3872. UK distributor: Chainsport Distributors, 595 Wandsworth Road, London SW8 3JD. Tel: 071-720 6755.

CycleBinding, The Shellburne Corporation, Box 158 Route 7, Shelburne, Vermont 05482. Tel: (802) 985-8045.

Descente America Inc., 601 Madison Avenue, New York, New York 10022. Tel: (212) 888-7710.

Diadora (see Gita Sporting Goods Ltd, US distributor). UK distributor: Carati Sport, Unit 49, Waverly Estate, Beaches Industrial Estate, Yate, Bristol BS 17502.

Expressline, 719 W. Ellsworth Road #4, Ann Arbor, Michigan 48108. Tel: (800) 521-0549.

Giordana (see Gita Sporting Goods Ltd). UK distributor: Carati Sport, Unit 49, Waverly Estate, Beaches Industrial Estate, Yate, Bristol BS 17502.

Gita Sporting Goods Ltd, 12600 Steelecreek Road, Charlotte, North Carolina. Tel: (704) 588-7550.

Lady Tommaso (see Ten Speed Drive Imports).

Nike, 9000 SW. Nimbus Drive, Beaverton, Oregon 97005. Tel: (800) 344-NIKE. In UK: Nike International UK, Consiton House, Washington Centre, District 4, Washington; Tyne & Wear NE38 7RN.

Paramount (Schwinn), 217 N. Jefferson Street, Chicago, Illinois 60606-1111. Tel: (800) 633-0231.

Pearl Izumi, 2300 Central Avenue, Boulder, Colorado 80301. Tel: (800) 328-8488.

Rohan Designs, 30 Maryland Road, Tongwell, Milton Keynes, MK15 8HN. Tel: (0908) 618888.

Saranac Glove Company, Corporate Offices, PO Box 786, Green Bay, Wisconsin 54305. Tel: (800) 558-7302. (Ask for 'customer assistance'.) UK distributor: C. L. Gaul & Co., 22 Baras Street, Whittlesey, Peterborough PE7 1DA. Tel: (0733) 204 526.

Specialized, 15130 Concord Circle, Morgan Hill, California 95037. UK distributor: Specialized UK, 14 Woodcote Drive, Crofton, Orpington, Kent BR6 8DB. Tel: 081-760 5065.

Sunbuster, 21601 66th Avenue W., Mountlake Terrace, Washington 98043. Tel: (206) 775-9346.

Ten Speed Drive Imports, PO Box 9250, Melbourne, Florida 32902-9250. Tel: (407) 777-5777.

10 *Shaping Up and Body Shape*

Since taking up cycling I am a lot more confident about my body and don't worry unduly if I seem to be putting on weight because I know I can lose weight by cycling instead of going on a diet.   Hilary Brooke, 26, Acomb, Yorkshire

With cycling I can accomplish many things, like long rides, that I never dreamed I could do. And it's fun. But most rewarding for me is I've lost 45 pounds without dieting. The pounds more or less 'fell' off; I didn't even realise it until all my clothes started getting baggy. I'm smaller now and in better shape than before I had my children. I really feel great. I'd like to lose about 10 more pounds, but I'm not on a diet per se. I know as I continue my riding, the weight will eventually come off. Biking has really given me a new, younger body!   Carol Nelson, 37, Chino Hills, California

I was amazed at the effect cycling had on my body in such a short time. My legs got very strong and had better muscle definition. My weight keeps very stable, cycling 3 miles each way to work and on weekends. And my circulation has improved tremendously. I also found that I became interested in other sports and outside activities.   Maura Thornton, 33, Clifford Park, Coventry

I eat as much as possible so I can train as hard as possible. This keeps the weight off!   Eve Wildi Hawkins, 37, Webster, New York

I now have more stamina and no longer 'give up'. I eat as much as I used to and weigh as much; but people say I look better . . .   Yvonne Fallows, 32, Whitburn, West Lothian

Since I've cycled regularly I feel more confident about myself and my body. I feel fitter and more able to cope generally. I've lost half a stone [7 pounds] without dieting and don't seem to feel as hungry or as bothered about eating.   Judith Stuuter, 22, Wymondham, Norfolk

About two years ago I went through a depression and lost my appetite. Vigorous cycling was the only thing I could think of to stimulate it. It worked and I very quickly put weight back on. Now my weight has stabilised since three months after I began cycling.   D. Hamilton, 29, Abingdon, Oxfordshire

If weight control is one of your goals, can cycling help?

Possibly it can. Certainly we know that dieting without exercise can be frustrating, as metabolism slows and the body burns calories more slowly. The emotional tension is terrific, and the dieter is often easily distracted, agitated, perhaps depressed. She may deny her hunger often enough that she becomes out of touch with how it feels to be hungry. Then when temptation finally overpowers her and she dives into one of her 'forbidden' foods, she may 'binge' far beyond the point of satisfying hunger. She thinks, 'Well, I've already broken my diet for today, so what's the difference?' Researchers Janet Polivy and C. Peter Herman, in their book on the dangers of dieting, *Breaking the Diet Habit* (Basic Books, Inc., New York, 1983), call this the 'what-the-hell effect'. They point out that dieting generally precedes episodes of binge eating, often by many months.

By contrast, exercise is a much safer way to initiate weight loss. Why?

Exercise, as we've seen, is often the body's great regulator. Here, too, in the matter of weight control, exercise can start us rolling in the right direction. Everybody knows that exercise burns calories while you're doing it.

But what most people don't realise is that it can also have a beneficial effect on your *basal metabolic rate* – that is, the rate at which your body burns energy during its resting state. Riding for a half-hour or an hour, for example, will stimulate the thyroid gland to produce a substance called *thyroxin*. Along with adrenalins produced by the adrenal glands, thyroxin increases metabolic activity during exercise and, though to a lesser extent, for hours afterward. Exercise is almost like money that never stops earning interest, since it's possible to have as much as a 25 per cent increase in basal metabolism for fifteen hours *after the exercise is over*.

And even a small change in the metabolic rate can have a significant role in weight control. (Interestingly, for individuals whose basal metabolic rate tends to be too high, a condition often associated with tension, exercise can help to lower the metabolic rate.)

Survey Findings: Cycling and Weight Control

The total sample size for this question was 583 women.

Q. Do you find that a combination of the exercise of cycling and eating nutritious, balanced meals is sufficient to allow you to maintain a weight you are satisfied with?

A.	78.7%	Yes
	4.6%	Yes, when combined with other exercise
	16.6%	No

Q. Do you use other measures of weight control?

A.	23.8%	Moderate calorie restriction
	1.2%	Crash diets
	0.3%	Liquid diets
	1.0%	Diet pills or related aids
	1.4%	Fasting
	0.3%	Weight Watchers
	0.3%	Overeaters Anonymous

Note: 1.4% Indicated they don't try to lose weight and watch out for excess weight loss.

Exercise helps in yet another way by gradually helping to build muscle. This not only tones the body but also raises metabolism. Why? The body's fat cells are basically inert storage tissue, but muscle is working tissue that is always burning calories to maintain itself. More muscle means more calories burned.

A recent study by Doctor Grant Gwinup, an endocrinologist at the University of California at Irvine, demonstrated that cycling or walking at least thirty minutes a day can foster significant weight loss even without cutting calories. In a six-month test of overweight women who exercised up to an hour a day by walking, swimming, or riding exercise bicycles, the group which rode bicycles were most successful, losing 12 per cent of their body weight – while continuing to eat normally.

In my own survey of North American women cyclists, over four-fifths of the women who responded (83.3 per cent) indicated that the exercise of cycling (and other sports for those in multiple activities) along with a nutritious, balanced diet, is sufficient for maintaining a weight they are satisfied with. Inherent in the notion of a balanced diet for some respondents is moderate calorie restriction, as 23.8 per cent of all participants indicated they restrict calories moderately. Only a very small percentage of all women responding use more extreme measures of weight control. (See chart for details of survey findings.)

In our diet-conscious society, these findings testify to two things, I think:

- the beneficial effects of cycling for regulating weight
- a strong level of self-confidence in these women.

And if that's so, do we take up cycling because we happen to be confident, positive types, or do we feel better about ourselves and our bodies as a result of our cycling? While I don't exclude the first alternative, it's clear that most of the respondents in my survey feel better about their bodies (and themselves) as a result of cycling. The majority (57.6 per cent) feel 'much happier' about their bodies since starting to ride; another 27.9 per cent feel 'somewhat happier'; and 13.8 per cent feel 'about the same as before'.

If your goal is weight loss, along with cycling, should you restrict calories? That's for you to decide, but if you choose to, your smartest bet for good health is to cut fat consumption and especially saturated fats and dietary cholesterol. That's good advice for cancer prevention and for your heart, and it targets the food group that packs the most concentrated calories and the calories that are hardest for your body to burn. If you need to, see again the chart in chapter 5, A Long and Healthy Life.

Now, a word about expectations. If you take up cycling to lose weight or shape up your shape, what can you expect?

At 42, Lou Hotton is five foot two inches worth of cycling muscle and drive. Her powerful legs (in pink leopard print tights) have stoked the tandem she shares with captain Patti Brehler, 37, to two impressive records.

Survey Findings: Cycling and Body Image

As indicated in the text, the vast majority of women participating in my survey stated that they are happier with their bodies since taking up cycling: of the total, 57.6 per cent are 'much happier', 27.9 per cent are 'somewhat happier', and 13.8 per cent feel 'about the same'. It should be noted that women indicating no change in feelings may nevertheless be quite happy with their bodies, as a number did in fact comment. Only 0.5 per cent indicated any dissatisfaction, noting that their legs had got bigger or the muscles became more defined than desired.

It was interesting to note that the women who grew up with the least athletic experience indicated, as a group, the most improvement in their feelings about their bodies after taking up cycling.

With the following question, survey respondents were asked to describe their background:

Q. How did you feel about sport activities before you began cycling?

- 'I grew up enthusiastic about various sports.'
- 'I hated organised sports and gym class in school.'
- 'I've been pretty inactive until taking up cycling.'
- Other (Write-in answers turned this category into:) 'I'd become active previously in recent years.'

A fifth group also emerged, of women who both 'hated organised sports and gym class in school' and had 'been pretty inactive until taking up cycling'.

It was this fifth group which indicated the most improvement in body image: 90 per cent feel 'much happier' with their bodies. It was as if this group had really found themselves. The responses for all five groups appear below.

	much happier	somewhat happier	same	less
Hated organised sports/pretty inactive	90%	6.6%	3.3%	–
Hated organised sports	71%	21.7%	7.2%	–
Pretty inactive	63.2%	27.5%	9.1%	–
Grew up enthusiastic	52.2%	30.5%	16.3%	0.9%
Previously active in recent years	48.5%	32.3%	19.1%	–

On September 19, 1986, the Pink Leopard Cycling Team set a world record for the women's 24-hour tandem event, clocking 422.518 miles. That means they rode their custom-made 'bicycle-built-for-two' round and round a 16-mile course over rolling hills and through a night cloaked in patches of heavy fog. As the hours wore on, the same hills seemed to get steeper, and Patti and Lou's speed dropped from an initial 22 mph to an overall average of 17.6 mph. But that was to be expected, and they outperformed even their own goal of 400 miles.

The Pink Leopards – Lou Hotton (left) and Patti Brehler – not long after setting their 24-hour marathon record in 1986 (*Craig Gaffield, Daily Tribune*).

About a year later, the Pink Leopards took on the last phase of another challenge. Lou and Patti had not only qualified for, but they completed cycling's best known 'recreational' marathon event, the 750-mile Paris-Brest-Paris. Originating in 1891 and now held every four years, P-B-P is a bike race from Paris to the coast of Brittany and back. Thousands participate. The clock runs nonstop, and riders must complete the distance within ninety hours to be counted official finishers.

The route is difficult, with an estimated 1,250 climbs (especially challenging for tandems), but the French love a bicycle race, and even in the middle of the night people stand cheering by the roadside. Lou and Patti, shown on TV and featured in French newspapers as the only women's tandem team, received special attention from spectators. As even the press noted, Patti and Lou were exuberant and projected their enjoyment of the race, despite a total of just four hours' sleep. Understandably the event remains Lou's favourite: they finished in seventy-nine hours, forty-three minutes and were greeted with a huge bouquet as the first women's tandem team ever to complete P-B-P.

A former marathon runner turned cyclist in 1980, Lou Hotton must burn calories the way my furnace burns coal in the winter. She not only rides a bike, she runs, swims, plays soccer, skis in winter, and works out with weights. How does she feel about the results?

To my survey question about whether cycling exercise and nutritious, balanced meals are sufficient for maintaining a satisfactory weight, the ultra-distance cyclist and mother of two checked 'yes'. In the margin she added, 'Pretty much – although sometimes my expectations are unrealistic'. And therein lies a sharp appraisal of the position women find themselves in today.

WOMEN AND BODY IMAGE

It is not simply that one woman might have unrealistic expectations. It is the expectations of an entire society regarding women and body image that have become unrealistic. In recent years we've seen a disturbing mass obsession among women with food and thinness. The tide is turning now, at least in America, and women are less driven to be ultra-skinny.

But now there's a new image. According to a recent Gallup Poll conducted for *American Health* magazine and reported in 1988, the average woman would like to trade in her soft body tone for a more muscular, fitter silhouette. Yes, she'd also like to drop about 10 pounds, so the thin ideal hasn't completely disappeared. What's going on? Are we more concerned with being fit or with looking fit? Are we simply subscribing to another stereotypical (if possibly more natural) image of beauty? Are we freer to be ourselves these days, or must we now all have designer muscles?

In a consumer age in which women's bodies are constantly being utilised to sell goods, girls are taught early in life to regard their appearance as currency for getting what they want. In the process, we ourselves become the sales targets of advertising media in general, and the diet and beauty industry in particular. To win love, friends, and fortune, society tells us we must look a certain way. Most particularly, the 'in' body type is dictated by a barrage of media messages as if body size and type were a hemline we could raise or lower at will. Not to have the fashionable shape can produce an inhibiting self-consciousness, a sort of 'body insecurity'. As long as any single silhouette is in vogue, to the exclusion of other naturally occurring body types, many women will suffer under a dreadful burden, attempting to fit the fashion.

The notion of an ideal body type is nothing new. The flat-chested flapper was the image of the 1920s. Then from the 'thirties through the 'fifties, voluptuousness and curves, narrow waists and large breasts were the ideal feminine attributes.

The slimming of the modern ideal began in the early 1960s with English model Jean Shrimpton ('the Shrimp'), writes the British feminist psychotherapist Susie Orbach in *Hunger Strike* (W. W. Norton and Company, 1986). The media soon brought us the exploits of the Jet Setters, who could not be too chic or too thin, and whose thinness came to connote freedom and high style. Later, fashion model Twiggy came out of a working-class background to democratise the trend. In America in the 'sixties the Establishment witnessed a youth rebellion on many fronts. Consumer advertising soon capitalised on it, pairing with thinness the struggle against aging.

In the 'seventies, as women were asserting themselves in the workplace, seeking a larger role and comparable pay, was it a coincidence that fashion should demand this threatening figure to shrink further? To try to live up to the body image ideal, to become thinner and thinner, requires tremendous reserves of a woman's time and energy – resources that must be turned inward instead of outward for other accomplishment.

The 'eighties have seen the fitness boom. Muscles are 'in'. We've also seen a disturbing increase in anorexia and bulimia among young women. And we see adolescent and pre-adolescent girls who are now so attuned to popular adult conceptions of beauty that normal weight girls take up crash dieting and purging.

In fact, in one recent study of 271 adolescent boys and girls, almost half the girls believed themselves too fat although 83 per cent of the girls who made that judgment were, in fact, normal weight for height. More than half of the girls had dieted, and 15 per cent had induced vomiting to lose weight. By contrast the boys who thought themselves overweight, tended to be so. Only 14 per cent of the boys had tried dieting, and fewer than 1 per cent had tried purging for weight loss.

One of the dangers of dieting is that it can actually lead to longterm weight *gain* through slowed metabolism and deprivation-induced binge eating, as Polivy and Herman point out.

Their research, they note, supports the theory that each person has a setpoint, or 'natural weight range' as they prefer to call it, below which weight loss is extremely difficult because of many natural defences of the body.

On the other hand, they say, if an individual has put on weight above her natural weight range, theoretically the body should put up less resistance to losing it. Even then, however, weight loss ought to be gradual and exercise has a key role to play in helping bring it about.

In this short space it's easy to oversimplify the issue. But I wanted to put expectations about weight control into perspective. Society encourages women to worry too much about their appearance. A belief that changing our looks will solve all our problems is a trap that's easy to fall into.

Perhaps a more realistic and worthwhile aim is to improve our fitness level, feel better, and have more energy for the things we do throughout the day. These goals seem to be shared by women who take up cycling and stick with it. Fitness was the number one reason survey respondents gave. The next two most frequent reasons had to do with enjoying the sport. (See Survey Findings: Reasons for Involvement with Cycling.)

Survey Findings: Reasons for Involvement with Cycling

Respondents were asked to check off their reasons for taking up cycling and keeping it up. 'Fitness', chosen by 84.7 per cent of the women, ranked highest. 'Weight control', selected by 45.8 per cent, ranked only fourth. Reasons appear below in descending order of frequency in selection.

84.7%	Fitness
73.7%	Recreation, seeing the countryside
46.5%	An activity to enjoy with friends or club
45.8%	Weight control
36.1%	Cycle touring
25.3%	Because boyfriend or husband rides
24.1%	Local transportation, commuting
12.8%	Competitive racing

If we want to lose weight and firm up in the process, that may happen too. And if it does, I hope you will feel as good about it as the women whose comments introduced the chapter . . . and not regret it if you don't manage to look like the bodybuilder models pumping iron in TV commercials.

'As women we need to move away from what a sport can do for our appearance, and into a pure appreciation for how our preferred activity makes us feel,' writes one very perceptive cyclist. 'Only if we accept that form follows function will we have the freedom to search for and discover the sport that is uniquely right for us as individuals.'

I couldn't agree more. And a perfect example of that is Karen Dowie, 30, from Des Moines, Iowa. 'The best part of biking is my self-confidence,' she writes. 'All my life I've had a short, stocky body – very muscular. I've always hated my build. Finally I found a sport I'm built for! My large, powerful legs are great for passing all kinds of cyclists on hills,' she observes, and she should know. Recently she did the popular cross-Iowa ride (known as RAGBRAI) with about 10,000 other cyclists. And Iowa *does* have hills.

'I love hills,' Karen goes on. 'The best part of my ride is hills, the bigger the better. If my muscles aren't burning at the top of a hill, it wasn't challenging enough.

'Biking has done wonders for my self-image. I've finally found a sport that "fits" me and I'm good at!'

11 *Building Fitness*

If you followed the tips in chapter 7, Out of the Garage and on the Road, you've reacquainted yourself with cycling. You've familiarised yourself with your new bike (or one languishing in your garage), you've established the beginnings of good riding technique, and refreshed your memory on the rules of the road. It's time now to set your goals and start riding toward them.

GO-FOR-IT GOALS

A satisfying goal, in cycling as in anything else, is one you think you can meet but you have to stretch yourself at least a little bit to do it. It should be performance-related and specific, so you know when you've done it. And it should fit your idea of cycling fun and accomplishment. So be creative: it doesn't have to centre on speed or on competing with anyone else. Consider, for example, Amy's goal in her first year of riding.

Last year I promised myself I'd cycle to Pratt's Falls, a local park, and back before summer's end. Though it was only 26 miles, it would be my longest ride and a new destination. There's something a little scary about riding to a new place. But then bicycling in general is a real adventure – on a small scale, with small delights and surprises. Afterward I feel I've really accomplished something.

On this early Sunday morning ride, the sky was cloudy and a storm threatened, but I decided to go anyway, telling myself I could always turn back or find shelter.

On the way out I bought bagels at a drugstore that opens early on weekends. On Woodchuck Road I passed three deer who were as startled to see me as I was to see them. I came upon a deserted green field canopied with brightly striped tents (the site, I later learned, of a fair about to take place).

At last at the falls, I ate a bagel and then headed home. En route I had a dazzling view of a local lake as I sped down a steep hill.

Considered singly, these things might not seem like much, but it was all new to me. This sense of being able to try something new and succeed spills over into other parts of my life. It's great!

Amy Hubbard, 33, Syracuse, New York

Many riders like having a big goal to climax the riding season – something to work towards. I do. Typically I'll sign up early in the season for a big group ride, or a bicycle tour, or even a triathlon in August or September. It's no coincidence that in the US September is Century Month, with many clubs holding these 100-mile challenge rides.

At the same time it's good to have a series of goals to meet throughout the season, so you have a regular success 'fix' and proof of improvement. These short-term goals should be compatible with a gradual increase in mileage, so that your endurance builds naturally and you don't ask too much of yourself too soon. The year I trained for my first European cycle tour, one of my intermediate goals was to ride alone from my city to another (a distance of about 55 miles), on a Saturday, carrying clothes I needed for a weekend visit with my parents; they had indulgently promised to drive me and my bicycle home afterwards. Like Amy I enjoyed the adventure. It involved map reading and finding my way along surprisingly scenic back roads. I didn't even mind that it rained most of the way; it gave me a chance to try my new rain suit.

Racers also confirm the importance of intermediate goals. Olympic gold medalist Connie Carpenter Phinney says that as she came up through the ranks, she set goals a week or a month ahead. Not until she neared the top in 1982 did she let herself dream of the gold medal.

Having well-thought-out goals needn't rule out spontaneity, though, as Toni's example proves. Toni Childs-Gray, 27, had just been introduced to a 'terrific guy' who, like her, was interested in cycling. He asked her to join him for a ride and picked a devilishly hilly route in their Sacramento, California area.

Toni says,

I think I surprised him by being able to keep up until the last killer hill. I really struggled but made it.

A week later he asked me to ride again on the same course. This time I was prepared. I'd worked on hills all week. You should have seen the look on his face as I called, 'On your left,' and passed him near the top! From then on it was a sweet ride downhill to the jacuzzi.

I suggest you set a goal for each month of this season. For new cyclists here are a few ideas:

- First month: explore your area and find three different routes you like. Ride at least twice a week.
- Second month: find a local cycling club or other group that welcomes new cyclists on short rides. Join them for a 25-miler.
- Third month: treat yourself to a weekend bike tour in some area you'd enjoy discovering. Pick a low-mileage, organised tour (35-miles/day maximum) with pleasant lodgings.
- Fourth month: select a challenging organised ride that strikes your fancy. Prove what you can do.

105

MAKING THE MOST OF YOUR TRAINING

Don't be put off by the word 'training'. If you choose to ride regularly, regardless of the level of intensity, you *are* training and you'll experience benefits.

A few principles lay the foundation for any training programme. Once you understand them, you can tailor the suggestions that follow to meet your needs. By the way, if your interests are divided between cycling and other pursuits, you may substitute other aerobic activities for some cycling sessions. Such 'cross-training' is fine so long as your goal is to be well-rounded rather than the best cyclist you can be.

All cycling training programmes begin with *aerobic* conditioning. That is, you set a moderate pace at which your muscles can be fuelled by the oxygen you're burning. Racers resuming training after a brief winter layoff begin with many miles of steady, aerobic riding in low-to-medium gears before they sharpen up with more demanding speedwork. For more casual cyclists as well, aerobic conditioning is the key for developing endurance. In the process muscles and joints are also strengthened.

Finding your heart rate. To ride aerobically, what you want to do is ride with a brisk cadence at a steady pace, raising your heart rate high enough to create a training effect but not so high that you wear yourself out too quickly.

How fast is that? After a while you'll be able to tell simply by how you feel. You should feel your rate of breathing increase, but you shouldn't feel so breathless that you can't talk. The most casual of cyclists may find this a sufficient guideline and not concern themselves with formulas or pulse taking.

Learn to Take Your Resting Pulse

Your resting pulse is one indicator of your fitness level. Racers typically take their resting pulse each morning and record it in their training diaries. You can keep track of your resting pulse too by writing it on your training calendar or diary. Over a period of time you should see a gradual lowering of your resting pulse as your fitness improves.

Resting pulse is usually taken just after waking in the morning while still lying quietly in bed. Take your pulse for fifteen seconds and multiply by four to determine your resting pulse for one minute.

However, if you'd like to be sure you're within your *target heart range* you can use what exercise physiologists refer to as the Karvonen formula.

Step 1. Subtract your age from 226 (for women; 220 for men) to compute your Maximum Heart Rate (MHR).
Step 2. Subtract your resting pulse (see box) from your MHR.
Step 3. Multiply that figure by .60, then add your resting pulse rate, to calculate the lower limit of your target heart range.

Step 4. Multiply that same figure from Step 2 by .85, then add your resting pulse rate, to calculate the upper limit of your target heart range.

226 – Your age = MHR
MHR – resting pulse x .60 + resting pulse = lower limit
MHR – resting pulse x .85 + resting pulse = upper limit

For example, let's say Jennifer, 30, has a resting pulse of 77.

226 − 30 = 196 (Jennifer's MHR)
196 − 77 × .60 + 77 = 148 bpm (beats per minute)
196 − 77 × .85 + 77 = 178 bpm

Jennifer's target heart range is between 148 and 178 bpm. She should achieve training benefits if she keeps her heart rate within that range as she rides. Theoretically, she would improve more quickly if she trains somewhere in the upper portion of that range during at least some of her rides. However, she must also be guided by which level of exertion feels comfortable to maintain.

How do you know your heart rate when riding? Many racers – like British Olympic team member Maria Blower – cycle with a heart rate monitor. 'I use it when riding on a relatively flat route to keep my pace constant,' she says, 'and when riding on my trainer indoors.' Many recreational cyclists also use cycle-computers with a heart monitor.

Some riders manage instead by taking an exercise pulse. If you can ride no-handed, it's easy, and you can take a pulse at your wrist, which is preferable. If you need to keep one hand on the bar, take a pulse at your neck while coasting briefly during a workout. Press your neck *lightly*, just enough to feel the pulsations. Use your fingers, as the thumb has a pulse of its own. Take the pulse for six seconds only, then multiply by ten to obtain your rate per minute.

If you feel shaky trying it while moving, stop your bike and take your pulse at your wrist for six seconds. Do it immediately or the pulse will drop, making your measurement inaccurate.

Quickening your cadence (rpm). You've already been thinking about cadence, so by now you shouldn't look as if you're pedalling in slow motion. A lively cadence raises your heart rate, makes your legs more supple, and helps you avoid sore knees that can result from pushing too big a gear. Try for a cadence of 80 rpm, or 90 if you can.

If you haven't treated yourself to a computer with a cadence function yet, you might want to: it lets you check cadence frequently, and you'd be surprised how your rpm can lag when you aren't thinking about it. Or wear a watch which shows the seconds. Count revolutions of one pedal for fifteen seconds and multiply by four to get your rpm.

Do you ride with a friend? Now and then you could call out 'Count!', then each count your own cadence for fifteen seconds 'til you call 'Stop!' Don't cheat by suddenly speeding it up; you want to know what you're habitually doing. If her cadence tends to be closer to the desired rpm than yours, then watch and try to match hers.

107

This pacing work goes best on level terrain or gently rolling hills. On bigger hills your cadence will drop as you run out of low gears to shift into. Remember to choose gears according to which one allows the desired cadence. And if you feel the need to coast on level terrain to rest your legs, you should gear down.

Joanne Ernst, the American triathlete who won the 1985 Iron Man, says short-term goal-setting has always been important for 'staying on track toward a long-term goal. Positive feedback from meeting short-term goals keeps me from getting lethargic' (*David Epperson*).

A fast cadence may not feel natural when you first try it. In fact, you may have difficulty keeping your upper body still as you spin your legs. But make a conscious effort not to bounce around.

Now a few thoughts on other equipment matters that can affect cadence: first, if you find your legs rubbing the sides of your saddle as you pedal, your saddle may be too wide and need replacing.

Second, if you don't have toeclips and straps or one of the newer strapless pedal binding systems, it's time to think about adding them because they make pedalling more efficient. Good cyclists pedal 'round', but without a system to fasten your shoe on the pedal, you can only push away and down. In cycling lingo we call that 'pedalling squares'. Efficient riders also pull up on their pedals. To have a brisk and *smooth* pedalling cadence, you must be able to pedal 'round'. You will particularly notice the difference as you concern yourself with cycling hills.

Admittedly, the thought of strapping your foot on to the pedal brings out every new cyclist's fears. You worry you'll fall over because you can't get your foot free. And it seems to happen to everybody – once – sooner or later. Usually you bruise your ego and that's about it.

On the other hand, holding the shoe on the pedal prevents another possible mishap – having your foot slip off the pedal which then catches you in the back of the heel as it comes around. And that hurts.

Maria Blower says, 'I can't imagine riding with nothing holding my feet on the pedals.' This is particularly true for racers because of their very fast cadence in a sprint, which could be anywhere from 120 to 180 rpm. But recreational riders who get used to straps or other pedal binding systems say the same thing.

If you choose to start out with toeclips and straps, which are inexpensive, you can wear the straps loose enough to pull your foot out, until you learn to remember you're wearing them. Experienced riders who use clips and straps often keep the straps loose for stop-and-go riding in town.

It Happens . . .

'Some accidents are just funny. After a long ride a friend and I reached an intersection controlled by a traffic light. It was red for us. We stopped and did track stands, waiting for our arrow. Then boom! My friend fell over. He just lay there like a turtle on his back, both feet still fastened into his Look pedal system and his bike salvaged in the air. I laughed so hard I fell right on top of him. And there we both lay in the middle of a busy intersection on our backs, laughing hysterically!'

Maripat Boland, 24, Norman, Oklahoma

By the way, here's the secret for slipping *into* your toeclips or pedal system without wobbling as you start out. Before mounting up, put one foot in, then step down on the pedal as you always do. Seat yourself on the saddle and continue pedalling for a few revolutions before trying to engage the other foot. Having this momentum helps you keep your balance.

Now to pedal 'round', visualise this: at the top of the pedal stroke, extend your leg forward from the knee. As your foot moves down, gradually add power from the thigh. Keep pressure smooth and even.

Just before the bottom of the stroke, start bending your leg at the knee and pull back on the pedal; the movement is like scraping mud off your shoe on one of those old-fashioned boot scrapers. As the pedal travels upward, you don't have to pull up very hard (except ascending a hill). Just let your leg float up in a smooth motion.

Begin gradually. What this means in terms of miles and pace will vary with each person. The idea is to start with short enough distances and in moderate terrain so you don't feel wrung out and discouraged at the end of a ride. Your body needs to become accustomed to this new activity, especially your knees. This means moderate gearing and gradual increase in mileage.

If you've been riding, a good rule of thumb is to add to your weekly mileage by no more than ten per cent each week.

If you're really new to cycling, begin with rides every other day at first, or three times a week. If commuting is feasible, it's an ideal way to work in some bike miles on a regular basis. After a week or so, you should feel ready to take at least a short ride five or six days a week if you want to. Allow yourself one rest day per week.

Inevitably among many of us the problem arises, 'But I can't ride three or four days during the week.' And if that appears to be so, then you must look for ways around the problem (and a real problem it is for busy women who work full-time and often don't have daylight hours at home for cycling). Buy yourself a stationary bike, trainer, or rollers and pedal indoors. It's not as much fun as riding *al fresco* but you can beat the boredom and build strength by doing intervals. (Apply what you learn about such speedwork in chapter 16, Fitter and Faster.)

Especially in winter, many busy cyclists run during their lunch hour or before or after work instead of riding that day. You'd not be using precisely the same muscles, but it's a good aerobic workout nonetheless. If this is your choice, begin with low running mileage – say, 2 miles – and gradually increase to avoid overuse injury. Figure 1 mile of running roughly equivalent to 3 miles on your bicycle. If you are not up to running, then walk briskly, swinging your arms.

Easy day/hard day. A widely accepted rule for everyone who rides almost daily is to alternate 'hard' workout days with 'easy' days which let your body rest. In the beginning stages of conditioning, 'hard' means longer distances. (Later on, it could also refer to efforts of higher intensity.) Do shorter rides on 'easy' days.

For example, if you do your longest ride over the weekend, then Monday and Friday are good choices for easy days. If you want to take a somewhat longer ride during the week, do it mid-week. You'll build endurance more quickly if you vary the lengths of your rides this way instead of always cycling the same distance. In fact, as soon as you feel up to it, make your long ride twice the length of your regular training rides.

Following such a plan, you can start with very low mileage and increase surprisingly quickly. A new rider's schedule might look like the one opposite. This is fine for most purposes – fitness and recreational riding as well as conditioning for touring.

Keep in mind that you don't have to increase every week if it seems like too much effort. You might hit a comfortable plateau that feels good and suits the time you have available.

This schedule is just a sample. You can make up your own, following these principles. Many riders devise their training programme based on time rather than miles. This works especially well for cyclists who ride on hills one day and on the flats another. In this case, effort is more easily gauged if you measure it in time.

	miles/ week-day	miles/5-day week	miles/ weekend	maximum total/week
April				
(Week 1)	2–5	10–25	6–12	37
(Week 2)	*	*	*	40
(Week 3)	*	*	*	45
(Week 4)	*	*	*	50
May				
(Week 1)	4–7	20–35	10–20	55
(Week 2)	*	*	*	60
(Week 3)	*	*	*	67
(Week 4)	*	*	*	73
June				
(Week 1)	6–9	30–40	20–40	80
(Week 2)	*	*	*	88
(Week 3)	*	*	*	97
(Week 4)	*	*	*	100
July				
(Week 1)	8–11	40–55	40–60	105
(Week 2)	*	*	*	115
(Week 3)	*	*	*	125
(Week 4)	*	*	*	137

* Increase mileage according to your preference within the established pattern, to meet the week's total.

HOW TO STICK WITH IT

Look for scenic routes. Experiment with your daily schedule to find the time you most enjoy riding. For many cyclists, like Vivien Turnbull, 51, of Harwich, Essex, that's when others are sleeping.

> I ride in the early morning when few people are about, along country lanes where wildlife abounds or down to the beach, sparkling with the rising sun. On such a morning in late spring, I met a horseman. As we passed, he called out to me, 'Look at that! Over there! The first swallow of summer!' I followed his gaze and there it was, swooping low over the glistening meadow . . .

A magic moment like that can make your whole day.

Tell someone else your goal. When that person shares your expectations, you'll have two reasons to live up to them. Gail Johnson, 29, of Fergins Falls, Minnesota, took this idea a step farther by involving her entire family:

> During my first summer of serious cycling I would ride once a week to my parents' house, 27 miles away. It would take 2½ hours each way and was quite a feat for me. I'd ride up, take my younger brothers swimming, then ride home. It made for a rather full day, and I really felt good about myself. Nobody else in my family exercised at the time, so they were rather impressed. They also thought I was nuts, but they're coming around now . . .

Keep a training diary. It's satisfying to see the miles add up and witness your progress. In fact, you'll find a training diary excellent motivation to keep up your cycling at those moments everyone experiences when they're tempted to call it quits. Even more important, a diary is a valuable tool for learning how your body responds to training – the reason why most racers keep a diary. Use a simple format and record the date, miles (or hours) ridden, and the weather. Add where you rode and with whom, and how you felt. If you time a ride to judge your progress, record that too. Your very first entry for each day will probably be your resting pulse, if you take it. You may want to add more details to describe special rides.

Prove what you can do (*Dan Burden*).

What can you learn from your diary? You'll see patterns. You may find that an increase by several beats in your resting pulse means you're coming down with something, a cold perhaps, or it may correlate with a sudden increase in training mileage and a feeling of tiredness a few days later.

If you've never kept a diary like this before, you may be surprised how much you can learn about your body from it. Look your diary over from time to time, to see what seems to benefit your cycling most. And if one of these days you suddenly feel as if you have cement in your tyres, check your diary to see what might have you dragging.

Find a riding partner or partners. For most of us it's more fun to have company. Even if you're a self-starter, it's great to have somebody else to suggest meeting for a ride. And you have extra motivation knowing you don't want to disappoint your partner by wimping out at the last minute.

If you have a choice of riding companions to divide your training time with, you could do well to ride one day with someone a little faster than you so that you work harder. And, riding with more experienced cyclists, you pick up better riding technique almost by osmosis. On another day train with someone at your own level. Unless you're the highly competitive type, riding catch-up all the time can be discouraging.

Get to know yourself and what motivates you. What puts me off might bring out the best in you. Consider the case of Karen Bell, 26, of Mystic, Connecticut:

> After I took up cycling I began riding with competitive women in the area. Because of my pride, I seemed always to be in so much pain just to keep up . . . and sometimes I couldn't even do that. I read cycling magazines, dropped 10 pounds, cross-trained with swimming, and developed a better attitude. A male cycling friend convinced me to try a time trial so I could gauge my improvement.
>
> On time trial day I was only a little nervous. I'd been doing pretty well on the road for the last month, so expected to do okay. As it turned out, I took first place in the women's division. I even beat the two women who used to drop me only four months before! As a full-time working mother, I felt well rewarded to be competitive with women who train all the time and are responsible only for themselves.

You will improve, so tell yourself that when a ride gets tough. And find ways to measure your progress. Don't race against a stopwatch for every ride; that's too much pressure. But you might time yourself once a week or every other week on the same route and keep a record of it. Or take a gamble and try riding the club's time trial. Who knows what you can do until you try?

12 *Fuelling the Engine*

I was about 75 miles into a century, when all my technique and form just fell apart. I'd been riding with a small group in a paceline, and then a couple of us were dropped. The least little hill was an ordeal, my cadence was slowing. No matter how hard I tried, I had no power, so I was shifting to lower and lower gears. I kept losing ground even to the friend who was riding with me – he'd wait for me from time to time at the top of a hill.

I was starting to wonder whether I was going to complete the 100 miles. Then I fished a cookie out of my pocket and ate it. In a few minutes things came together for me, and I finished strongly.

Ellen Dorsey, 45, Bethlehem, Pennsylvania

Successful completion of a challenging ride depends not only on training and comfort on your bike, but on something seemingly so simple as what and when you eat and drink. Here Ellen Dorsey has described the draining experience endurance athletes call 'hitting the wall'. In a way, it's like running out of gas. But savvy riders like Ellen know how to pick themselves up out of an energy slump – better yet, how to prevent one – and so will you. And this doesn't apply just to 100-mile efforts. For some, a challenging ride might be considerably shorter.

To continue the automobile analogy, not only must we fuel our muscles, but we have to be mindful of our 'cooling systems'. We need to drink plenty to keep fluid levels up, or stay *hydrated*. In this chapter we'll talk about these aspects of nutrition and the way training and exercise intensity affect how energy is burned, or *metabolised*.

FOUNDATIONS OF GOOD NUTRITION

How you must fuel your engine is not terribly complicated.

The first important thing to understand is that the basis for good nutrition for sport in general and cycling in particular is a well-balanced diet. This is the same sort of nutrition which is recommended to promote heart health and ward off cancer – a diet in which the majority of calories are provided by complex carbohydrates, and dietary fat is kept to a minimum. This, in fact, is the same principle behind the smartest way to curb calories for weight loss, if that is one's goal.

While on the subject of fundamentals, I'd love to let the air out of a couple of myths about protein: Myth 1 – Some dieters still cling to the notion that high-protein/low-carbohydrate diets are the path toward weight-loss. Myth 2 – Some athletes believe that eating more protein enhances performance. The fact is there are a number of problems with high-protein diets, and one is that protein in food is hard to get without taking in fat at the same time. Fat has twice the calories of carbohydrates (9 calories per gram compared to 4), and fat calories are harder for the body to metabolise.

As for the myth that athletes need more protein, the typical Western diet, even that of vegetarians if they eat nutrient-dense, complex carbohydrates, includes ample protein to build and repair muscles. And protein provides little energy during exercise. But a diet low in carbohydrates robs us of energy needed for daily activities and most certainly for exercise.

Therefore, nutritionists recommend that almost half of the calories you take in come from complex carbohydrates. According to nutritionist Ann Grandjean, Ed D, a healthful regime for the average person would break down as follows:

- at least 55 per cent carbohydrates, of which no more than 10 per cent comes from refined sugars (table sugar, honey, jellies, etc.) and 45 per cent or more comes from complex carbohydrates plus the sugars in milk and fresh fruits.
- 15 per cent protein
- a maximum of 30 per cent fat, of which 10 per cent is polyunsaturated, 10 per cent is monounsaturated, and 10 per cent is saturated. Even better is limiting dietary fat to 25 per cent, by eliminating half of the saturated fats. (In this case, total carbohydrate consumption would rise to 60 per cent.)

Experts encourage us to base our meals on whole foods as much as possible, and according to a food group plan, such as the Basic Five, that meets our needs for vitamins, minerals, fibre and other good things. These three dictums are the key to good nutrition. What do they mean?

Complex carbohydrates. These include the food group known as 'starches' – whole grain breads, pasta, dried beans of all kinds, rice, potatoes – plus vegetables. These are rich in vitamins and minerals and are a good source of fibre. They fill us up and help us feel satisfied. Complex 'carbos' provide long-lasting energy because they metabolise in a slow, steady burn. And they are not fattening – until we slather butter or margarine on our bread, or make our potatoes into chips (French fries). Well-planned vegetarian meals (which provide excellent nutrition) draw heavily on complex carbohydrates.

Simple sugars. *Monosaccharides* are found naturally in fruits and honey, while the slightly more complex *disaccharides* include table sugar. Both forms of sugar are broken down quickly in the body and provide a quick burst of energy (followed by an insulin reaction that lowers blood sugar levels). Athletes can use simple sugars to stretch performance, as Ellen did.

115

Whole foods. Assuming you structure your food plan in the above proportions, nutritionists Frances Sienkiewicz Sizer and Linda Kelly DeBruyne say there are two 'absolutely unbreakable rules' which, if followed, ensure a good diet. The first is to eat mostly whole foods – foods that are as fresh from the garden as possible. This is the state in which they offer the most vitamins, minerals, fibre along with the calories they supply. For example, fresh asparagus, lightly steamed, is much more nutritious (not to mention tasty and appealing) than the same vegetable out of a can; to serve, merely pour on a few drops of balsamic or herbed vinegar – delicious! A creative touch with salads – a crisp toss perhaps of mixed greens, sprouts, shredded carrots, apple slivers, toasted sunflower seeds, and thinly sliced onion with a light splash of vinaigrette – adds nourishment and eye-appeal to your table.

Now let's be realistic. I don't grow my own broccoli, green beans, and asparagus, for good reasons (like lack of space and time) which many of us share. But I do buy my vegetables and fruits fresh from a local farm market or greengrocer's. My husband and I have found a few quick, easy ways to prepare them that we enjoy. Sure, we open a can of something once in a while, like whole tomatoes that we use in cooking. But a daily regime of supermarket micro-wavable entrées, canned veggies, and fast food on the run provides fewer nutrients and more fats and simple sugars than do fresh fruits and vegetables and your own home-cooking.

The Basic Five. Variety is the soul of good nutrition – that's Sizer and De Bruyne's second rule. If you build your meals from the Basic Five food groups, you'll select foods of sufficient variety to provide the vitamins and minerals, proteins and carbohydrates you need. The US Department of Agriculture's Human Nutrition Information Service recommends these guidelines as 'a pattern for daily food choices'. It is for individuals who regularly eat foods from each group. For the average woman (I'm not presuming to advise the diabetic) the following comprise a balanced diet:

- *Meat; poultry; fish; and alternates (eggs, dried beans and peas, nuts, and seeds).* Two to three servings daily will give you ample protein to build and repair muscle. To minimise saturated fats, choose lean cuts of meat and skinless poultry. Fish has less fat, and *legumes* (dried peas, beans, and lentils) have even less – and it's unsaturated. If the latter are new to you, a good vegetarian cookbook will show you how to turn dried peas and beans into flavourful, inexpensive dishes that diversify your menus.

  What's a 'serving'? It's not a steak that covers your plate. For cooked, lean meats, 5–7 ounces is recommended. Servings of fish and poultry are usually a little larger, and with beans larger still.
- *Milk; cheese; yoghurt.* Two to four servings a day. The USDA recommends three servings for teens and all women up to age 24 as well as women who are pregnant or breastfeeding, and four servings for pregnant or breastfeeding teens. Skimmed milk and skimmed milk products – cottage cheese, low- or non-fat yoghurt are most highly recommended. A serving is

1 cup of milk or cottage cheese, 8 ounces of yoghurt, or 1½ ounces of natural cheese. Dairy products are important, but not the only, sources of calcium, an important nutrient discussed later in this chapter.

- *Bread; cereal; pasta; rice.* Would you believe, six to eleven servings daily? These are the complex carbohydrates you need. Select whole grain bread (rich in fibre and B vitamins); if you want to spread something on it, a little jam is no sin. Pasta can be served with sauces that win raves but are still low in fat. This group isn't fattening unless you make it that way with butter, gravy, or other fatty toppings.
- *Fruits.* Eat two to four pieces or servings of fresh fruit a day. These are high in fibre and vitamins C and A. Hint: a good start to the day is topping a bowl of whole grain cereal with sliced bananas, peaches or berries and pouring on the skimmed milk; it tastes so good I don't even add sugar.
- *Vegetables.* At 3–6 ounces a serving, eat three to five servings per day. All veggies provide valuable fibre. The dark green, leafy ones provide nutrients like vitamin A, folacin (a B vitamin that helps to make red blood cells and haemoglobin), iron and magnesium that tend to be low in most diets. Deep-yellow vegetables also are rich in vitamin A. Starchy vegetables, like potatoes, corn, green peas, and dried peas and beans, offer B_6 as well as folacin, iron and magnesium.

The USDA recognises a sixth group, *Fats, Sweets, and Alcoholic Beverages,* which provides little nutrition and should be consumed in moderation.

This is the basis of good nutrition for sport. (If you want further information on the dietary guidelines, write to Eating Right, USDA, Washington, DC 20250 for a list of helpful, inexpensive publications.) For cyclists whose mileage is modest, there isn't much more to it, except understanding how energy is metabolised and timing the refuelling.

Cyclists with demanding training schedules require more calories, and to a point can supply these by increasing the quantity of complex carbohydrates in their daily diet. However, some athletes can eat their fill of beans and rice and still not get enough calories. Additional refined sugars and sometimes fats are required to meet the need. These can supplement the wholesome foundation we've been talking about.

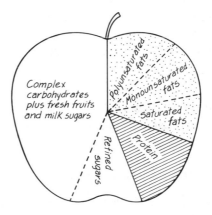

Fats 25-30% of Total calories
Protein 15%
Carbohydrates 55-60%

Fig. 14
Bite into this regime for good daily nutrition.

ENERGY FOR EXERCISE

Just how are our human engines fuelled for cycling? By now you're familiar with the concept of pacing yourself – riding at a speed which lets you go the desired distance on a particular day. You've discovered, maybe by trial and error, that you can make an intense effort for a relatively short distance or go long distances at an easier pace. What you're doing in pacing yourself like this is calling on the appropriate energy system for the type of effort you've chosen to make.

Any exercise lasting more than about two minutes draws on two fuels for the muscles, *glucose* and *free fatty acids*, both of which require *oxygen* brought to the muscle via the bloodstream for the fuel to be utilised. Where do these fuels come from?

Glucose comes mainly from *glycogen*, which is stored carbohydrate. At most our bodies hold about 3 to 4 pounds of this fuel in reserve, most of it in the muscles, with about ¾ of a pound of glycogen stored in the liver. How much glycogen is stockpiled in the body depends on how much carbohydrate we eat. Cutting down on the percentage of carbohydrate in the diet will reduce the amount of this precious fuel we have to draw on.

By contrast, free fatty acids are provided by the body's fat stores – which we could never deplete, no matter how long we exercise. We needn't try to increase the fat content in our diets because we have plenty to meet energy needs. If we could only burn enough fatty acids to fuel the entire effort, our endurance would be greatly increased. But it doesn't work that way.

Exercise intensity – how hard you're working – is an important factor in determining which fuel is being burned. At or below 50 per cent of maximum effort (measured in terms of oxygen consumption or VO_2max) fat is the chief source of fuel while glycogen is used in lesser proportion. As this leisurely pace is increased to above 70 per cent of VO_2max – for example, in a training ride or a race – glycogen becomes the main fuel.

If you ride long enough at this faster pace, glycogen is gradually depleted and the body has only fat for fuel. However, because fatty acids require more oxygen for metabolising than glycogen does, the transition is not easily made. Fatigue sets in, muscles stiffen, and thinking may get hazy as even the brain runs out of glucose.

FIGHTING OFF FATIGUE

The informed cyclist has these weapons in her arsenal for fighting fatigue during endurance efforts.

Conditioning. A gradual conditioning programme that includes long rides, as recommended in chapter 11, Building Fitness, helps muscles improve their ability to use free fatty acids as fuel. The body slowly adapts so that the trained cyclist can use fat for energy at a higher work intensity than can an untrained rider. As the riding season progresses, you may notice enhanced endurance as fat metabolism becomes easier.

Carbo loading. At the same time, cyclists preparing for endurance events can store extra glycogen by increasing carbohydrate intake up to 80 per cent of the total for three days prior to competition. By emphasising grains, starchy vegetables, fruits, and low-fat milk, you can meet protein and other nutrient needs while loading in the needed complex carbohydrates. A few extra slices of toast with jam would also be in the spirit of things. This method of glycogen enhancement is called *carbo loading*.

The usual approach is to do a fairly strenuous *depletion* ride 5–7 days before the endurance event. The idea is to ride hard in the time allotted (even a good, intense hour could be enough) so that towards the end your legs feel pretty tired. This would be your last hard ride before the big event. The depletion ride uses most of your existing glycogen stores so muscles are hungry for the glycogen provided during the 3 days of loading. Then the muscles really pack it in.

On those days after the depletion ride but before you begin loading, train moderately. Then during those three carbo-loading days limit cycling to a few easy miles. Be sure to drink plenty of water during this time, as glycogen production requires water. In fact, it causes water to be stored in the body, to be released later as glycogen is broken down during your endurance event. Don't be disturbed to notice yourself several pounds heavier as a result of loading; it is the water weight.

When should you carbo load? Don't bother for an event shorter than 1 hour, for example, as normal glycogen supplies should be ample. In contrast, century riders often carbo load, as do marathon runners.

Energy in your pocket. Ellen's well-timed biscuit, a bunch of grapes, a sweet juicy plum – any of these or other snacks which contain simple sugars can give a boost after you've been riding for an hour or so and your energy starts to flag. Indeed, Ellen probably should have been nibbling regularly all along. The maxim in cycling is, 'Eat before you are hungry; drink before you are thirsty.'

This is why cycling jerseys have pockets: in long races a rider's support crew hands up a *musette* (bag with a long strap) containing fruit, biscuits, sometimes little sandwiches; the racer slows just enough to grab the musette, slings it over a shoulder and pedals on, stuffing the carbo-rich snacks in the back jersey pockets.

Even if you don't race or ride centuries, take a few tips from the racers. They learn from experience which foods digest most easily while riding and when to eat. So can you. If you start off on what is, for you, a long ride, pop one of these snacks in your bike bag. Or have in mind a spot where you can buy food when you might need it.

One of my friends, Reg Tauke, 50, of Bath, Pennsylvania, remembers a ride on which she reached the 60-mile point and just had to stop for something to perk her up. 'There were only 10 more miles to go,' she says, 'and I probably would have made it okay. But I said to myself, "I'm not enjoying this. I just don't have the energy to turn the pedals." So I went into one of those gas station convenience stores and bought a 32-ounce cola – one of those 79c mini-mart specials – and drank it. In a few minutes I was fine.'

The caffeine/sugar combo in her cola is an old pro's trick often used near the end of a race to coax extra performance from tiring legs.

119

If you're riding all day, experts advise that frequent, small snacks are more easily digested than one or two belly-buster meals. And they suggest avoiding foods high in fat, as they take longer to digest. Experiment to see what works best for you.

More miles to the gallon. The most important ingredient you can put in your water bottle is water. However, in one form or another you can add a little sugar to that water for longer rides when you think your glycogen is likely to run low. A tablespoon of sugar or a half-cup of fruit juice added to a pint of water creates an inexpensive, homemade energy drink. If you expect to exert yourself steadily for three hours or more, you may want a drink with higher sugar content. Of course, you can experiment with increasing the amount of added sugar in your own drink. Or you can buy a commercially prepared sports drink. Look for one with a 5 to 10 per cent concentration of carbohydrate. Although there are drinks with considerably higher concentrations, current research indicates those higher concentrations cause nausea for some riders. Even within the 5 to 10 per cent range, you may find you tolerate, say, a 6 per cent drink better than one with more carbohydrate. Obviously, you should experiment with the drink when training rather than during an important event. You may try several different drinks in order to find the one that agrees with you and tastes best.

To replenish blood glucose stores to forestall fading, carbohydrate researcher Edward F. Coyle, PhD, advises you to start guzzling the sports drink from the very beginning of the ride. Coyle, who directs the human performance laboratory at the University of Texas at Austin, says to drink lots – 150 to 250 millilitres every fifteen minutes. (Figure a standard water bottle to hold 590 ml.)

Coyle's research shows that this sort of fortification lets you postpone fatigue during a long ride about forty-five to sixty minutes longer than if you simply drink plain water.

It's important to realise, by the way, that research in this area is ongoing. Scientists don't have all the answers about these metabolic processes. And the advice that circulated about five years ago is now out of date. For example, earlier it was believed that carbohydrate concentrations higher than 2.5 per cent would not empty from the stomach quickly enough for the sugar or the water to be used efficiently by the body. Subsequent studies have shown that, while stomach emptying is slowed somewhat, the important cooling processes seem to be unhampered.

Another widely-held concern a few years back had to do with taking in sugared drinks or foods immediately before the start of a ride. Normally (except in the case of diabetics), consumption of sugar causes insulin to be released into the blood stream. Since the insulin response lowers blood glucose levels, it was reasoned, in combination with the stress of exercise it could actually cause a *hypoglycemic* effect and interfere with performance. It might cause shakiness, irritability, and a reduction of energy.

Whether this actually happens and how common it is remains a matter of controversy. Coyle believes that most cyclists never notice such effects and that the benefits for fending off later fatigue are more significant. True hypoglycemics, however, could experience more serious effects signalling insulin shock, such as headache, confusion, cold sweat, hallucinations, convulsions, even coma. Real hypoglycemia is the exception, not the norm, and sufferers should already have their own dietary guidelines; and they should avoid ingesting sugar before starting to exercise. As for the more typical individual, if you feel you are affected, naturally you can avoid taking in sugar until after you've begun riding.

Another tip: don't mistake these sports drinks for 'health' drinks to be sipped any time of day under any circumstances, especially if you're counting calories. These drinks are designed for use while exercising to prolong endurance. You may also quaff your Gatorade or Pripps Plus immediately after a tough event, since the muscles are hungry for glycogen and will pack it in. Particularly, stage racers and tourists with day-after-day long rides can benefit. Otherwise, if you want a health drink, how about carrot juice . . . or water?

Remember the cyclist's maxim: eat before you're hungry; drink before you're thirsty (Dan Burden).

BEATING DEHYDRATION

Whether you drink plain water or rely on the water in a sports drink, wet, wonderful water is the main thing a cyclist needs to avoid dehydration. That's especially true if weather is hot or, worse, hot and humid, as humidity makes us perspire even more.

121

In both conditions the body can lose a great deal of water in sweat – as much as a couple of quarts or more per hour. We may not feel it on a bicycle because wind dries perspiration as we ride. And thirst is not a reliable indicator. By the time we feel thirsty, we're already on the way to dehydration.

That can be dangerous. 'I could have died if a motorist hadn't found me,' says Janet Noll, 38, speaking of the day the heat got her on a training ride. She was living in Palm Springs, California. An experienced cyclist, Janet knew the importance of staying hydrated and carried two water bottles on her bike. On this June day it wasn't enough.

With temperatures routinely above 100 degrees that summer Janet tried to start early on her rides – often by 7.30 am but always by 9.00.

That morning I started late for my two-hour ride and foolishly left my helmet behind. Several miles before the end I felt fatigued and stopped to refill my water bottles. I remember little after that, except that about a mile from my house a man found me lying in the street. I'd passed out on my bike. As he helped me up my thinking was fuzzy. He offered to drive me home, but we had an awful time finding it although it wasn't far away. Even as we pulled up to the house, I wasn't sure I recognised it!

Janet was lucky: she had a good bit of road rash and a gash in her head that required twelve stitches in the emergency room, but she's here to tell the tale and to remind us to drink up.

According to research cited by Sizer and DeBruyne, dehydration resulting in a 2 per cent loss of body weight hampers the body's ability to regulate temperature and reduces aerobic endurance. Water losses of 5 per cent of body weight cut the muscles' capacity for work by 20 to 30 per cent. A dangerous rise in body heat can cause heat stroke and even death.

As a journalist covering cycling events with five-hour road race stages, I've seen highly conditioned racers pass out on their bikes from heat exhaustion. I've stood around outside the 'drug control' van, notebook in hand, for a half-hour and longer, while the parched stage winner inside drinks glass after glass of water, still unable to urinate for the required drug test before being interviewed by the press.

It happens these racers were men, whose races are longer than women's typically are. Even so, it's possible to feel the effects of dehydration within ninety minutes of exercise on a hot day. Seasoned women racers know they, too, must make an effort to remain hydrated. As British Olympian Maria Blower says, 'Drinking is really important. Start drinking fifteen minutes into the race, even if you're not thirsty.'

Drink mostly water or your sports drink. Either of these will empty from your stomach and lower intestine and go where it's needed more quickly than anything else, especially when it's hot and you really need to put fluids back into your body. Beer, fruit juices, coffee and tea take longer for your body to assimilate.

If you are going to be riding several hours in the heat, you could add a half-teaspoon of table salt per pint of water (if you are not using a sports drink) to replace salt lost in sweat. This is the most important of the electrolytes that sports drinks replenish, and if you follow this formula you'll obtain similar benefit. For shorter rides don't worry about replacing salt; our normal diets contain plenty of it. Furthermore, with training, our bodies acclimatise and lose less salt in perspiration.

Don't take salt tablets, even for long days in the saddle. They deliver a much bigger dose of salt than anyone needs. If taken without water, they can hasten dehydration dangerously.

Know the signs of dehydration: if you feel lightheaded, dizzy, as if you might faint, or have nausea, or even (despite the heat) chills and goosebumps, you need water and a cool place to sit or lie down. These are the symptoms of *heat exhaustion*. Take them seriously.

If you don't, it's possible that body temperature can rise dramatically, that sweating will stop, you'll have trouble thinking and speaking clearly, and may lose consciousness. These are the symptoms of *heat stroke*, which is life-threatening. If you observe them in yourself or a companion, get immediate emergency help.

However, this need never happen. If you are sensitive to heat, ride in the cool, early part of the day. Wear lightweight clothing that breathes. And drink, drink, drink . . . water – throughout the day – before, during, and after riding. If you approximate this schedule, you should never have a problem and, in fact, it should help prevent other complaints women sometimes experience such as bladder infections, which may be related to problems of dehydration.

When?	How much?
2 hours before your ride	About 3 cups
10–15 minutes before	About 2 cups
During, every 10–20 minutes	½ cup
After	2 cups water for each pound of body weight lost

Source: SPORTS NUTRITION (Chicago, American Dietetic Association, 1986).

Some riders need to take extra care. Cyclists who use blood pressure medication (which causes frequent urination) or diuretics should realise that they may already be slightly dehydrated. Riders who are overweight should be aware that their bodies have less efficient 'cooling systems' – fat works to keep heat in. Discuss any problems or questions with your doctor.

MEETING A WOMAN'S NEED FOR CALCIUM

Most vitamins and minerals that play a role in athletic performance are provided in good supply in a well-balanced diet of nutritious foods. That's often not so, however, with calcium, necessary for muscle contraction as well as for building strong bones. Many women on reduced calorie diets, for example, don't take in enough calcium. In that case, calcium needed for daily activity is taken from our bones.

The very fact that we're increasing our activity level by cycling is helpful in preventing bone-thinning, or *osteoporosis*. According to leading researcher Doctor Everett Smith, 'Bone is a living tissue and requires mechanical strain (through exercise) to maintain itself.'

Other factors can put us at risk for osteoporosis, however:

- Insufficient calcium intake. Although the RDA (recommended daily allowance) for calcium is 800 mg, many women take in only about 600 mg per day.
- High caffeine consumption. Five to eight cups of coffee (or the caffeine equivalent in diet colas and tea) will increase the amount of calcium excreted in urine.
- High protein intake appears to increase bone loss.
- Excess alcohol consumption reduces calcium absorption in our bodies.
- Cigarette smoking has been related to earlier menopause, at which time the protective effect of estrogen, which slows bone-loss, is lost.
- Genetic influences.
- Thin bone structure. A slightly built woman can afford less bone-thinning than one with thicker bones.
- Race. Whites and Orientals have a significantly higher incidence of osteoporosis.

The time to guard against osteoporosis is now. After about the age of 20, though our bones have attained mature size, they can still become denser and stronger if sufficient calcium is provided for them to absorb. If it is not, bones can start thinning even before the age of 40.

Although the RDA is 800 mg of calcium, the recent thinking among experts is that this minimum is too low. Now 1,000 mg of calcium are recommended daily for women under age 35; 1,200 mg for women 35 to 50; and 1,500 mg for women who have passed through menopause. Since this is still somewhat a matter of controversy, the USDA 'patterns' for women's consumption of the Milk/Cheese/Yoghurt group do not reflect these higher calcium-consumption recommendations. You can, however, increase your intake without overdoing dietary fat and cholesterol, if you meet these needs with low-calorie calcium foods such as skimmed milk, low-fat or non-fat yoghurt, and low-fat cottage cheese. The Vitamin D typically added to milk, (in the US) by the way, enhances calcium absorption. Also high in calcium are canned salmon and sardines (bones should be eaten), and various greens (but not spinach). Extremely high in this mineral, though not a staple in the typical Western diet, are various seaweeds.

Supplements may be advisable, but absorption rates are lower than when calcium is provided in a food source. In fact, research shows that some calcium supplements seem not to be absorbed at all. In recent studies by Doctor Ralph F. Shangraw at the University of Maryland some 80 different calcium carbonate supplements (the type generally considered most effective) were tested to see whether they would dissolve quickly enough to be absorbed by our bodies. Many did not.

According to Shangraw, if you're taking a calcium supplement, a simple test will show whether yours is likely to be effective: put your calcium tablet in 6 ounces of room-temperature vinegar. During the next half-hour, stir occasionally. By the end of that time, a good quality tablet will break up into small particles. This indicates it should dissolve completely in an appropriate period of time for absorption.

Although a simple X-ray will not show up bone loss, diagnostic measures do exist for cases in which osteoporosis is suspected or a woman's risk factors indicate reason for concern. Bone density can be measured by means of computed tomography (CT) scan or dual photon absorptiometry. Both methods are clinical tests which involve a dose of radiation.

High Marks for Calcium: A Sampling

Milligrams of Calcium

Milk, 8 oz or 1 cup		Leafy Greens (cooked)	
Skimmed	302	Beet greens (from fresh)	
1% lowfat	300	½ cup	72
2% lowfat	297	Chinese cabbage	126
Whole	291	Broccoli (from fresh) ½ cup	68
Yoghurt, lowfat, 8 oz or 1 cup		Collards (from fresh), ½ cup	179
Plain	415	Collards (from frozen),	
Fruit	345	½ cup	149
Flavoured	389	Kale (from fresh), ½ cup	103
Cheeses		Kale (from frozen), ½ cup	79
American, pasteurised,		Spinach (from fresh) ½ cup	84
processed, 1 oz	174	Turnip greens (from fresh),	
Blue, 1 oz	150	½ cup	126
Cheddar, 1 oz	204	Turnip greens (from frozen),	
Colby, 1 oz	194	½ cup	98
Edam, 1 oz	207	Fish and Other Protein	
Monterey, 1 oz	212	Oysters, raw, 7–9	113
Mozzarella, 1 oz	183	Salmon, with bones, 3 oz	167
Munster, 1 oz	203	Sardines, with bones, 3 oz	372
Swiss, 1 oz	272	Shrimp, canned, 3 oz	99
Cottage, 2% lowfat, 1 cup	154	Dried beans, cooked, 1 cup	90
Low fat Ricotta, ½ cup	335	Bean curd (tofu)*, 4 oz	145
		Other	
		Molasses, black strap, 1 tbsp	137

*Only if processed with calcium sulphate
Source: National Dairy Council (USA)

IRON WOMAN

The other mineral deficiency common among women, particularly menstruating women and teens, is iron deficiency. Female endurance athletes are especially vulnerable. During long, strenuous exercise iron is lost in perspiration and by way of blood losses in the gastrointestinal tract, compounding a tendency toward anaemia if your diet is routinely low in iron-rich foods. With anaemia comes a reduction of the concentration of haemoglobin in the blood. The blood's ability to carry oxygen is impaired, and you feel slow and draggy. In women, haemoglobin values below 12 mg/dl are considered to indicate anaemia.

Ann Grandjean, who as a sports nutritionist has worked closely with élite American athletes, says that competitive cyclists who are menstruating are typically encouraged to have their haemoglobin and their haematocrit evaluated twice a year.

She adds that female recreational cyclists – if they are going to their gynaecologists for their annual pelvic examination and cervical (Pap) smear, as they should – are probably already being screened through routine blood tests. If unsure whether these blood tests are being done, ask your doctor. For the casual cyclist a check once a year should suffice.

For racers, ultra-marathoners, or women who do extensive touring, the annual check may be sufficient also. But if a high-mileage cyclist experiences persistent fatigue, or if performance seems unaccountably below par, she should inquire about further testing to see whether a deficiency exists and needs to be remedied.

Nutritionists say that we ought not take iron supplements without previous testing indicating a need for supplementation. It's possible to take in too much iron, which is also harmful. Taking an iron supplement should be monitored.

Meanwhile, all of us could afford to consider whether we're eating enough iron-rich food in our daily diet. The RDA is 18 mg.

Iron from animal sources (such as red meat), called *haeme iron*, is more easily absorbed than *non-haeme* iron (from vegetable sources such as peas, beans, and some dark green leafy vegetables). Combine the two types – as in chilli con carne – and absorption of the non-haeme iron will be enhanced. Simmer that chilli in a cast-iron kettle or skillet for three hours and the iron content will rocket. The more acidic the food and the longer it's cooked in the iron pot, the more iron it will draw from the pot. Given that treatment, a half-cup of (tomato-meat) spaghetti sauce increases its iron content from 3 mg to 88 mg.

Breakfast can be a good time to boost your iron intake by means of a cereal enriched with iron. Since accompanying iron-rich foods with something high in Vitamin C increases iron absorption, enjoy a glass of orange juice or a slice of melon along with your meal.

Ouch-less Riding

13

Long training rides are important for building endurance, but it's hard to stay in the saddle if you're falling victim to the ouch factor. A tender backside, sore neck, and numb hands are among potential cycling discomforts, but you don't have to suffer from them. If you feel an ache or pain, find out the cause and fix it. Better yet, avoid it altogether. This chapter tells how.

ELIMINATING NECK AND SHOULDER PAIN

After a ride, if you have the feeling someone's just stabbed an icepick into your neck and shoulders, check your position on the bike, says Tricia Liggett. She ought to know. As *soigneuse* (masseuse and trainer) and now team manager, Tricia has accompanied some of Britain's best women racers to five Tours de France, where day after day she must help racers cope with the gruelling strains of racing hard, then driving in a cramped car to the start of the next day's stage. Comfort, training advice, and a good rub-down are her specialities.

If you were to complain of pain, Liggett would take inventory: are you riding the right size frame? Is the reach to the handlebars too long (or, less likely, too short)? Would a handlebar stem with a shorter extension fix the problem, or are you a candidate for a new bike, perhaps even a custom frame? (Refer to chapter 6, So You Want to Buy a Bike, and check bike fit.)

You should be able to reach the bars with a bend in your elbows, she notes. Straight arms are stiff arms, and tension travels up the arms to your neck. Try to keep arms and shoulders relaxed while riding.

Even with a properly fitting bicycle, tension during a long ride tightens muscles. Try these on-bike stretches from time to time while riding. Don't wait until you start to stiffen. As with any stretches, do them smoothly and slowly. Don't jerk or push to the point of pain.

- Stretch 1: roll your head slowly to each side (but not back beyond the shoulder, as you could pull a muscle).
- Stretch 2: to loosen shoulders, with your left hand on the handlebar near the stem, put your right hand behind your head. Move your right elbow up and backward, and hold the position for a few moments. Switch hands and stretch your left side too.

If you take a break and get off the bike, don't miss the opportunity to stretch.

- Stretch 3: stand with your feet shoulder-width apart, bend your knees a little and tuck your hips under. Pull your belly-button toward your spine while you reach overhead with your arms, holding this position for several seconds. Then lower your arms and reach out in front of you (as illustrated). Hold for thirty seconds.
- Stretch 4: work your fingers into the muscle that covers the back of your neck and the shoulder, as well as the inside of the shoulder blade, while you move your shoulder at the same time.

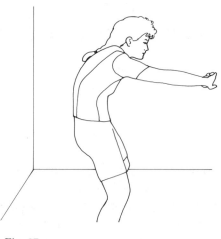

Fig. 15
Stretch 3

The way you breathe can also make a difference. When a cyclist is climbing or working hard to stay with a group of riders, she tends to catch her breath, trying to take more air in quickly. 'You tend to shallow-breathe,' Tricia says, 'and shallow breathing takes place in the upper thoracic area and lung area. That in itself causes tightness in your shoulders and chest. You then get a stitch and lose power.'

Tricia tells riders to regulate their breathing by counting a certain number of pedal revolutions on the in-breath and the same number of revolutions on the out-breath. The goal is deep, relaxed breathing with the diaphragm. When working hard breathe deeper, not faster.

BREATHING AND PERFORMANCE

It should be no surprise that breathing can affect overall riding performance, since breathing delivers oxygen that fuels the muscles. To be sure the out-breath gets equal time, Tricia often encourages riders to concentrate more on it than on the in-breath. 'It helps anyone who is asthmatic or suffers from stress-induced or exercise-induced asthma, which is quite common,' she adds.

Another interesting thing may happen when you think about your breathing: you may discover that you unconsciously hold your breath during intense effort, a habit you obviously want to break.

To facilitate deep breathing we must again consider position on the bike. If you've observed racers, you know that they often assume an aerodynamic position, bending low over the bars to reduce wind resistance. In doing so, a rider should be careful not to scrunch up her chest and hamper breathing. If elbows are held too close to the body and the back is humped, then the diaphragm is crowded. As for bike fit, the bony tops of your shoulders and the width of your handlebar should be the same. And for a racer (who typically has her saddle higher relative to the handlebars than other riders) the tops of the bars still should be no more than 2 inches below the saddle.

Tourists would probably be more comfortable with handlebars only 1 inch below the saddle or possibly with saddle and bars even. If needed, the stem on a bike can be safely raised to a point. (Look for the minimum insertion mark; 2 inches must remain in the steerer tube.) If that's not high enough because your frame is too small, the solution may be a stem with a longer shank, called a 'swan' stem.

As you know, when hill-climbing you need as much oxygen as you can get. That's why top road racers I observed in the Coors Classic in the Colorado Rockies ride with their hands on the brake lever hoods or on the handlebar tops, not on the drops. They sit up to climb, or stand on the pedals. For the latter, the brake hoods are preferred because the wider hand position gives better balance. Either way, to breathe freely, as Olympic gold medalist Connie Carpenter Phinney advises, 'Never climb in the drops; hold your head high, and keep your shoulders wide.'

HANDS-ON ADVICE

I remember well the fun of switching from my touring bike to my new Bianchi racer several years ago. It was like trading in a pickup truck for a sportscar – s-o-o-o-o much more responsive on the corners – and its lighter wheels made it easier for me to keep up on training rides. But compared to my touring bike with its laidback frame angles and the fat, foam rubber handlebar padding (which I'd added), my Bianchi transmitted much more road shock up the frame, through the handlebars, and straight to my elbows. Soon my poor elbows were really talking to me.

When you ride a drop handlebar bicycle, your hands bear a good portion of your weight. So hands and arms can suffer. But they don't have to.

I solved my elbow woes with some of the tips already offered. About that time I substituted a stem with a shorter extension to bring the handlebars a little closer to me. I kept reminding myself to ride with my elbows bent, which was now easier. And I relaxed as I became used to riding with a faster crowd.

'Cyclist's palsy' is another hand/arm problem that's no fun for cyclists. The *ulnar nerve*, which runs along the arm, enters the hand just above the wrist. Damage to the nerve (in medical terms, *ulnar neuropathy*) can occur in cycling, with symptoms of weakness, discomfort, or numbness. Smart cyclists avoid the problem with the following:

- Every now and then during a long ride, take one hand off the bar and give it a good shake to stimulate circulation.
- Change hand positions often to relax muscles and avoid numbness. Unlike other handlebar types, drop handlebars offer a variety of places for your hands to rest. Make use of them.
- When riding the drops, keep wrists straight and hold the curved, not the flat, part of the bars.
- The brake hoods offer several options. The most obvious choice is riding with thumbs on one side of the rubber hoods and fingers on the other. You can also rest your palms on the bend of the bars just above the hoods. I

prefer those two positions, but you might also try riding with three fingers on the outside of the hood, with index finger and thumb inside or, if you have large hands, you may like a position with two fingers on either side of the brake hoods.

- On the tops of the bars keep wrists relaxed and straight.

Make use of the options of drop handlebars

Fig. 16
left On the drops, riding with hands on the curved portion of the bars helps you to keep wrists straight.

Fig. 17
right A frequently used position on the brake hoods gives easy access to brakes, a position comfortable for your upper body, and stability for climbing out of the saddle.

Fig. 18
left A variation, with palms on the bars just above the hoods.

Fig. 19
right Hands on the tops of the bars provide the greatest stability for one-handed manoeuvres like signalling.

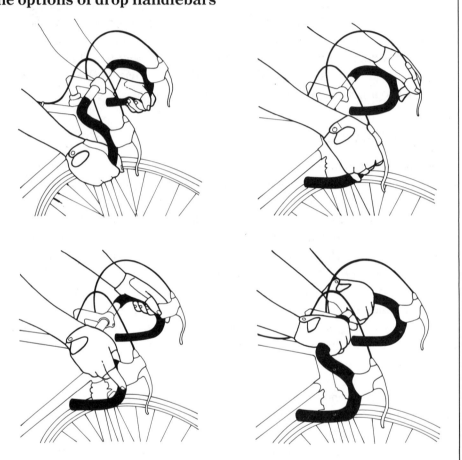

On other types of bikes bear the same idea in mind – don't put a lot of pressure on wrists or ride with wrists cocked.

If, despite good hand positioning, you experience symptoms, equip your bike with handlebar padding. Also, some cycling gloves have extra padding to help reduce road vibration. One brand even has a padded web between thumb and forefinger.

SOLVING SADDLE WOES

Even with proper cycling shorts, do you still find you can't get comfortable on your saddle? First, check to make sure it's level. A saddle tilted up in front will cause you to put extra pressure on the genitals, and that hurts.

130

Saddle type also makes a difference. One time I tested a bicycle and though I remember nothing else about it, I'll never forget the saddle. It was stylishly narrow and covered with a beautiful midnight blue suede – and I was in agony. What was wrong? It had to do with a rather personal measurement: the distance between my *sit-bones* (or the part of the pelvic bones we sit on called the *ischial tuberosities*).

Well, my sit-bones hung over the edges of that saddle, as would most women's, because our pelvises are a little wider than men's. Since my sit-bones weren't supporting me, some rather tender tissues were being crushed by my body weight against that gorgeous, blue suede torture device.

What a woman needs is a *slightly* wider saddle than a man requires. 'Not one of those *really* wide saddles,' cautions exercise physiologist and cyclist Christine Wells, PhD.

Since my blue suede experience the 'anatomic' saddles have come into being. A woman's anatomic saddle is a little wider and a little shorter than a man's saddle, and it provides a padded area to give good support to the ischial tuberosities. Some anatomic saddles have nylon foam inserts which form bumps of padding near the back of the saddle; other, newer versions use a special gel (elastopolymer) for cushioning. Generally there is a choice of women's and men's models in touring, racing, and mountain bike styles.

Many women, including myself, find these saddles comfortable. If you don't have one and need to make a change in your saddle, try one. For selecting and using your anatomic saddle Doctor Wells suggests:

- Some beginners make the mistake of rolling forward on their saddle so they're not sitting on their sit-bones. To feel what it's like to perch on your ischial tuberosities, sit on a curb. Those bones you sit on are the sit-bones.
- Bike fit matters. If the reach to the handlebars is too long, you tend to sit forward on the saddle and not where the sit-bones have good support.
- It's okay if the flesh of our buttocks hangs over the saddle so long as our sit-bones are comfortably perched.
- Don't think of your weight as being fully supported by the saddle and your arms. Think of yourself as straddling the saddle and putting some weight on the pedals as you spin them.

Anatomic saddles do not suit every woman, however. Some experienced riders prefer a good quality leather saddle in a women's model by Brooks or Ideale (available in North America and in the UK). After about 500 miles or so of riding and occasional applications of a leather dressing to the underside, the leather conforms to the rider's shape. (Use just a small amount of the leather dressing, and wear black shorts for a few days after treatment, as dressing can seep through and stain shorts.) Don't buy a cheap, poor quality leather saddle because it will never break in and feel comfortable.

Sometimes a woman can't get comfortable on either an anatomic or a good leather saddle. I talked to Susan Notorangelo about something she's come to call 'smash', a term for 'swollen genitals'. As a pioneer ultra-marathon cyclist, Susan made her first record-breaking transcontinental US ride in 1982. With about 1500 miles still to go, Susan had smash in Kansas. At first she thought she might not be able to continue. But she and Lon Haldeman, who managed her support crew on the ride, went to work on her saddle. (Lon is a well-known marathon cyclist and now Susan's husband.) 'We took an Avocet anatomic saddle and sliced a little box out of it to avoid contact there,' she remembers.

'I sat on it for 20 miles until I squashed something else. We tried a variety of things, including a sheepskin saddle cover, and the pain finally went away when I was distracted by something else.'

What causes this problem? A woman's pelvic structure is different from a man's in yet another way: the arch of the pubic symphisis is shallower in women. As we lean forward on the saddle, that pubic arch may compress tender genital tissues against the seat.

Today Susan believes the problem is related to bike set-up. 'If your bike is set up properly *for the way you want to ride,* you shouldn't have that problem,' she says. Back in 1983 she realised she couldn't ride the drops comfortably, so she had a stem with a shorter extension put on her bike and raised the handlebars as high as safety would allow.

'Through the years I've developed tolerance of a very low, aerodynamic position. That takes time, a concerted effort, and a bike that fits you so that it handles well.' Good flexibility at the waist helps too.

Susan also relates saddle complaints to fitness level. 'I think it's not just the saddle,' she says, echoing Christine Wells's advice. 'It's that you're not really *riding* the bike, not really putting weight on the pedals.'

That said, if none of the above remedies the situation, try modifying a saddle as John Forester recommends in *Effective Cycling.* Sit in riding position on the saddle and determine what portion of it you're pressing against that's causing pain. It's probably an area along the saddle's centreline approximately a third of the way back from the nose. Forester says to cut a slot by making many holes with an electric drill (literally a perforation), and then file the edges smooth. The slot, he suggests, would be rounded on each end; the front end about 12mm wide, the back about twice that. It would be about 70mm long, and the front end of it would start about 90mm back from the saddle nose. John recommends a plain plastic saddle for this, which he admits may feel hard.

The woman who used the saddle further modified it by drilling out a small circle where each of the two sit-bones would rest; she then covered the entire saddle with a

Fig. 20
A do-it-yourself saddle modification for women

piece of supple 'upholstery' leather, adhered with contact cement. With use the leather naturally formed depressions in each of the three holes. It provided cushioning and protected her shorts from any wear the holes might have caused.

Regardless of your choice of saddle, getting up off it once in a while relieves saddle pressure entirely, stretches your legs, and allows a cooling breeze. Every half hour, at least, stand up and pedal for thirty seconds or so.

WHAT YOUR KNEES NEED

Among female athletes the most common injury complaint is knee problems – usually a result of over-use, or stress, caused by forces applied in a repeated movement such as running or pedalling.

By comparison, because it's a non-weight-bearing activity, cycling is much kinder to knees than jogging. The many runners who take up cycling while sidelined by injury from running can tell you that. In fact, a number of my survey respondents noted that cycling has actually helped them strengthen legs and knees as they were recovering from running injuries.

The knee is a complex and wondrous joint, and I won't sidetrack us by trying to explain why women are vulnerable to knee injuries except to say that a woman's wider pelvic bone, compared to a man's, directs the stresses of exercise toward the knee cap at an angle. So there's likely to be an uneven distribution of weight, more pull and tension on the ligaments and muscles around the knee, and more potential for wear and tear on a woman's knees. This anatomical difference is just an additional reason for women cyclists to take care to avoid knee injury. Both male and female riders experience over-use problems frequently enough for the term 'cyclist's knee' to be recognised along with 'tennis elbow' and the like. The first symptom is often a stinging sensation.

As with other discomforts, the best treatment for knee problems is prevention. In cycling this means proper bike fit, gradual conditioning, and good flexibility.

Bike fit. Correct saddle height and fore/aft positioning of the saddle are critical for efficient operation of the knees. (See chapter 6, So You Want to Buy a Bike.)

Racing shoe fit. Don't overlook correct placement of cleats or base-plates, or you'll be asking for knee trouble. (See chapter 9, Dressing the Part.)

Conditioning. John L. Beck, MD, and Byron P. Wildermuth, PT, in a symposium on 'The Female Athlete's Knee' observed that injury rates are lower among well-conditioned women athletes than among less trained females. Beck and Wildermuth also cited studies of highly trained athletes, confirming that women are capable of the same leg strength as their male counterparts when measurements are corrected for lean body mass. Don't let anyone tell you, Beck and Wildermuth said, that females are inherently weaker.

That's good news. Getting in condition is much easier than changing our anatomy!

So let your legs catch up with your enthusiasm. That's why coaches encourage a gradual programme of conditioning – high cadence and low gears – before tackling speedwork, big hills, and high gears.

This warning isn't just for racers. A few years ago I joined a group bike tour in Brittany on the northwest coast of France. One of our party was a friendly but hard-driving Wall Street lawyer. She had plenty of gusto but lacked cycling experience. Unfortunately, she took the advice of a man in the group to ride all the time in high gear. After two days her knees gave out, and she rode the rest of the route in the sag wagon. A month of training before the tour and use of moderate gears would have made all the difference.

If you expect a lot from yourself as a cyclist, train year-round. That's why more and more women are buying indoor trainers. Or in the winter substitute another activity that exercises cycling muscles. Cross-country skiing is ideal. Also good to supplement lower cycling mileage are circuit weight training, aerobics, and vigorous ice skating. Andy Pruitt, a former racer and certified athletic trainer who's worked with élite and recreational women cyclists in the US, warns that knee problems tend to bloom in the springtime after the first races. Women must learn that cycling strength is something they build over many years, he adds.

Flexibility. Cold, tight muscles are much more liable to injury than supple, warm ones. Make the first fifteen minutes of any ride a warm-up, in which you spin easy gears and get the blood racing. Likewise, the last ten or fifteen minutes of training should be at an easier, cool-down pace in low gear.

In addition, some top riders and sports medicine professionals emphasise the value of stretching to improve flexibility and relax muscles that might otherwise tighten with exercise. Personally, I often stretch my legs after a ride. Sometimes if I forget, I'm noticeably stiff later on. It takes only three or four minutes.

By contrast, Susan Notorangelo tells me that the warm-up and cool-down rides are usually sufficient for her. She doesn't stretch after cycling, she says, unless she felt pain during the ride. Susan adds, 'I just saw Mark Gorski (1984 Olympic sprint gold medalist) on television, saying he stretches for twenty minutes daily. I stretch only in the wintertime; as part of a weight workout I do strengthening exercises that involve stretching.'

What's best for you? If, like Susan, you don't need it, then fine. As Andy Pruitt points out, everybody's different. He also notes, however, that any sport requires a certain range of motion. Cycling requires flexible ankles and hamstrings, as well as good straight-leg hip flexion, for example. Besides, if one muscle group is tight, other muscles have to work overtime to compensate.

In this chapter you'll find some stretches which can help you maintain flexibility for cycling. They don't take much time and could benefit you.

YOUR BACK

As with knees, cycling is easier on the back than some other sports, so again athletes sometimes turn to cycling when back problems force them to give up their more punishing running or tennis. At the same time, cycling can cause back muscles to tighten. I experienced this myself not long ago when I increased my mileage rather suddenly. The back stretches which follow helped me improve my flexibility.

Since cycling exercises the back muscles but does not work the abdominals, back muscles may tighten too much because the abdominal muscles aren't strong enough to counter them. 'Crunches' are excellent for strengthening abdominal muscles.

They do it better than the old-fashioned situps you're probably familiar with – and they're easier to do.

In fact they're so easy you'll wonder if that's all there is to it: to position yourself for a crunch, lie on your back on the floor with knees bent and feet flat on the floor; lace your fingers underneath your head with your arms flat out on the floor. Now you're ready. Lift your upper back no more than 30 degrees from the floor, keeping your spine straight and your head in line with your spine; at the same time breathe out and contract your abdominal muscles. Maintain this straight body alignment as you lower your back to the floor; inhale in the diaphragm while doing so.

Do fifteen to twenty-five of these three times a week (perhaps right after your ride). You'll not only derive 'back benefits' but you'll also have a firmer abdomen.

STRETCHES FOR CYCLISTS

Work these stretches into your day whenever you choose – even while watching television – although just before or after a ride is best. A mere ten minutes a day spent on these will let muscles work together efficiently without overworking any one muscle group.

Remember, stretching motions should be smooth and sustained, not bouncy or jerky. It's fine to stretch until you feel it, but don't overdo it to the point of real pain. Expect your flexibility to improve gradually over a few weeks, and recognise that there are individual differences in potential.

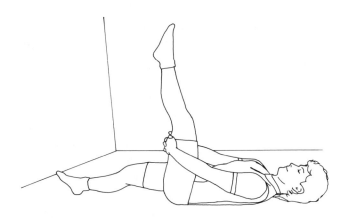

Fig. 21

- For hamstrings, lie flat on your back. Keeping your right leg on the floor, raise your left leg, clasping the back of that leg with your hands. With your knee straight, press your leg against your hands for a few seconds. Then relax the knee and pull the leg towards your chest. You should feel a stretch in the hamstring in the back of that leg. Hold for ten seconds. Then repeat the entire procedure; see if you aren't a little more flexible during this repetition. Now start over in reverse position to stretch your other leg.

Figs. 22–27

- To stretch the calf and the Achilles tendon (to improve ankle flexibility), lean against a wall, stepping forward with the left foot and bending the right knee. Keep that right heel flat against the floor and feel the stretch in the right calf and the ankle. Hold for thirty seconds, then reverse position with the right leg forward to stretch the left calf and ankle.

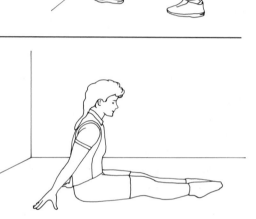

- For the top of the foot and ankle area, sit down (remove shoes if wearing them). With legs extended, point toes of both feet and hold the stretch for ten seconds.

- In this position you can do another stretch to improve ankle flexibility if you like: flatten your feet (so soles are perpendicular to the floor). Reach out and grab the toes with your hands and gently pull toes toward you. It's okay to bend your knees if you need to.

- For hip flexors and fronts of thighs, stand with feet shoulder-width apart and take a long stride forward with the left foot. Both feet should point straight ahead. Bend knees slightly, tucking hips under and keeping heels as close to the floor as you can. Do you feel the stretch in the front of your right thigh and through the hip? Hold for thirty seconds, then reverse for opposite leg.

- For the iliotibial band (the ITB, which runs along the side of the thigh and tends to tighten while cycling), do the 'human pretzel'. Sit with your back straight and left leg extended. Cross your right foot over your left knee and set it on the floor. Now, keeping your back at a 90 degree angle to the floor, pull your right knee toward the left side of your chest. Feel the stretch near the right hip where the ITB inserts. Reverse position and stretch the other side.

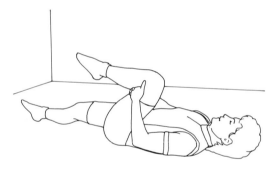

- Here's one for your lower back: lie on your back with legs out flat and relaxed. Bend your right knee, bring it up and clasp your hands around the back of your thigh. Pull knee to chest, at the same time pulling abdominal muscles in. Reverse position and stretch again.

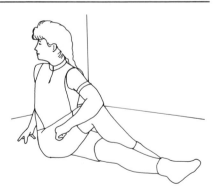

- To improve lateral flexibility in lower back: sit up straight with legs extended in front of you. Cross your right foot over the left leg and rest it on the floor. Reach your right hand behind you and brace your left elbow against the outside of your right knee, while keeping spine erect.

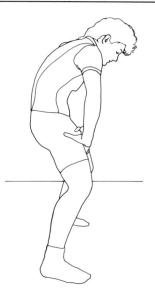

Fig. 28

- For upper back: stand with feet shoulder-width apart, knees slightly bent, and hips pulled under. Pull your belly-button toward your spine and, with hands resting on thighs, gently separate your shoulder blades.

FOOT COMFORT

If you've ever felt when riding as if your feet were on fire, Maria Blower knows just what you mean. 'I recently changed to Look pedals (a strapless pedal system), and I love them,' says the British Olympian. 'Before, to get my toeclip close enough to my shoe, I had to wear my toe strap up fairly high on my foot. It was painful because your feet swell in the heat.' Even without straps, lacing your shoes too tight can have the same effect, she warns. Loosen them at the first hint of discomfort.

Not quite ready to switch to a new pedal binding system? Riders using clips and straps for long rides might try leaving the straps just a fraction loose until you need to pull them tight for a big climb.

Another trick is using two straps on each pedal. One goes in the usual spot, and the other is threaded through the forward part of the pedal cage, and over the toeclip. With double straps, neither has to be quite so tight, and again you can snug them up when you need to.

And if you're still trying to make do with running shoes or – worse – trainers, you probably need a good pair of touring/fitness shoes. 'Because they're too flexible, trainers are terrible,' Maria reminds us.

Tuning Up Your Technique 14

In bike racing and recreational cycling, the best riders demonstrate technique as well as strength and endurance. It's the old story of using grace, form, and brains to supplement brawn. Women cyclists not only need to do this, but possess a special affinity for it. Don't we often think our way around a problem instead of simply muscling through? Here we'll talk about improving efficiency in dealing with wind resistance, improving climbing skills, making the most of our gearing, and more.

CHEATING THE WIND

Even when the air seems fairly still, a lone cyclist expends about 30 per cent of her energy merely overcoming wind resistance. So it is that Silvia Sivret, 39, of Claremont, New Hampshire, noticed such a dramatic difference in her first experience with 'drafting':

> Once my husband realised my commitment to the sport, he made an effort to teach me more technique. On a training ride we did some paceline work (he pulled the whole way), and it demanded my greatest concentration to stay as near his wheel as I dared and shift into the gear ratios he asked for. Aside from the concentration involved, our speed thrilled me. No wonder he and his cycling buddies have such fun! After the one-hour, eleven-minute ride, I felt less tired than I do following a ride with my friends at a touring pace and doing our own pulling.

As Silvia says, *paceline* riding takes concentration, as you must respond to the cues of the rider in front. But it isn't difficult. You can learn to do it and experience a new exhilaration in cycling as you speed along in the slipstream, part of a well-tuned group of riders, or *chaingang*, as it's called in Britain.

Drafting (riding closely behind) another cyclist benefits you by reducing the wind resistance you'd normally have to overcome. Thus you can go 2 to 3 mph faster than if you were alone. The closer you can stay to that rider's wheel, the more energy you save. And the larger the chaingang, if working efficiently, the faster you can go.

As aerodynamics expert Chester Kyle, PhD, points out, even several bike lengths behind another cyclist you can take advantage of the slipstream, 'if you can find the wake, or "bubble"'. For example, when another rider passes you on the road, if you move over into her wake you'll get a boost in speed. Turn on a burst of effort and you may be able to catch up and draft her.

139

Paceline Pussycat

'My funniest, sickest, and grossest riding experience occurred on a cycling vacation in the Florida Keys, where my husband Tom and I failed to imagine the consequences of the many cats Ernest Hemingway had introduced to the area.

We began a beautiful ride with Tom in the lead while I practised drafting close to his wheel. Because of crosswinds and tractor trailers on the road we weren't talking much. And to stretch out after driving for two days, we were moving pretty fast. Suddenly without warning, Tom veered off the shoulder of the road. And what did he leave me to face? There on its back with all four feet sticking straight up in the air was the largest, deadest, stiffest cat I ever hope to see. It was big enough to do some very big wheel damage, I'm sure. I missed it, but I'm still not letting Tom forget that one.'

Pamela Gill, 34, Cheverly, Maryland

Paceline riding is a skill any cyclist can use. A group of bicycle tourists may find themselves with long mileage to do or a stiff headwind; a paceline could be the answer. For recreational riders whose regular training rides take a familiar route, working together in a paceline keeps it interesting. Of course, in competition use of the slipstream is integral to most race strategy.

You could begin learning, as Silvia did, by drafting one experienced rider who's willing to *pull* (ride at the front) and who can maintain a steady pace. The lead rider must remember never to stop suddenly, and to give warning if a pothole or other road hazard should suddenly need dodging, since you may not see it. (Usually the rider in the lead points a finger at the offending pile of glass or whatever.) Go over matters of communication with your riding partner before you start.

My patient friend, Ellen Dorsey (a top Veteran racer at the time), taught me that way. A smooth, strong rider, she could be trusted not to make a dangerous move. So I quickly got the hang of it. We didn't bother calling out gear ratios, but you could. Here's the technique:

- Try to follow a foot or two behind the wheel in front of you.
- Ride an inch or so to one side of the wheel in front, so you have space to manoeuvre if there's a sudden slow-down. This gives you a better view of the road ahead, too.
- Don't overlap wheels. A swerve by the rider in front of you could take you down.
- Use peripheral vision to monitor the distance between your bike and the wheel preceding you, while you look at the road ahead.
- Don't brake if you can help it. That destroys the smoothness of the paceline and requires extra work to accelerate again. Instead, if you're gaining on your partner, briefly ease off pedalling. As the gap widens to the correct distance, smoothly resume normal pedalling.

Those are the basics. Usually riders share the work by taking turns pulling. To change the lead, the front rider looks back to make sure no cars are coming; this is also the signal to you behind. Then she speeds up a little and moves over a few feet (to the left in North America, to the right in the UK). She eases her pedalling while you maintain a steady pace. Don't accelerate; if you had riders behind you, it would open up gaps in the line. When she is alongside you (or alongside the last rider if there are more), she accelerates a little and moves over to catch the draft. Now she can rest.

How long does a rider stay at the front? That depends. At race pace the front rider works very hard, so racers may relieve each other every ten pedal strokes or sooner. On your ride a stronger cyclist may pull longer than a weaker one; thus riders of varying abilities can ride together and each get an appropriate workout. Or you can agree that each pull for a certain distance or, say, a minute apiece.

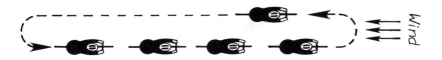

Fig. 29
Single paceline

If riding with a larger group, like six or a dozen, the same principles apply.

With rapid turnover at the front, you'll see a *circular* flow of riders, with one line moving forward, the other back. Lines should stay close together to take best advantage of the slipstream and not use too much of the road.

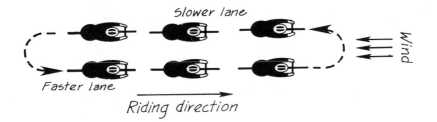

Fig. 30
Circular paceline

If traffic is light, a large group can make a *double paceline*. This works like two pacelines riding side by side. To change the lead, front riders swing out to either side. They drift back and pair up again at the rear.

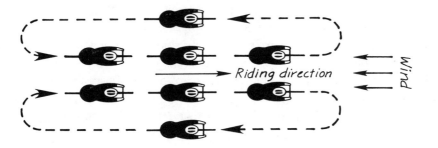

Fig. 31
Double paceline

141

In a crosswind, the standard paceline is less effective than the *echelon*, a diagonal formation across the road. That's because the pockets of still air are diagonally to the rear of each rider. When riding with a partner, you can use echelon technique if the road is wide enough, but larger groups should not unless the road is closed to traffic, as in a race.

Fig. 32
Echelon

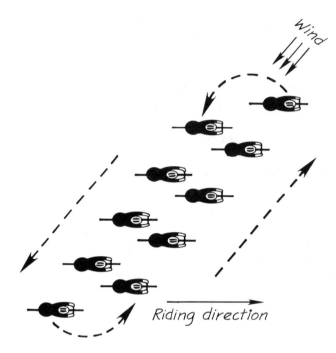

CLIMBING TO THE TOP

One of my friends calls hill climbing 'the moment of truth' for cyclists. Some find it our true call to glory. 'Steep and long, bring 'em on!' say the natural climbers – typically slender, muscular, and aerobically fit types. Others of us see hills as penance we do for the other pleasures in riding – like the view at the summit and the stand with homemade ice cream on the other side. Hills are gargantuan bumps in the way of where we really want to be.

If that's how you feel, hang in there. As you continue to ride and improve your fitness, climbing will get easier. Surprisingly soon some of your best memories will centre on how you made it to the top. But don't wait for it to happen: good technique, practice, and determination will speed your progress.

For example, every June there's a one-day ride from London to the seashore resort of Brighton, which is shared by about 30,000 cyclists. Anyone who's joined in this 56-mile bit of mass hysteria knows there are plenty of hills and that they loom higher and steeper as you progress toward the coast. There's one real stinker about 6 miles from the finish, when your legs have just about turned to cottage cheese. I walked up the infamous Ditchling Beacon myself last year.

142

Understandably, to the stalwart regulars Ditchling Beacon becomes a point of pride and test of determination. After the ride, another partaker, Helen White, 24, from South Hatfield, Hertfordshire, reported cycling all the way up two years running. She was so determined to cycle up it in 1988 that she 'even rode over a £10 note someone had dropped! There's determination.'

So you supply the determination; here are some tips.

- Your bike must be geared low enough. Unless you have a low gear down around 35 to 40 inches, look into modifying or replacing your bicycle – or all the determination in the world won't take you up much more than a pimple. Of course, the lighter the bicycle, the easier climbing becomes. A bike weighing more than 30 pounds will handicap you.

- Exploit downhill momentum. I love rolling hills because they vary the ride and let you take advantage of gearing. After you've crested one hill, you shift into high gear and pedal down. You may have to level out some before your pedalling actually makes a difference, but as soon as it does, pedal rapidly to maintain speed as long as possible.

  If the hills are gentle rollers, you may ascend the next with a snappy cadence and surprisingly little effort. If not, shift down and keep pedalling. If you've just a short distance to the top, you could stand on the pedals for greater leverage. Once you're over the top, shift again into high for the next downhill. This sort of terrain is a joy to ride and an excellent opportunity to work on technique.

  This approach also applies to long descents. If you shift into high as you start down, when you resume pedalling, you'll be in the correct gear.

- Use cadence as a guide while you experiment to see which climbing style suits you best. Some cyclists do much of their climbing out of the saddle; others sit and spin.

  Let's say you usually ride at a cadence of 85. On a short climb, remain seated as you try to keep your cadence up. With hands on the tops of the bars or on the brake hoods, pull a little on the bars as you pedal, but otherwise keep your upper body relaxed. Pull up on the pedals as well as pushing down. (Toeclips or other pedal binding system are essential.) Remember to breathe deeply in your diaphragm.

  As your cadence drops below 80, grip the brake hoods and get up off the saddle to pedal. Lean forward, centring yourself over the pedals. This makes use of your full body weight to turn them. Put muscle into it. With each pedal stroke, pull with the alternate hand. You'll feel the bike sway a little from side to side, which is expected. But keep the bike moving straight ahead; don't weave.

  You may find yourself gasping for breath because the effort becomes *anaerobic* (requires more fuel than the oxygen you breathe in can provide). Slow your pedalling if necessary but keep going to the top; you'll catch your breath on the descent.

143

Fig. 33
This technique is especially good for 'honking' up a short hill: with hands on the brake hoods, get up off the saddle; rock the bike from side to side in opposition to each pedal stroke.

Beginning climbers, if you must stop on the climb to rest, then the next time you do this hill or a similar one, forget about cadence. Simply try to make it up the hill without stopping. Do it by gearing down and then pedalling at a slow cadence. In fact, the first time, go as slow as possible without wobbling the bike, even if you feel you could go faster. It will probably feel easier to climb seated, but stand up if you need to. Don't worry if other riders are passing you. If you reach the top without feeling out of breath, than you'll know you can go faster the next time. Practise on some hills like this once a week, going slowly enough to avoid really heavy breathing. You'll develop a sense of pacing and how much you can push yourself. When you improve, you can then concern yourself more with cadence.

- Pace yourself on long climbs. Begin conservatively if you're not sure what you can do. If you start in an easy gear and you feel capable of more by the time you're halfway up, you can always shift higher. Try to keep your cadence up. Ride seated until you tire, then stand to use different muscles. Alternate the two positions.

  If you must slow your cadence, it's no great sin. Remember to use deep, rhythmic breathing. Be patient with yourself and keep going. If you can take in the scenery while keeping an eye on the road, it's heartening. Just today I enjoyed a view of barns and fields in a patchwork valley and watched cornstalks drop behind me as I pedalled up a long hill. Simply watching the road, you feel you're going much slower than you actually are.
- A full stomach hampers you on a long, strenuous climb.
- When the going gets too tough, sometimes the smart stop going. It depends. If you have a competitive streak, you may battle your way to the top regardless. On the other hand, tourists have the perfect excuse for stopping during a climb: to better admire the view. You'll find a one- to

three-minute rest long enough to catch your breath, maybe even snap a picture. Then climb back on and pedal. Try it. If it's too much, you can always get off again and walk.

You *will* improve.

DOWN THE OTHER SIDE

Some riders don't mind climbing hills but tremble at descents. To me downhills are one of cycling's great bonuses. With correct technique they can be a very safe thrill.

Whether you descend fast or slow, here's what *not* to do: don't simply apply the brakes and keep them on 'til you reach the bottom of the hill. Why? The sustained friction of rubber brake pads against your rims can melt the pads so they glaze over and aren't effective for stopping. Tyres are also vulnerable to heat buildup in the rims; air inside tubes or tubulars can expand, causing a blowout.

Instead, as your speed exceeds the point where you feel you have control of the bike, apply the brakes briefly but firmly enough to dampen your speed, then release them. Coast until you want to slow again. Brake again briefly and so on.

Body position will also affect your speed. To slow your descent, sit up to increase wind resistance, keeping hands on the brake hoods ready for braking. (If you have difficulty operating brakes from this position, check with your bike shop to see whether levers are mounted in the proper spot. Or perhaps you need smaller levers, now available.) Don't count on auxiliary brake levers, if you have them. They come out of adjustment easily, and that hand position is not secure: if you bounce on an imperfection in the road, you could go over the handlebars.

The hands-on-hoods body position has other advantages, too. Compared to riding the drops, you see the road better and breathe more freely – helpful when you're recovering from the effort of ascent. If the road is winding and bumpy, though, riding the curved part of the drops gives you the most secure grip and the levers are right there for you.

Give yourself room on the road. Don't hug the edge on a descent. Having checked for traffic, I move out into the lane far enough to avoid sand or gravel that accumulates near the edge, and so that I can move either way to avoid rough spots. On a long, fairly straight downhill (where I can be seen from a distance) I take the centre of the lane. Should a driver approach from the rear, I may hold the centre if I'm travelling about the speed limit, or I can move over to let him pass.

On a long downhill, pedalling in high gear even if you are spun out keeps legs from chilling and stiffening.

Cornering on a descent is the challenge, particularly at speed. But as you develop competence, you'll love that feeling of mastery. Here are the basics:

- Whether going fast or slow, it's better to brake before instead of during a turn. At the apex of the turn, where you'll be leaning most, be especially careful not to brake, or you could cause your tyres to slide.

145

- Remember in a turn to keep your inside pedal up to avoid scraping; on a right turn, that's right leg up. At the same time, put pressure on the left (outside) pedal and lean hard to the inside of the turn. The bike goes in the direction it's being leaned. (If you're a downhill skier, it's the same technique.) Weight the outside arm and grip the handlebar a little tighter with that hand.

- As in normal cornering, pick in advance the line you'll take through the turn. Traffic permitting, the ideal line follows an 'outside/inside/outside' orientation. That is, you approach the turn near the outside edge of the road and gradually move toward the centreline at the apex of the turn. Then as the corner eases, you gradually move toward the outside again.

Fig. 34 For faster downhill cornering, the idea is to 'straighten out' the curve as much as possible. The dotted line shows the path a cyclist would take on British (or other) roads where traffic keeps to the left. Here, on a road not closed to traffic, the safest, fastest line through a right-hand turn begins at the outside near the shoulder, angles toward the centreline, then moves back to the outside.

Bear in mind that racers take downhill corners (and descents in general) faster than you or I might. Sometimes that's because they've familiarised themselves with the race route. In 1983 Rebecca Twigg won the Coors Classic, America's biggest stage race, held in Colorado. In the mountainous 'Tour of the Moon' stage the road winds through sheer dropoffs of 1,000 feet to rocks below. There Rebecca's daring descent helped cinch victory. Earlier she and her coach, Andrezj Bek, had scouted the course. She rehearsed the descent, which at its trickiest wound around a sharp curve and entered two back-to-back tunnels. It was dark in there.

Rebecca's toughest competitor, Maria Canins from Italy, had outclimbed her and had begun the descent with another rider. But Rebecca, cornering more efficiently, caught them on the downhill and then broke away just before the two tunnels. With that bold descent she finished a minute and a half ahead of her rivals.

Before attempting such riding, we must develop proficiency. After mastering the basic skills, one way to improve downhill technique is to follow a good bikehandler who's willing to help you practise descents. Trace his or her path from a dozen yards behind.

Connie Carpenter Phinney, a contributing editor to *Bicycling* magazine, tells how in her first year of bike racing she was having trouble in practice with downhills on the world championship road race course in Italy. Repeatedly, her coaches drove her back up the road and had her follow the more experienced Miji Reoch through the sharp, difficult turns. The technique drill paid off: Connie was one of the first to complete the descent on race day.

She adds that if you have any doubt about your bike's frame and wheel alignment, have it checked out. It can make a difference.

A hill requires all your concentration, as Joy Crays, 30, from Banks, Oregon, learned the hard way. 'Let me tell you about the time I got my fancy new bike computer!' she laughs. 'It was so fascinating I couldn't keep my hands and eyes off it, which was a mistake. On my first fast descent I was checking my computer for speed while I should've been checking the road for turns. When I did see the turn, it was too late. I hit a blackberry patch and ruined a perfectly great jersey.'

Ouch! Take a quick peek at your computer if you like, but do it on a straight stretch of road.

GETTING THE MOST FROM YOUR GEARING

Shifting remains a murky matter for months or even years for many riders because they're unclear about the shifting pattern on their derailleur bicycles. Some cyclists are under the mistaken impression that all the lowest gears are on the small chainwheel and that shifting over to the big one gives you the remaining higher gears in nice, orderly sequence. I wish it were so!

But you don't have to fumble around in a gearing fog. You'll know exactly how to make the most of your gearing if you plot your gears. Begin by counting the teeth on your chainwheels and rear sprockets. (If the tooth numbers are engraved on your chainwheels, you won't have to count them.) Removing the rear wheel (see chapter 17) makes counting sprocket teeth easier.

On a piece of paper write down the number of teeth on each sprocket from smallest to largest, running down on the left. Write the two (or three) chainwheel-tooth numbers across the top. For example, my Terry 'Despatch' bicycle has chainwheels of 40 and 48 teeth. Its freewheel sprockets have 13, 15, 17, 20, 24, and 28 teeth. Here's my chart:

	40T	48T
13T	(83) inches	99½ inches
15T	72 inches	86½ inches
17T	63½ inches	76 inches
20T	54 inches	64½ inches
24T	45 inches	54 inches
28T	38½ inches	(46) inches

To figure the gear inches for each combination, I referred to the gear number chart at the back of the book. As you can see, the 28 × 40 combination gives me a lowest gear of 38½ inches.

147

Now let's look at my shifting pattern. First, I put parentheses around the 83 inch (13 × 40) and the 46 inch (28 × 48) gears because they are unusable. These are the small/small and big/big combinations, or 'cross-chain' gears, which we avoid because they put the chain at an exaggerated angle that speeds wear on the gear teeth. They also make an annoying rubbing sound which tells me if I've shifted into one of them accidentally.

It turns out I have a very simple shift pattern known as *crossover gearing*. Here's how I use it to shift up through the gears.

If I start in the lowest (38½ inches) I can stay on the small chainwheel as I shift up through 45, then 54, then 63½, then 72 inches. That is, I shift only my right lever.

To go still higher, I shift to the big chainwheel, or *cross over*. This gives me access to three more gears: 76, 86½ and 99½ inches.

In running through this progression I've had to *double-shift* (shift both levers) only once. That was when I crossed over from the 72- to the 76-inch gear.

That was easy, and so is down-shifting from the highest gear. With the chain on the big chainwheel I shift from 99½, to 86, to 76. I can cross over to 72 (double-shift) and continue to shift lower on the small chainwheel. Or I can continue down on the big chainwheel to 64½ then 54, and then cross over.

You've figured out by now that creating crossover gearing necessitated a couple of duplications. In effect this bicycle has only eight different, usable gears. But that's plenty if they're well-chosen. In fact, racers use crossover gearing because a missed shift can be a costly error. Crossover gearing, which can be created using many different combinations of chainwheels and rear sprockets, is useful for most other riders of twelve- and fourteen-speed bikes, too. Its main drawback is that it doesn't work well for truly wide-range gearing for loaded touring.

You can figure your own gears and shifting pattern similarly. If some of your chainwheel/sprocket combinations aren't on the gear chart, here for your convenience is the formula we used.

$$\text{Gear inches} = \frac{a}{b} \times c$$

where
a = number of front chainwheel teeth
b = number of rear sprocket teeth
c = rear wheel diameter

You may not have crossover gearing. If that's the case, you'll have a more complicated shifting pattern. To learn to use it efficiently, tape your chart to your handlebars and spend some time on your next rides practising. Shift in sequence from low to high, for example. For some shifts you'll probably need to double-shift; do this sequentially rather than trying to shift both levers at the same time. Also, using the chart you have just made, practise making the most efficient shifts to keep up a constant cadence over varying terrain. (And don't be embarrassed about having your chart on the bars. A little kidding is a small price to pay for your new skill.)

You may have a number of double-shifts. In fact, you may have some very awkward double-shifts which take you two or three gears away from where you want to be before you move the second lever to finish the shift. If after much practice, you decide that your shifting pattern is too troublesome, you could consider changing to crossover gearing. If you have a ten-speed, it would require changing your bicycle to at least a twelve-speed. A shop mechanic can advise you on it.

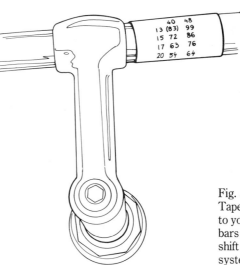

Fig. 35
Tape a gear chart to your handlebars to help you shift systematically.

CONSIDER YOUR WHEELS

If you've stuck with it this far and intend to keep working on technique, you deserve a bike worthy of the effort. Assuming you already have a derailleur bicycle that fits you well, if there's anything likely to be holding you back, it's heavy wheels.

Sherry Biddison, 41, of Bainbridge Island, Washington, discovered this by accident – literally:

'I followed my husband for four years – he, on his Lotus eighteen-speed touring bike and me with my Nishiki ten-speed, heavy steel rims and all. Last year my front rim got bent and was replaced with an aluminium one. If I had known it made that much difference, I would have done it years ago! I always felt like a wimp. I didn't know I was lugging around a handicap . . .'

What Sherry demonstrated so clearly to herself is the old maxim: 'a pound off the wheels is worth two pounds off the frame.' If you have an inexpensive derailleur bicycle with steel rims, the least costly way of perking up its performance is by switching to lighter aluminium alloy rims and better tyres. You would lighten your bike by about 2½ pounds. Furthermore, lighter wheels respond more quickly when you accelerate and when you brake.

With aluminium alloy rims, you'll also be rewarded with much surer braking in rainy conditions when rims are wet. And in case you're wondering, alloy rims are plenty strong enough in any normal riding conditions.

New rims will require new tyres. You'll want high-pressure clinchers (at least 90 to 100 psi). The 27 × 1 inch or 700 × 25C tyres are lighter and have less rolling resistance than the wider 1⅛ inch or 28C tyre, so they'll be more responsive. They're ideal for training rides, day tours or even 'credit-card touring'. At the same time they should be sure-footed enough for you – just don't go with a treadless tyre.

If you envisage putting loaded panniers on the bike for touring, then a wider 1⅛ inch (28C) or 1¼ inch (32C) tyre would be better.

The mechanic at your bike shop can advise you on rim and tyre selection if you describe your intentions.

149

15 *Sharing the Road*

The image we, as cyclists, present is extremely important!
Patti Brehler, 34, Clawson, Michigan

Other cyclists who don't follow the rules of the road are one of Patti Brehler's pet peeves. You probably agree, though whether you feel as vehemently about it as Patti does may depend on where you live. The flagrant violations of traffic code so common in Anytown, USA, by both children and adults are relatively infrequent in the UK because cycling figures more importantly as transport. Lacking the big yellow school bus, as an English friend puts it, British children and teens often cycle to school. In the elementary schools, bicycle safety is typically a part of the curriculum. And violations of the highway code by cyclists are taken more seriously by the police than they are in the States.

So British cyclists might be surprised to hear that, among North American women participating in my cycling survey, more are troubled by careless cyclists than by hills, or bad weather, or lack of equal opportunity, or even harassment from men. Seeing an irresponsible cyclist give the rest of us a bad name with motorists disturbs many riders in the States.

Equally worrisome, a wrong-way cyclist coming head-on in our road space is a genuine danger – and not an unlikely situation. Of course, this is not the only cause when two riders collide. Among skilled cyclists, collisions with other bicycles happen just as frequently as collisions with cars. (Each of these accident types – bike/bike and bike/car – accounts for about one-sixth of the total accidents occurring among trained cyclists, according to a study by Jerrold A. Kaplan, published in his *Characteristics of the Regular Adult Bicycle User*, Washington, DC, Federal Highway Administration, 1977. Although I lack figures for the UK, I suspect that bike/bike accidents are more frequent than most cyclists suspect; the tendency among cyclists everywhere is to overestimate the danger from automobiles and underestimate the frequency of other kinds of accidents when cycling.

At the same time, maybe we ourselves could sharpen up on a point or two to improve our own relationships with drivers. Or perhaps we need to master some in-traffic techniques to build confidence and make the going easier. (Developing road-use skills cuts cycling accidents by about 80 per cent among adult cyclists, Kaplan demonstrated. Once we have these skills, the evidence shows, cycling is a reasonably safe activity, contrary to loudly proclaimed opinions of a non-cycling establishment which often attempts to deny us access to the road.) In actuality, the risk of a fatal accident in a lifetime of cycling is about the same as in a lifetime of travel in cars.

Additionally, we may have concerns about harassment on the road – how to prevent it or deal with it. The tips in this chapter will help you be a more competent, assertive, and – possibly – more considerate cyclist in traffic.

THE GRACIOUS CYCLIST

'I train and cycle-commute in the Detroit area, which is motor city,' says Patti Brehler, half of the marathon team, the Pink Leopards (see chapter 10). 'When I started wearing a helmet, I noticed I was getting more courtesy from drivers. I decided that the image I projected made a difference in the way they treated me.'

She became conscious of cycling habits – her own and others'. 'I'm bothered by some cycling clubs I observe around here on rides. They go through red lights and disregard other traffic laws, ruining it for everyone,' she adds. Although Patti's own commute home takes place at midnight, she says she stops for red lights even then. 'I think, "What if someone saw me?"'

The ripple effect works both ways. One rude or stupid act by a cyclist causes motorists to think a little less of all of us. Efficient, courteous riding helps drivers recognise that bicycles can be part of an orderly traffic flow.

Bearing in mind the power inherent in the word, I suggest that we be *gracious* cyclists. That is, let's remember we have a right to be on the road but be thoughtful in using it. We covered a few basics in chapter 7. In addition, put yourself in the driver's shoes to see why you would appreciate the following:

- Keep left (right, in the US and Canada).* As a motorist, you would be irritated by bicyclists in the middle of the road for no obvious reason. If the shoulder of the road is clean and unobstructed by vehicles, potholes, drain covers, or other hazards, it makes sense to use it. However, you need only ride as far left (or right) as is practicable. It's better not to ride at the far edge of the shoulder, but about 3–4 feet away from traffic where you can still be seen by vehicles entering from a side road. When the shoulder is not clean, you'll save your tyres by riding just to the inside of the road edge, since car tyres will have swept that area free of debris.
- When you stop to read a map or wait for a companion, pull well off the road. You'll avoid riling drivers and save your own skin in the bargain. Be especially careful in taking a breather at the top of a hill, where a motorist may have a tough time seeing you. I repeat, get completely off the road.
- On a busy road, leave the gabbing for later; don't ride two abreast, causing traffic to back up or cars to veer dangerously wide around you. If a string of cars slows behind you even though you're riding singly, pull off the road briefly to let them pass. In this situation a group of cyclists should break up

*Exceptions to this rule are discussed later in the chapter.

into sub-groups of three or four riders, leaving a few car-lengths of space in between these small groups to facilitate passing.

- Remember intersection etiquette. We've already talked about respecting traffic signals (and one-way streets). Furthermore, save the *track stand*, the racer's balancing technique, for the track. It's not that much hassle to disengage a toe strap or binding and put your foot down, and it's much better for public relations than if you ride in circles in front of a motorist waiting for a red light. The other alternative, leaning on somebody's car, might really raise the driver's hackles, especially if it's newly waxed.
- Don't block a turning lane. If the law permits a turn on a red light but you're going straight, stop just on the inside of the straight-ahead lane so cars can go by to turn.

DEFENSIVE TACTICS

Most of my cycling is concentrated in London, and actually I quite enjoy battling with the traffic. It's exhilarating. You've got to keep awake and concentrate quite hard to foresee things that are likely to happen, like cars pulling out of junctions, turning across you . . . it's good for your reactions.

Julia King, 32, London

As experienced motorists ourselves, we know the necessity for being alert to traffic patterns around us and anticipating errors other drivers might make. In our cars we're not so much afraid as we are ready, say, to give a warning toot at another driver about to pull out without looking. We call it 'driving defensively'.

A cyclist must be similarly wary. Even when you have the right-of-way, you should scan driveways and side streets for drivers who fail to look for you. Get in the habit of noting if a motorist is looking in your direction, and make eye contact if you can. If you can't, a good, loud yell ('Hey!'), gains the driver's attention and is better than a bicycle bell (not loud enough in traffic) or a whistle (requires you to take one hand off the handlebar or ride with the whistle always in your mouth). Your voice will serve to warn a pedestrian about to step into your path. (Say 'Heads up,' 'Watch out,' etc.) Maintain your pace but be ready to make an emergency turn to avoid collision if a driver/pedestrian in a total fog fails to yield. (A quick turn is a manoeuvre that takes practice. It is covered in the next section.)

Eye contact is a great help in many situations. I also look for a car's turn signal or note which way the wheels are turned if, for example, I'm stopped at an intersection and want to proceed straight on while making sure a driver doesn't turn into me. If I do make eye contact, the motorist may motion me to proceed: I will check to make sure no other traffic is coming (never assume the driver has done this for you), then nod my thanks and go on.

Remember, the sounds around you provide important cues. Don't wear your personal stereo when riding outdoors.

Keep an eye peeled for hazards in your path – before you get to them – so you have time to decide your course of action. And perfect your dodge (chapter 7). *Half* of the accidents among experienced adult cyclists in Kaplan's study were falls in which no car, dog, or other bike was involved. Just in case you don't recognise these as dangers:

- Don't ride over gratings with slots parallel to the road edge (a bicycle wheel will get caught in there). These are often near the curb – another reason not to ride too close to it.
- Beware if there's an uneven surface where road and shoulder meet, often there's a slight drop-off to the shoulder. If you happen to drift off the road, you can't simply drift back. Your wheel would catch, knocking the bike out from under you. You must cross back over the unevenness at a fairly wide angle. Or stop and place your bicycle back on the road.
- Some bridge-expansion joints are wide enough to be wheel-swallowers. Sometimes you've no choice but to walk your bike through.
- Water-filled potholes can be treacherous; water may camouflage a deeper hole than you think.
- Railway tracks and cattle grids usually require you to slow down, since as a rule they protrude and hitting them too hard can dent your rims. A little extra insurance for protecting your wheels in this situation is to get up off the saddle and crouch with knees and elbows flexed, centring your body weight evenly between the two wheels. Tracks that angle across the road necessitate extra caution or they will throw you: experienced cyclists change course to encounter the tracks at a right angle – just be careful not to weave into traffic.

Be wary of the inexperienced cyclist on the road – as noted, more of a problem in America than in the UK. Merely passing such riders can be risky, since you've no way of knowing whether the individual might swerve into you: many a careless rider, as you've observed, often doesn't ride in a straight line on the road, or could veer into you by making a turn from the curb. Alerting this cyclist to your presence doesn't guarantee that he'll know how to let you pass safely. The wise course of action is to treat him as you would a larger, slow-moving vehicle in your lane, as Myrna Meyer, a certified Effective Cycling instructor from White Plains, New York, advises. That is, you change lanes to pass, after using the backward scan as discussed above. If necessary, slow down behind this cyclist until it is safe to make the lane change.

Note, please, that often the least safe place to ride is a cycle path, partly because the mix of users may include inexperienced cyclists as well as walkers, joggers, skateboarders, roller skaters and more! (Of course, the mass ride is another situation which brings riders of all ages and experience levels together; it's ripe with opportunities for crashes with other cyclists. The safest place is the front of the pack if you should go on one.)

Mixed usage, as on this British cyclepath, creates additional challenges. A bell is useful for such riding – just loud enough to let pedestrians or other cyclists know you're approaching from behind (*John Tauke*).

EMERGENCY MANOEUVRES

Like any other emergency, we respond best to traffic emergencies with advance preparation. You may not need these moves often, but even a single use in your cycling lifetime is worth the practice.

The panic stop. Every now and then there's a situation when you want to stop very quickly. To do a proper panic stop, you must strongly apply the front brake, which has double the stopping power of the rear. Here's how to do that without pitching over the handlebars: as you're squeezing the front brake lever hard, apply the rear brake lightly and at the same time, move back on the saddle to place more weight over the back wheel. As the rear wheel starts to skid (your clue that it's about to lift off the ground), ease your pressure on the front brake.

Try this at slow speed in a traffic-free area like an empty parking lot. Remember to use light pressure on the rear brake, or else you'll make the back wheel skid too soon. In your repeated practice stops, try increasing your force on the front brake a little bit each time, until the back wheel actually does begin to lift off. Immediately, release the front brake lever.

Of course, you know by now not to depend on auxiliary brake levers for this sort of a manoeuvre if you happen to have them on your bicycle. The most secure hand position for the panic stop is with hands on the curved portion of the bars, although if you are riding the brake hoods when a true emergency arises, you won't have time to switch. You'll just have to hold tight.

The quick turn. What can you do when a thoughtless motorist makes a turn so close in front of you that you have no time to brake? To avoid ploughing into it, you make a 'quick turn' in the same direction with the car.

Since this requires a sharper turn than in normal cornering, you must modify your technique. Say you need to make a quick turn to the left: you begin with a momentary turn of the handlebars to the right (away from where you want to go); this causes your bicycle to lean left. Then you can steer left. (In other words, it begins like the dodge, chapter 7. If you don't do any correcting, you'll find yourself leaning into a sharp turn in the opposite direction.)

Practise this in that empty parking lot. Do it slowly at first while you develop a feel for it. Gradually increase your speed with repeated practice. As you do, you'll see you don't have to steer so sharply to make the turn. Work on it during a few practice sessions and you should have mastery of it; then practise it from time to time. Do it now so you'll be ready if you ever need it.

CITY STREET-SMART

It's quite a jungle out there. Motorists are a mixed bunch. Some of them are quite tolerant and will sit behind you until there really is enough room to go past. But more often if they think they can get through a gap, well, they'll try it and see. And sometimes they can't. I'm not a cyclist to take risks. I won't go into a gap that I see is going to close up. I'll always cycle within my own limits and the limits of my machine, and I know what they are. Having said that, I suppose I'm quite pushy.

You've got to have the courage of your convictions. There's no use going out there thinking, 'I'm going to be scared by this traffic'. Because you'll wobble and you will get knocked off your bike. Or you'll try and ride too close to the side of the road and somebody will open a car door on you.   Julia King

An overly-cautious crawl through traffic is not only maddeningly slow, it's also risky. Maintaining a brisk pace and riding the proper portion of the road makes it easier for drivers to see you and helps ensure that they'll yield right-of-way when traffic law requires. Your part is to be defensively aware but at the same time, not to hang back in fear.

While you should keep as far left (or right) as is practicable, you have the right to use as much of the road width as your safety prescribes. You already know not to weave in and out among parked cars because doing so makes it hard for drivers approaching from behind or coming into an intersection ahead to see you. And you realise you must give yourself room in case a car door should be flung open in your path. (Would you believe you might even be held liable for damage to the car?) Hugging a curb too closely also makes it easier for a driver to pass you and then cut you off by making a turn immediately in front of you. Curb-huggers appear to be, and usually are, riding slowly; motorists are more likely to disregard them.

Where, as is often the case, a one-way street has two lanes, the best way to avoid being squeezed between parked cars and moving traffic is to move far enough into a lane so that drivers are required to pass you in the other one. Check for traffic behind you before moving over. Then once you do, proceed in a straight line on the road. As a general rule, the proper place for you is the left lane (in England), since the vehicle code decrees that slower traffic keep left. In the US and Canada, the opposite applies, since slower traffic stays to the right.

Any time you change lanes, like a car, you must yield to traffic already occupying the lane you want to enter. Thus the novice cyclist's biggest bugaboo – in England, the righthand turn. (Americans and Canadians, read 'lefthand turn'.) Mastering it will make riding in traffic much less worrisome for you. The intent is to position yourself, as a vehicle would, for the turn. So you must cross a lane of traffic, possibly two or three.

For the sake of example, let's say you'll cross two traffic lanes. This is a four-step procedure. Begin some distance back from the anticipated turn so you have time to complete the manoeuvre:

- First you must gain the cooperation of a driver behind you to cross your own lane. Give a clear hand signal and scan quickly over your shoulder. (If you can't signal and scan backwards at the same time, signal first and then scan. Glance quickly so you remain alert to what's in front of you as well.) Repeated glances may be required until there's a sufficient break in traffic or the driver behind motions you over; then move across your own lane.
- Next you signal and scan again for help from the driver in the next lane so you can just cross over the line.
- Repeat signal and scan to cross that lane. Move to the far side of the lane; or, if the lane is a turning lane, simply merge with it.

- Continue to signal the turn even as you wait for your light; make the turn when it is safe to do so.

The key to all of this is communication. Most drivers will cooperate if you make your intentions clear. (You'll find other situations to use similar technique, such as when you need to merge into another lane to pass a vehicle double-parked in your own.)

If overtaking traffic is coming on too thick and fast to turn like a vehicle, then your alternative, at a four-way intersection for example, is to ride straight through the intersection, then dismount and walk your bike across like a pedestrian.

Your choice of roads makes a difference in the kinds of traffic conditions you'll encounter. Obviously this is a judgment call that's up to you. And your decision may be affected by restrictions that prohibit bicycles from certain roads. As a rule, however, if you wish to move quickly through a city or other built-up area, main streets will have fewer stop signs than will intersecting side streets. Traffic lights will be timed in your favour. Although traffic volume is likely to be heavier, the compensation is wider lanes with longer sight lines where you'll be more visible. And you can expect fewer encounters with incompetent cyclists on these streets. Bear in mind, the fewer the intersections, the faster and safer the going. If main streets and highways are your choice, the optimum speed is a snappy pace, but leave yourself some reserve to accelerate if you need to.

If you prefer a more scenic route and slower going, back streets may be the better choice. In either case, if this is a route you'll use often, some map-study or suggestions of other cyclists may be of help.

CYCLING THROUGH STALLED OR SLOW TRAFFIC

One of the many advantages of the bicycle is that it lets you keep moving when motor vehicle traffic is stuck in a traffic jam. But proceed with caution and, of course, continue to obey traffic lights and other signals as you normally would. Ride slowly – slowly enough to stop in time – in case an unwitting driver should open a door in front of you. And beware of another cyclist, hidden by a vehicle ahead, who could pull into your path.

If a single car or truck stops in your lane in front of you for no obvious reason, take extra care because the driver's course of action is unpredictable. Wait for the vehicle to move on, or pass it on the right (in the UK; left in North America), allowing plenty of room to spare.

Consider that for every stopped vehicle there are both a blind spot and a safety zone. For example, you have no worry next to the rear wheels since they can't move sideways – only forward or back. You are also positioned where the next driver back can see you. As you roll towards the front of the car, you pass through a blind spot. Observe the angle of the front wheels; if they are turned to pull out, or if you hear the engine rev up, wait by the back wheels until the driver makes his move.

Be especially wary where you see driveways or parking spaces along the road which the stopped motorist might pull into. Slowly move laterally away from the vehicle you want to pass, into the open space, and scan back before you come in range of its front wheels to see whether the driver has noticed you. Before moving away from the back wheels in this situation, some cyclists rap on the back window to catch the motorist's attention.

If you need to cut across a lane of traffic in front of a stopped vehicle, signal and catch the driver's eye first for assistance. Then check to make sure the car in front is not likely to roll back into you. (The most probable cause for this is on an incline as a traffic light is changing. Also a driver who's protruding too far into the intersection might back up without looking for you.) When you determine it's safe to cut across, before entering the next lane, remember to scan back for another cyclist who might be approaching.

If your lane is clear (no cars behind you) but traffic is stopped in the next lane (a turning lane perhaps), move over in your lane for extra 'breathing space' and watch for any turned wheels that suggest a driver might pull out into your lane. Don't hesitate to give a yell if you need to warn that driver of your presence.

When a bus or truck is stopped in the curb lane, don't try to pass it on the left (UK; right, North America). You run the risk of hitting passengers or drivers who may step into your path. Allow yourself plenty of room and pass on the right (UK), moving cautiously in case you encounter a passenger coming around the bus.

Bearing these cautions in mind, you can keep moving safely in stalled traffic while all those drivers sit fuming at the wheel. If traffic isn't fully stopped but merely crawling at a few miles an hour, you can still navigate through it. But be even more wary. Pass only when cars have nowhere to go but straight ahead. Stop and wait at a vehicle's rear wheels if its front wheels are turned, indicating the driver may pull out into you. Watch out for long vehicles that might be turning; don't let yourself get caught between a bus or a truck and the curb.

ASSERTING YOURSELF ON NARROW ROADS

Lightly travelled, two-lane country roads make lovely cycling, but we must be alert nonetheless – especially when they are narrow, as they frequently are. The first rule to remember is to avoid the inevitable squeeze play that occurs if a car passes another at the same point on the road where you are riding. For any number of reasons (the drivers are distracted and forget to watch out for you, or a driver pulls back over too soon after passing you to avoid hitting a car head-on, etc.) you could be hit or forced to leave the road.

You must take the initiative to prevent an unsafe situation. Do so while cars are still far enough away that they have time to respond to your action. For example, when you become aware of traffic approaching from in front of you, scan back to see if any is coming from behind you. Let's say a car is coming which you determine will reach you just about the time the oncoming car will also be passing you. Usually your first action is to move out closer to the centre of your lane; if you monitor the driver's approach with a quick backward glance, this signals your awareness of him. As the car nears, use a hand signal (arm extended downwards) that says 'hold back' to the driver behind you, indicating he should slow and follow you. After the oncoming car has passed and you can see the road is clear for him to pass in safety, move back to your usual position near the road edge and wave by the waiting driver.

Are you worried the driver will misunderstand and be furious at having to slow down? Remember, you are simply requiring the motorist to do what the law requires, to reduce speed when passing is not safe. About nine out of ten drivers will perceive you as helpful and, in Myrna Meyer's experience, wave to thank you, waiting until you signal them to go on. Myrna, who cycles all the time on these kinds of roads, says the other odd driver 'will ignore my signal and pull madly around me'. She wears a helmet mirror and finds it useful for monitoring a driver's reaction in a situation like this. If she sees she has a hothead back there who may not slow down, she's prepared to leave the road in a hurry. I agree, this is a situation where a helmet mirror could be a life-saver. (It's important to realise though, that you can't depend on a mirror when a backward scan is required. Like a car mirror, a cycling mirror has a blind spot and you could fail to see a car behind you if it happens to be in that spot. By the way, adjusting the mirror can be tricky, but many club cyclists use them, so you probably know someone who can help you.)

Keep a watchful eye for all oncoming traffic on narrow roads, especially if curves entice drivers to take their half out of the middle of the road. With a line of oncoming cars, beware of drivers who pull out to pass; sometimes they don't see you, or they

Here's how *not* to ride. Because their wheels are overlapping, if the front cyclist swerves, the rear rider is sure to crash (*Dan Burden*).

159

underestimate the distance they need to pass safely without endangering you. If necessary ride off the road.

When curves limit visibility, it's in your best interest to deter a driver behind you from attempting to pass you where it would be unsafe to do so. Why? Because if that driver rounds the bend and finds herself face to face with an oncoming car, she won't hesitate to pull back over – whether you're in the way or not. To prevent this, operate as above: as you approach the curve, scan backwards to make sure you've room, then pull toward the centre of the lane, again using a hand signal to slow the driver behind you. Remain in this controlling position until passing is safe again, then pull back to let the motorist by.

On these kinds of roads simply being seen is always a concern for cyclists, which is why we commonly wear brightly coloured clothing. Furthermore, on roads that are rolling or hilly, we must remember that – bright clothing or no – after we've crested a hill, we disappear for the driver approaching from the rear. Bear that in mind and don't dawdle at the top. In fact, your safest action is to speed up near the top and make a quick start on your descent. Your out-of-the-saddle, side-to-side movement and the bobbing of your brightly helmeted head as you crest the hill should catch the driver's attention before you drop out of sight. Your speedy descent will help put some distance between you.

HANDLING HARASSMENT

I was riding on an isolated road in Tampa when a vehicle with three teenage boys passed very close. One boy slapped me hard on the backside. I noted the licence plate number as they sped away, and being a private investigator, I was able to obtain the name and address of the driver. I called the police, who found the culprits at their parents' home in my neighbourhood. The boys' father apologised to me, then made his son do the same. They will think twice before slapping another female again!

Alison Boh, 33, Temple Terrace, Florida

I find it extremely frustrating that because of harassment I talk myself out of taking overnight trips or short tours alone. It stops me from doing what I really want to do. Randy Lee Jablin, 30, Brooklyn, New York

A rude slap or loud horn blast right in your ear is not only disconcerting, it can be dangerous, possibly causing you to lose control and have an accident. Even worse are the offenders who throw bottles, shove a cyclist off the bike, or try to run you off the road. And women cyclists aren't the only victims. Last June a news clipping made the rounds of the (largely male) *Bicycling* magazine staff, and I heard nothing but derision for a 31-year-old Texan named Eddie Vega who 'apparently leaned out the window of his truck to slap the backside of a woman bicyclist and fell on to the road'. He was run over by his own pickup truck and killed. I have to admit, it seemed like poetic justice.

A beer can in his hand gave away ''ie fact that he'd been drinking. The cyclist also fell, but fortunately was uninjured.

Of the women I surveyed, quite a number volunteered accounts of slapping or shoving in answer to a question about their 'worst cycling experience', and 22.7 per cent of all respondents indicated they found harassment from men disturbing. The first time I ever had my rump thumped, I was too outraged and surprised to respond as Alison Boh did. But the second (and last) time, just a few days later, I paid attention to the licence number and wrote it down. Sorry to say, when I called the police and reported it, they refused to call and reprimand the driver unless I was willing to press charges. That seemed ridiculous at the time, so I dropped the matter. (I didn't want to retaliate, I just wanted to make them think.) I congratulate Alison for getting her point across.

Of course, we want to put a stop to this sort of thing and try not to let it intimidate us. Thanks to a great arsenal of responses, Patti Brehler says she can't remember the last time somebody assaulted either her bottom or her eardrums. This sort of individual is courting a reaction, Patti says. 'So when it used to happen I'd call, "I love you!" Instead of flipping them off, laugh it off,' she advises. 'You don't solve anything by getting upset, you just stress yourself.'

She believes improving her own cycling skills has made her a less vulnerable-looking target. If you feel confident and project that, it makes a difference – that's something she's learned in her job as a journeyman grinder in an otherwise all-male shop. 'I do all the maintenance on our bikes. If women can take care of themselves, it shows,' she says.

Good cycling skills offer another benefit because when you cycle like a vehicle driver, motorists do not have to deviate from obeying traffic law to accommodate you. Therefore, when somebody in a car *is* doing something unusual, it's easier for you to recognise that, and more quickly. Then you can take action sooner if you have to.

Patti has found that wearing a helmet mirror helps. 'There've been times I've gotten off the road because I thought I'd better. Either the car looked like it was trying to get too close, or I saw that arm out the window.' And the helmet itself helps disguise one's sex.

Sometimes, but not always, dress can be a factor. Patti and her partner, Lou Hotten, generally avoid halter tops or short crop tops, plus anything that's going to show cleavage as they lean over the handlebars. 'We wear outrageous things – bright pink leopard skin tights and obnoxious neon green jackets – but there's a purpose in those,' Patti says: for safety's sake they want to be visible to drivers.

By contrast, Myrna Meyer is somewhat less optimistic than Patti. Even her grey hair (at 55) doesn't spare her. She's had kids riding straight at her on bikes, trying to play 'Chicken', and verbal harassment which she finds highly annoying. What she wears seems to make little difference, and she isn't easily scared.

Occasionally she's caught up with the troublemakers. Once a kid screamed at her from a summer camp bus, which she later overtook at a light. 'I got in front of the bus and went through very obvious motions of writing the licence number down,' she recalls. 'I told the bus driver he was responsible for the actions of his passengers and that if it ever happened again I would get the lawyers in our bike club to go after the camp. I made an impression on him and he apologised.'

Myrna suggests that riding with a partner might cut down on the problem, but that usually she prefers to ride alone and continues to do so.

How much should you worry about harassment? I've talked with many cyclists who experience little trouble with it. I myself have had next to no difficulty with it in recent years. Admittedly, I often ride with my husband or with a friend, but I do not fear cycling alone.

I think the extent of the problem can vary widely from one area to another. Says Myrna, 'It has its ups and downs. Twenty years ago the attitude was, "You don't belong on the road." Then as more people began cycling, the heckling and so on subsided. Today cycling is a yuppie thing and there's a backlash. Out of resentment, I think harassment is on the rise again.'

In her locale Patti thinks it's on the decline, as more drivers themselves cycle now or have friends who are cyclists.

Should it become a problem for you, I think among the ideas given here you can find a solution.

True Grit

'My husband and I are both triathletes living in a small town in Wyoming. We are definitely freaks around here and take a lot of abuse from the local ranchers. We do much of our riding on a narrow two-lane highway leading to the Uinta Mountains. Ranchers who live along the route always haul long horse trailers or large semis full of cattle and just about push us off the road most of the time. We fought over space all last summer. However, by fall their attitude began to change. They realised I wasn't just a city-slicker with a fancy bicycle and strange clothes when I was still out there in November in 25-degree weather, riding along enjoying the Wyoming countryside. A few of the ranchers even waved!'

Linda Prater, 36, Evanston, Wyoming

Further Reading

John S. Allen, *Street Smarts* (Rodale Press, Emmaus, Pennsylvania, 1988). This helpful booklet covers traffic situations not dealt with in this chapter. It's offered as a public service to groups, at $.25 each plus shipping and handling, for a minimum order of fifty. Contact Rodale Customer Communications, 33 East Minor Street, Emmaus, PA 18098. For individuals in North America, $1.00 each covers booklet and mailing. For UK requests £1.00 each covers booklet and surface mail; £2.00 air mail.

Fitter and Faster 16

Last month I rode a 10-mile criterium and captured third. I've never felt more proud and exhilarated.

I remember hoping that since I was ten years older than the rest of the field, strategy – not strength or youth – would win the race. Then I noticed a two-member team signalling each other. They worked their way to the front, and one of them took a flyer. Everyone else was meek enough to let the teammate hold them back, but I went for it. I tried to catch the breakaway rider but failed. The pack swallowed me up, and I decided to settle for placing. (Heck, she could always crash.)

I planned my strategy for the final lap. I would come around the last corner in somebody's slipstream. When I was close enough to sprint, I'd take her!

Amazingly, everything went as I'd planned. I set myself up perfectly. I began my sprint. My thighs had never burned like this before. My throat was parched, my breathing laboured. I was gonna throw up! I'd never pushed myself this hard.

The finish line was just meters away . . . when reality struck. The teammate had used my strategy – on me! How dare she! She squeaked past me and claimed second by half a wheel.

But I was still ecstatic. I'd almost thrown up! *I'd kicked butt that day!*
Barb Tanner-Hury, 34, Altamonte Springs, Florida

There are many measures of satisfaction in cycling, and sometimes they centre around making a greater effort, finishing a certain distance, achieving a particular speed, entering a first race, or winning in competition. In some way you see proof of your progress toward being a fitter and faster cyclist.

This is not to say that fast is always best or that fast is everyone's ultimate goal. It may not be. But even a recreational rider can use some speed in her legs – if only to cross a busy intersection more quickly and safely. Or on an organised ride when an efficient paceline speeds by, maybe you'd like to jump into overdrive and catch it. We'll talk in this chapter about ways to improve your speed that you'd probably even enjoy.

We'll also cover more structured kinds of training, along with some road racing strategy from three of Britain's top women cyclists. Of necessity this will be a superficial treatment of the subject – there are entire books on race training and competition. However, I think you'll find some worthwhile insights.

STARTING SPEEDWORK

I'm assuming you've built a good foundation of conditioning with a couple months of 'spinning' in easy gears (described in chapter 11). Now, to improve your speed, there's a variety of approaches you might take. Each approach has certain things in common:

- Developing leg speed. It's this simple: if you can turn the pedals faster in the same gears you're using now, you will go faster. Over the last decade in world cycling competition, leg speed has increased among the very top competitors in every event.
- A gradual increase in training work load. Training involves stressing the body and giving it time to recover. As we know, this allows the body to adapt by becoming stronger. To continue to improve, you must continue to push your body past its current limitations by small increments. If you've not been doing any speedwork, start with one session a week. After some weeks, you could increase it to two sessions. And so on. And remember, the more you push your body, the more essential rest becomes.
- The importance of 'active rest'. The day after a long ride or a hard training session, for example, it's better to go out for an easy ride using low gears than it is to sit at home with your feet up. The spinning and increased circulation help keep your muscles supple.
- Begin each speedwork session with a warm-up; end with a cool-down.

There are some important differences, too, among the various approaches to speedwork. Some might be better suited than others to your cycling goals. Some, such as interval training, require a fairly high level of motivation and are most likely to be used by the competitive cyclist. Others can be enjoyable and productive for the broader spectrum of riders. Suggestions in the first two sections which follow may be useful to anyone who wants to improve.

GROUP PSYCH

One of the best things a woman can do is ride with stronger cyclists, which could mean riding with men. As British Olympian Lisa Brambani puts it, 'You could learn a lot from going out with the local lads, riding on the back . . .' This is common practice among racers, sometimes because there's a shortage of competitive women to train with.

But you don't have to be a racer to benefit. You simply need a group of strong riders willing to let you ride at the back. For a woman it's almost like motorpacing: you ride in the shelter of the paceline and really work on keeping a high cadence, say around 110 rpm or higher. The idea is to use the same gears you're using now but to spin the pedals faster, increasing the cardiovascular demand.

'Joining a group works best if you have the cooperation of the guys,' says my friend, Ellen Dorsey. She prefers to stay on the back of the paceline and let the rider who's dropping back (after his pull) slip in front of her. 'I tell them to pretend I'm not there.'

You need to be comfortable with your bikehandling, and with drafting (covered in chapter 14, Tuning Up Your Technique), so you can conserve energy. 'I seem to know where to go to get the best draft,' says Ellen. 'My bike just seems to go there.'

Like Ellen, Nancy Neely, 24, of Macungie, Pennsylvania, keeps fast company on weekly rides with a group of male track riders – some of America's best – drawn to our area by the existence of the Lehigh County Velodrome. (Nancy herself has eight track racing seasons under her belt and was silver medalist in the points race at Nationals in 1987.)

The frequent presence of another woman on these training rides helps make it less intimidating. The ride begins at a moderate pace, and Nancy takes her turn at the front or, she says, 'some guys will tease you if you don't'. Usually the other woman is in line behind her, so each takes a short pull. After a while they simply *sit in* (ride at the back) and stay with the men as long as possible. Eventually the group breaks up as the pace increases.

This is the point many women fear – and the reason why having another rider of your ability level on the ride helps. 'I've been dropped so many times out in the middle of nowhere,' says Nancy. 'As one of the guys jokes, "Bring along some money and a map, and you'll be fine."'

Typically riders regroup at an established halfway point, and everyone has another chance to try to hang on.

This sounds like work, but I know from my own training rides with a mixed group that it's exhilarating and fun – you're motivated to put forth something extra, and you get results. If you aren't used to riding at this pace, once a week is plenty. The following day an easy 'recovery' ride would be ideal.

To be race-ready, train with a group so you're prepared for elbow-to-elbow contact in the pack (*David Epperson*).

165

FARTLEK

Another approach is to incorporate *fartlek*, or 'speedplay' into your training. On some group rides, for example, there's almost an unspoken pact that everyone sprints for the 'town limits' signs. You can do fartlek when training by yourself, too, by picking up your speed for portions of a ride.

What distinguishes *fartlek* from other kinds of speedwork is that it's unstructured. And you can have a good time with it. 'There are so many games you can play,' says Nancy, crediting her coach with making it fun. Nancy's coach happens to be Patrick McDonough, seven times an American national champion in cycling and a 1984 Olympic silver medalist in team pursuit.

I'm all in favour of fun, and Pat McDonough's an old friend. So I asked him to share pointers. As coach at the Lehigh County Velodrome, he's been working for a competitive edge by studying technique and training methods not only of top cyclists around the world, but also those of the élite in swimming and in track and field.

McDonough tells me he's convinced the trend in racing training for cycling must be in the direction of more time spent on speedwork (already seen in recent years among world-class runners and swimmers). He's taken this tack with his riders, and with impressive results – just last year they netted twelve US national championship titles.

Group fartlek sessions are useful, he explains, to simulate many different situations that might occur during a race. These simulations are a terrific confidence-builder for the real thing, and they spice up a group ride.

One of his favourite simulations he calls 'Indians'. 'I'll pick a couple or more Indians,' he says. 'They'll take off from the pack, which is moving fairly slow. We'll let them get fairly far away, and then the pack will try to catch them.'

Both the Indians and the chasers now have a chance to practise working together in their respective groups. This is just like in a race, where in a breakaway or in a chase group, riders join efforts regardless of team affiliation.

'I demand that the groups work in paceline or echelon formation,' he says. 'So you're practising many things besides just speed training. The Indians are thinking, "I'm going to go out there and make an attack and try to make it stick". The chasers are trying just as hard to reel them in.'

Such speed games are great preparation for racers and give riders who're thinking about racing a taste of it. 'It's unstructured, but it's fun and,' he says laughing, 'it can hurt like hell.' As Nancy attests, in the heat of the chase, you don't mind so much.

Even a pair of riders can make use of a chase, by the way, for some speedplay. If one is stronger than the other, always let the weaker one take off first.

INTERVAL TRAINING

By contrast, interval training is best done alone, since it's unlikely that two riders will be at precisely the same fitness level. 'If you start doing intervals with your friend, one of you will get more out of it than the other,' says McDonough.

Instead he encourages riders to monitor their intervals in some way, using their training diaries to keep track of speeds attained or an improvement in the length of the work period or cadence, as appropriate. 'Besides that,' he adds, 'I can guarantee the intervals will help you because many times, as my riders can confirm, the race will seem easy compared to training. If you do intervals right, they hurt.'

A rider who wants to do intervals, or at least give it a try, must decide first of all what her goals are – because there are many different types one might do.

Pat McDonough categorises intervals according to which of the various energy systems is being trained.

The aerobic system. For example, a rider wanting to improve her speed at a steady pace would be training her use of that energy system which draws on both glycogen and, to a lesser degree, free fatty acids (described in chapter 12, Fuelling the Engine). These intervals are done with a relatively moderate output of energy but with short rest periods. The work periods might be five minutes or longer; the rest would be five minutes or usually shorter, maybe half that.

'I call them *pace* intervals,' says McDonough. 'I say to myself, "What sort of pace would I be doing in a road race?"' He assumes it would be an aerobic pace but probably faster than one he'd normally keep up when training alone because he doesn't have the competition to keep him going. Using these intervals, he can get an aerobic workout if he keeps it up long enough. Generally he recommends a 1½-hour session to his riders – and that takes discipline.

The lactate system. This is an anaerobic system, fuelling efforts that use more energy than oxygen can sustain. Within your body, it involves the conversion of glucose into the fuel known as *ATP* (adenosine triphosphate). In the process *lactic acid*, or lactate, is created; as it builds up in the muscles, it causes a temporary but painful fatigue. Eventually your blood carries the lactate away to the liver. There, when oxygen is available, the lactic acid is converted into glucose.

This amazing cycle can provide energy for more intense efforts that might last from a half-minute up to about three minutes. In track, road, and criterium racing, all of which involve bursts of speed – and often repeated bursts of speed – this system is key. McDonough's racers do a variety of intervals to train it. A criterium racer, for example, might use a heart monitor and do her speedwork at about 80 per cent of her maximum heart rate (MHR), or right around her *anaerobic threshold*, the point at which muscles must start depending on the lactic acid system for energy.

'You're trying to train your body to operate with a certain amount of lactate, and also to ultimately put off producing lactate until you're at a higher speed. In other words,' McDonough explains, 'you're trying to push back your anaerobic threshold.'

To do this, the cyclist rides at about 80 per cent of MHR for about five to ten minutes, so long as the heart rate is being maintained and speed (mph) does not drop more than about 3 per cent. When the speed drops, the work period is ended, followed immediately by five minutes of *rolling rest*, spinning low gears but keeping the heart rate up to 100 or 110 beats per minute. This active rest, McDonough explains, keeps circulation up and speeds removal of lactic acid from the muscles via the bloodstream. If you stopped completely, you would load up even more with lactate.

In this manner, work sessions alternate with rolling rest. A cyclist would start with two five- to seven-minute work periods with ten minutes of active rest in between. Gradually she might increase to four work periods of ten minutes each with seven minutes of active rest in between. It takes time and conditioning to build up to this level, as each succeeding work interval is more difficult because of the accumulation of lactic acid.

The ATP-PC system. This is the system that kicks in for those photo-finish victories. In the muscles we have limited amounts of a substance called *PC* (phosphocreatine) which can be transformed instantly into ATP for very short bursts of intense speed, usually less than thirty seconds. Maximum speed workouts are important for track sprinters and for road racers or criterium riders who want to improve their finishing sprint, for example.

The work interval is at most fifteen or twenty seconds, an all-out sprint, with at least six minutes of rolling rest in between, probably more like twelve minutes, suggests McDonough. He recommends doing this sort of workout about once every two weeks, with a minimum of four work intervals and a maximum of eight.

To sum up, a racer who prefers to be well-rounded rather than specialise in a certain event must train all systems. Too many cyclists think of their training only in terms of quantity. 'If you spend 80 or 90 per cent of your time riding slow and steady, that's how you're going to ride in the race,' says McDonough. 'And with the exception of the Race Across AMerica, there aren't too many races that are slow and steady!'

HILLWORK

Just as you can improve your speed, you can better your climbing by devoting one day a week to repeat efforts on a hill. For example, pick out a hill that's challenging enough but that you know you can climb sitting down. Devise a short, circuit route that lets you climb that hill a half-dozen or so times. Put your bike in a gear low enough to use all the way to the top, and try to keep up a high cadence as long as you can.

In the succeeding weeks, when that hill starts to feel easy, practise attacking near the top. And begin looking for another hill more worthy of your efforts.

Why We Do It

'There was a man picking up his entry packet at a local mini-triathlon at the same time I was. He was obviously amused at the grey-haired woman entering a triathlon, and he didn't try to conceal his contempt. I had the pleasure of passing him as he struggled up a steep hill near the end of the bike portion of the triathlon. "You're looking good, son," I said "encouragingly" as I spun by.'

Myrna Meyer,
54, White Plains, New York

GOING THE DISTANCE: CENTURY TRAINING

For me, completing my first century ride was a real adventure. I'd been riding year-round for four years and had had a century as my goal for about a year. This spring I began a ten-week training programme which would culminate in a century ride of my own – not a group or club event – just my own personal goal.

The whole training time was exciting. My first 40-mile, then 50-mile, then 70-mile rides were real peaks (and valleys!) The adrenaline rush was surprising to me. How good I felt after a long ride surprised me, too – though I did move slower for a day or two. The most depressing thing was bad weather – cold and rain – for the 40- and 50-mile rides.

The century itself was truly a climax, a perfect day except for a brutal south wind that blew me home, since the last part of the ride went north. I feel really good that I could do it, and more confident than ever about riding anywhere I want to go.   Susan Ripple, 43, Rapid City, South Dakota

In the States *centuries* (organised 100-mile rides) are popular events, giving cyclists a goal to shoot for during the season's riding. Some clubs sponsor less daunting *metric centuries* (100 kilometres, or 62 miles). In either case, decorative patches are often awarded to finishers, who usually keep a record of their times. If it's a race at all, it's a race against yourself.

The principle behind preparing for any long ride is to gradually build endurance through regular increases in mileage, including one long ride each week. Here we'll talk about preparing for a century, but if your goal is of a different length, you can apply the principles to create your own training plan.

Some experienced riders, already fairly disciplined in their training, may not need a highly structured schedule to prepare for 100 miles. Such a cyclist is my friend Ellen, who says in her racing years she typically rode 20 to 25 miles a day on weekdays, and in the last couple of months before a century she'd 'try to do some 50-mile rides' on weekends, and work in a 65-miler a couple weeks before the event. You don't need to do the entire 100 miles in training in order to complete it on century day – save the thrill of accomplishment for the big day.

Many riders do benefit from a schedule. The two offered here cover the preceding ten weeks. You can achieve some real improvements in performance over this period of time and yet it's a short enough span that you don't feel you're giving a lifetime over to training. (And you may enjoy it so much that you'll find yourself elevated to a new standard in your cycling.) As these schedules have appeared in *Bicycling* magazine, many cyclists have already found success with them.

Schedule 1 is for first-timers and those who've been cycling about 45 to 50 miles per week. If you've been doing a little more, you could increase distances slightly.

Schedule 2 is for cyclists already training over 75 miles a week. It should ensure a comfortable finish or a new best time.

In both, 'easy' refers to a leisurely ride; 'pace' suggests riding at the pace you expect to keep during the actual event; and 'brisk' intends that you'll exceed your

169

SCHEDULE 1   # Goal: To Ride 100 Miles

WEEK	MON. Easy	TUE. Pace	WED. Brisk	THUR.	FRI. Pace	SAT. Pace	SUN. Pace	Total Weekly Mileage
1.	6	10	12	Off	10	30	9	77
2.	7	11	13	Off	11	34	10	86
3.	8	13	15	Off	13	38	11	98
4.	8	14	17	Off	14	42	13	108
5.	9	15	19	Off	15	47	14	119
6.	11	15	21	Off	15	53	16	131
7.	12	15	24	Off	15	59	18	143
8.	13	15	25	Off	15	65	20	153
9.	15	15	25	Off	15	65	20	155
10.	15	15	25	Off	10	5 Easy	Century	170

SCHEDULE 2   # Goal: A Century with Strength to Spare

WEEK	MON. Easy	TUE. Pace	WED. Brisk	THUR.	FRI. Pace	SAT. Pace	SUN. Pace	Total Weekly Mileage
1.	10	12	14	Off	12	40	15	103
2.	10	13	15	Off	13	44	17	112
3.	10	15	17	Off	15	48	18	123
4.	11	16	19	Off	16	53	20	135
5.	12	18	20	Off	18	59	22	149
6.	13	19	23	Off	19	64	24	162
7.	14	20	25	Off	20	71	27	177
8.	16	20	27	Off	20	75	29	187
9.	17	20	30	Off	20	75	32	194
10	19	20	30	Off	10	5 Easy	Century	184

Source: *Bicycling* magazine, August 1988.

century pace. By the way, you might want to use one of your 'pace' days to do the aerobic pace intervals described earlier. In this case, you would ride the work period about 1 mph faster than your intended century pace, and do the 'active rest' period at about 1 mph slower than your intended pace.

You'll note that the long ride of the week (crucial for building endurance) is planned for Saturday – a good idea, so if that day should be rained out or otherwise impossible

Riding for Weight Watchers team Britain's Lisa Brambani, 22, won the 1989 ten-stage, 358-mile Ore-Ida Women's Challenge. The Idaho event is a top-ranked women-only bike race with hilly courses that put to good use Lisa's training at home in the Pennines (*Ore-Ida Foods*).

On Lisa's handlebars (she's wearing no. 5) note the heart monitor she uses in training and racing (*Ore-Ida Foods*).

for riding, then you have another chance on Sunday. Observe, too, these schedules assume century day is a Sunday. If yours is on Saturday, shift that entire week's programme accordingly so that the day off, for example, is Wednesday.

Schedules look dreadfully uncompromising, but use your good sense. Suppose heavy pressure at work, for example, creates such stress that trying to complete every ride one week according to plan feels like too much. In that case, ease off a little on training.

To some extent, you can also shift things within the schedule. On a particular day, even after you've ridden some warm-up miles, you may feel tired and sluggish. But a 'brisk' ride is scheduled. You'd probably better make this a 'pace' or 'easy' ride.

On the other hand, don't skip a day merely because you don't feel up to it. At least go out and warm up. Sometimes you'll be surprised how good you feel once you're on the bike. We have a lot more toughness and resilience than sometimes we give ourselves credit for. Finding that out is one of the great rewards of mastering the century.

For carbohydrate loading and other nutrition tips, see chapter 12. Likewise, for on-bike comfort review chapter 13. On century day, limit rest stops to ten minutes each so you'll be less likely to stiffen up; make each stop an opportunity to stretch as well as eat and drink. Even if rest stops will provide food, carry a few snacks in reserve in case you need an energy boost toward the end.

Go for it!

TIPS FROM THE PROS

If you're interested in racing, you'll want to learn as much as you can about race tactics from fellow club members, further reading, and the like. Maria Blower reports that her knowledge of team tactics and race strategy came from her (pro racer) father. 'I'm so familiar with it, I'm amazed when other girls don't know these things,' she says. Here she and two teammates, Lisa Brambani and Sally Hodge, share insights garnered in years of international racing.

Conditioning. *Sally Hodge*: Include speedwork in your training. When I started cycling, distance was all-important to me. Now I've learned about doing 'quality' work. I do more quality work and less distance now than ever.

Lisa Brambani: Increase your cadence. A lot of people fall into the trap of pushing big gears. You'll get the blood to your muscles quicker if you twiddle (spin) lower gears. In a race you can attack better if you twiddle, and you'll remain more supple.

Sally: I'm comfortable at 110 rpm on the Turbo Trainer. I'm not sure what I use on the road, but it's probably close.

Lisa: Increase your strength. Valerie Rushworth, my coach (a former national champion), is always going on about this. Your arms play a big part in climbing, and sometimes they do ache on a hill. I'm very weak in the upper body. I do have weights at home, but I really have to get psyched up to do it. So when I'm lifting this winter, I'll think about some miserable hill to get motivated.

Sally: Do circuit (weight) training in the winter, two to three times a week. I tend to do this more perhaps than the other girls because I have a track racing background. Circuit training is a good change of pace in the winter, and a change is as good as a rest.

Rest is important. I don't have a set rest day, but I use Monday as an easy day, with fewer hills, if it's been a hard weekend. I ride low gears and just enjoy looking around on the country lanes. If I took a set day off completely, then I might really need a rest day later on in the week and I'd miss two days. So I train seven days a week and make sure to take one rest day every two weeks.

On equipment. *Lisa*: The average person doesn't need to worry about internal cable routing and aerodynamic rims. That sort of equipment only matters at the highest levels. 'I'll show them I can beat them on my cheaper bike' – that was always my attitude. I started from humble beginnings. My bike was really rubbishy.

Learning to ride in close quarters. *Lisa*: Don't stick at the back of the pack all the time. If you're back there and there's a crash in the middle of the bunch, it's hard to avoid it. After a while you know the good bikehandlers. Try to stay with them.

If somebody's leaning on you, you've got to learn to lean back. If you lean the other way, you're bound to fall. Sometimes Val (my coach) will go out with me on her bike and rough me up a bit. She'll ride me into the gutter, elbow me and such, to accustom me to riding in a pack.

You're bound to crash at times. Try to think of it as just part of the glory.

Before the race. *Maria Blower*: When you get a race programme (or profile) write the information on your handlebars. Note, for example, where there's a hill – (the top is) a likely spot for a sprint, so you'd want to move up within the pack to be ready for it. Use your watch or cycle-computer to keep track of the mileage to these points.

It's really important to know the course. Know where the hills are, for instance. So if you're a weak hill climber, you try to dominate the pace and then on a hill, as you drift back through the bunch, there are some wheels left at the top you can sit behind and draft. If it's a really long climb, it's good to get behind a really steady climber. Otherwise, it's easy to get carried away and blow up.

Always check your gears before the race starts. If you discover a problem, with luck you can have it fixed. It's really demoralising to try to make a shift on a hill and have it not work.

If you have a jersey with pockets, don't pin the pockets shut when you put your race number on. It's hard to get the food in that way! If somebody else pins your number on, check to make sure they don't make that mistake.

Sally: A good warm-up is important. Races go from the gun – partly because they are shorter in distance than they need to be, and partly because better riders want to get out ahead of less experienced ones, to avoid crashes.

(If the road or track isn't clear for a warm-up, perhaps because of another race,) you can warm up on rollers. Also we might use them afterwards for a cool-down.

During the race. *Maria*: New racers, don't be afraid to attack. You might feel overawed, but the way to improve is to attack. The way to race is to race.

Don't stop immediately if you puncture. Sit on the back of the pack (until the support vehicle is near). Put your right hand up to signal you need a back wheel, your left for a front wheel.

If you crash, look around you to see who's getting it back together to chase. Try to ride back up to the pack as a group. Don't go racing off alone if you can help it.

When you sprint, always position yourself so your opponent has to sprint into the wind. Say the wind's coming from the left: sprint in the righthand gutter so if anyone comes by you, she blocks the wind. That's why it's really important to check out the finish before a race. Get out of the car and check to see which way the wind is blowing.

Energy needs. *Maria*: In a stage race it's important to eat right after the stage so you can get your glycogen replenished. If a race is short, you don't have to eat during the race.

On drugs to enhance performance. *Maria*: I've never been in a situation where I've been offered drugs. But I wouldn't do it if I were. I want to win on my own. And I don't want to change my body. I want to have children some day. Besides, what would it do to my family, my grandparents, my friends? What a stigma! If you're caught cheating once, people think you do it all the time.

Further Resources:
If you want to race, you'll need a racing licence. Also inquire about training camps and clinics through your federation.

British Cycling Federation (BCF), 36 Rockingham Road, Kettering, Northants., NN16 8HG Tel: 0536 412211

Canadian Cycling Association (CCA), 333 River Road, Vanier City (Ottawa), Ontario K1L 8B9

United States Cycling Federation (USCF), US Olympic Training Center, 1750 E. Boulder Street, Colorado Springs, CO 80909 Tel: (303) 578-4581

Nothing Flat – And More Repairs You Can Do Yourself

17

I know how to make minor adjustments to my bike such as seat height and pump up the tyres . . . If anything else needs doing, I consult a repair book. Oh yes, I did adjust the gears successfully after my husband had tried and failed . . . Jillian Doylend, 40, Weymouth, Dorset

Learn at least basic repairs such as punctures and always carry tyre levers and puncture kit/spare tube, so that you're not forced to ask strangers for help. Susan Richardson, 32, Liverpool

I have a few friends who do my repairs. I haven't a clue myself. My boyfriend does most of it. He tries to show me how, but I think I'm a little too lazy to learn, as he will do it for me. Naughty, eh! L. J. Widger, 28, St Blazey Gate, Cornwall

When it comes to bike repair, many women like to take matters into their own hands. Literally. But not everyone.

If you're in the latter group, what do you do? The guise of feminine helplessness may work if you have indulgent friends or if you married wisely. Often husbands take over, even for women who used to do their own repairs before marrying. Maybe you can get away with finding something else to do when it's time to service the bike.

And there's always the bike shop. You may find it easiest, and relatively cheap, to drop in with the occasional flat tyre to be fixed.

Sooner or later, however, you'll find it's smart to learn at least the basics. These skills will give you greater freedom in your cycling. Otherwise, there's always a nagging fear that some time you might find yourself inconvenienced, maybe stranded, because of not knowing what to do.

Besides, to remain totally at a standoff with wrenches and chain tools, tyre levers and patch kits is to miss one of cycling's great benefits – the discovery of our mechanical aptitude. While some of us grew up learning to use tools, many of us did not. Fixing mechanical things often seems a male domain we don't dare enter. But we can! Bicycles just aren't that complicated.

In the first place, not too much goes wrong with a bike if you take care of it.

Second, many of the working parts carry on their duties in full view. While these clicking freewheels, moving chains, and swinging derailleur cages may appear complex, they aren't. And their very visibility makes things easy. Take time to observe how they work, and you'll discover there's no mystery to it.

In this chapter we'll cover the most common repair situations – fixing a puncture, putting your chain back on and remedying wheel wobble. We'll also talk about some good workshop habits and a schedule for maintenance. We begin with a bicycle safety checkup you should do right now if your bike hasn't been given a 'physical' lately.

SAFETY CHECKUP

Even if you don't consider yourself a technical whizz, this is a checkup anyone can do. If you find you need to head for the local bike shop, you'll be better prepared to talk about repairs. And if you're thinking about buying someone else's used bicycle, these same check points can help you evaluate its state of repair.

YOU'LL NEED:
- Some clean rags
- Bike lubricant available at a bike shop
- Tar remover
- Six-inch adjustable-end wrench (also called crescent wrench)
- Five mm Allen wrench (also called Allen key or hex wrench)
- Small screwdriver

It's also helpful to have a bicycle pump with a built-in pressure gauge – the type called a *floor pump*. It's made to stand on the floor and, using your body weight to push down, you can fully inflate your tyre more easily than with a portable frame pump. If you don't have access to a floor pump, you could take your bike to a bike shop to have the tyres pumped up. But don't use a gas station pump meant for automobile tyres or you're asking for a blowout. Do buy a floor pump soon so you can pump your tyres up to the correct pressure before every ride. Under-inflated tyres make for slower riding and invite flats and rim damage.

1. The bike's bound to be dusty, so give it a good wipedown with a clean rag. Ignore the chain and cogs for the moment, and dust off everything else. Remove any grease spots with a little tar remover on your rag. As you clean the frame, keep an eye open for dents, severe rust, loose welds or other damage. (If you discover damage to the frame, have it checked at a bike shop before trying to ride.)

Next squirt some lubricant on a section of the chain, and wipe off grit and excess lubricant by grasping the chain with another clean rag while rotating the crank backwards to move the chain past the rag. In this manner, clean the entire chain. A little lubricant will remain on it to prevent wear and make for easier shifting.

A rusty chain should be discarded and replaced.

(If the chain has come off the chainring, see 'Putting a Chain Back On' later in this chapter.)

2. Examine the tyres and remove any bits of embedded stone or glass. If tyres have sizable cuts, dry rot, odd bulges, or badly worn tread, they'll need to be repaired or replaced. Pump up the tyres to the correct pressure, which you'll find marked on the sidewalls. It will be given in *psi* (pounds per square inch).

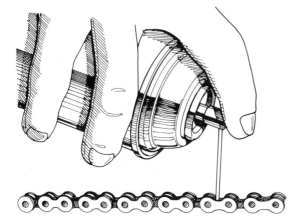

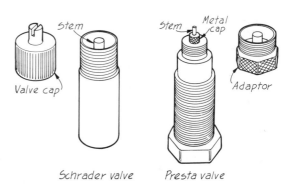

Schrader valve   Presta valve

3. Give the wheels a once-over. Feel each spoke to be sure there aren't any broken ones. Check rims for any dents. Rims should be round; they can be *trued* (have spoke tension corrected) in a bike shop if they appear not to be.

Are wheels mounted securely? If wheels are attached with nuts, test the nuts with your adjustable wrench to be sure they're tight. If wheels are attached with quick-release levers, test to be sure levers are snug in the closed position. (Some new riders don't realise that levers are meant to be flipped open and closed. They should be screwed only to adjust so that the lever flips closed with some resistance.)

Check for loose bearings in each wheel hub by grasping the wheel rim and wiggling it sideways. If there is more than a little play, have the bearings checked at a shop.

4. Check the brakes. *If you have a one-speed with coaster brakes*, ride the bike a short distance and brake by backpedalling. Pedals should rotate less than a quarter turn before braking action occurs.

If your bike has caliper brakes, typical of multi-speed bikes, start by checking that you have four rubber brake pads with plenty of rubber left on them. If your brakes have a quick-release system, check to be sure releases are in the closed position. Some quick-releases are found on the brake levers (see below). Others attach to the calipers. Brakes don't work normally when quick-releases are open.

Then spin one of the wheels and squeeze the hand brake that controls it. Both brake pads should contact the rim squarely and immobilise it. Spin the wheel again and look to make sure neither brake pad is rubbing when you aren't braking. If a brake pad is rubbing, check to see whether the wheel is centred. (Need help? This is covered later under Fixing That Flat.)

If one side is rubbing (despite centring the wheel), gently pivot the entire caliper (see figure 38) slightly to allow better clearance. To do this you may need to loosen the nut that holds the mounting bolt (and the entire brake mechanism) in position. Look for it on the opposite side of the frame from where the brake caliper is. Use your wrench or Allen key (as appropriate) to loosen the nut just enough to pivot the entire brake until the wheel rim is centred in between the caliper arms. Hold the brake mechanism in place with one hand while you tighten the nut with your other hand. If these adjustments don't fix the problem, have it checked at a shop.

Fig. 36
left Lubricating the chain: do this every week or so. And if you ride in the rain, lube your chain before taking the bike out next time.

Fig. 37
right Know which kind of valve you have, so you can buy the proper tubes. If you have Presta valves, you may need an adaptor for your pump.

177

Fig. 38
left This sidepull brake has a quick-release which flips up to open but is now closed. Note that the wheel is centred between brake pads with a little clearance on each side.

Fig. 39
right A brake quick-release on the lever is shown in the closed position. It flips open to the side.

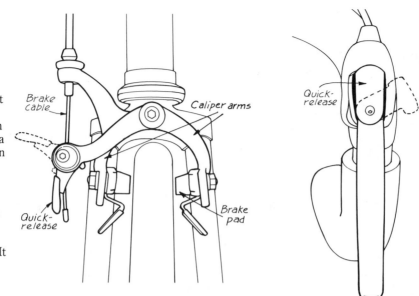

Repeat these steps with the other brake and wheel.

Finally, look over the brake cables (where visible) for broken strands or frayed cable where it enters the hand lever and where it fastens to the brake. Squeeze each brake lever and look into the opening for any fraying in there next to the end button (the metal bulb that holds the cable in the lever), the usual point of wear. If you find damage, cables need replacing. Spray a bit of lubricant into each end of the plastic casing on the cables.

5. Make sure the handlebars and stem are secure. Face your bike, holding the front wheel firmly between your legs and gently try to twist the handlebars left and right. If they move, the stem (which attaches them) is loose and the bolt on top of the stem needs tightening.

Then try to rotate the handlebars. If they move, the binder bolt on the stem part underneath the bars should be tightened.

Look the stem over. If you see a hairline crack anywhere, that's a sign of metal fatigue and means the stem needs replacement. Don't ride your bike until you have it checked at a shop.

6. Now for the saddle and seatpost. First, examine the seatpost for hairline cracks. If you find any (as with the stem), they signal a need for replacement.

Does the saddle need tightening? Try to twist it up and then down, left and then right. If it doesn't move, it's secure.

Next, for a comfortable ride, check to see that the saddle is level. If not, adjust it using the bolt under the saddle.

Finally, check saddle height. Find a wall or something else stable to hold on to while you sit on the saddle, or ask someone to hold the bike for you. Put your heels on the pedals. With your leg extended at the bottom of the pedal stroke, you should have a *very slight* bend in your knee. Dismount and adjust the saddle height if necessary. (You'll find the seatpost binder bolt on the back of the seat lug.)

178 If you're raising the saddle, make sure you don't raise it above the minimum insertion line; this is the safe limit for raising it. (If you need to raise the saddle higher than this, the bike is probably too small for you.)

Mount up again to make sure the height is right for you. The above rule of thumb is approximate. You can make small adjustments (¼ inch at a time) from there. Some riders prefer to have no bend in their knee when pedalling. If you find you're rocking from side to side when pedalling, you've raised the saddle too high.

7. Off the bike again, you're ready to check the gears now. Examine all visible gear cable for any broken strands or fraying, and check to see that the cable is attached firmly at a few points along the frame. Squirt some lubricant into each end of the casing, as you did with the brake cables. Check the gear shift control or levers to be sure it/they are securely attached to the bike.

If the gearing system passes this visual inspection, you can proceed. Suspend the bike (or ask someone to hold it for you) so the rear wheel is off the ground and can turn freely. Rotate the pedals to test the gears in each setting. Remember, with *a derailleur bicycle* you must rotate the pedals as you move the shift lever.

Does the chain shift smoothly in each position? Also, as you rotate pedals, watch to see if the lever moves by itself from one setting to another. (It shouldn't.) If you have two levers, test the gears with each one.

If the bicycle slips from one gear to another by itself, some adjustment is necessary. *Internally geared bicycles* – three-speeds and some four- and five-speeds – may have a problem within the hub that will need repair at the shop. You may be able to adjust *a derailleur bicycle* yourself simply by tightening the gear shift lever screw *slightly* with a screwdriver. Some bikes will have a D-ring here which can be turned to make the adjustment without a screwdriver. Then test again.

During this test if the chain should fall completely off the chainring, it's an indication other minor adjustments may be needed and are probably best handled in a shop.

Okay so far? Rotate the pedals backward again, this time watching where the chain curves around a sprocket at the rear hub. You're looking for any stiffness in the chain. Let any stiff link travel around to where you can get at it with both hands; then flex it sideways with your thumbs.

8. Examine the pedals and cranks. Watch out for any tiny cracks here or in the components that make up the bottom bracket. (See any? Show them to your shop mechanic before riding.) Do you hear any peculiar noises from the pedals when you turn them? Hold one crank in your hand and feel whether the pedal is attached securely. While the pedal should turn on the pedal spindle, you don't want the spindle to wobble where it attaches to the crank.

To check the cranks, grasp one in each hand and check for play by rocking them from side to side at several positions in the rotation of the crank. If there's any play, have the cranks checked at a bike shop.

9. Now it's time to test the bearings in the *headset*, which holds the front fork on to the frame. Lift the front end of the bike off the ground a few inches and drop it. If you hear a clank, the headset is loose and needs attention. Here's another check: stand beside the saddle and face almost forward. Lean on the saddle with your diaphragm to hold it in place, and squeeze the front brake lever tight to brake the bike. Try to rock the bike back and forth. Any movement would indicate play in the headset bearings. Have repairs made before you ride the bike.

10. Now a last look for anything that might be hanging loose. If there are mud guards or bike bags, check to be sure they aren't rubbing against the tyres. Is there anything sharp that could cut you if you brushed against it or if you fell? If the plugs are missing from the ends of the handlebars, for example, have them replaced.

11. Give thought to bike fit. We talk about it in detail in chapter 6.

Proper fit is important. Otherwise, you'll have unnecessary aches and pains – especially in shoulders, neck or back if the reach is too long for you – and a bike that is too big or too small is more difficult to control. So, whether it's your own old bike or someone else's, if it doesn't fit you, don't put time and money into fixing it up.

12. Consider the saddle – the most important point of contact between you and the bike. If it seems your saddle was not designed with your anatomy in mind, see chapter 13 on saddles, and make a change. Many saddles are too narrow for women's 'sit-bones'. The wrong saddle can be torture and will limit your riding potential.

That's it. If your bike failed inspection on any of these points, take it to a shop for repair. Tell the mechanic what you've found in your checkup, and ask for an estimate of costs before you leave the bike. This will help you make sure the bike is worth repairing. If costs are high, you might want to invest in a new bike instead.

Don't feel intimidated because you are a woman. Bike shops depend on return business from their customers – all of their customers, including you. As Caroline Della Porta, 30, of London, puts it:

> Don't be afraid to ask about repairs or parts in bike shops. Before your bike is repaired, make note of the work to be done and check it when you pick the bike up. Have a quick cycle round the block and come back if anything feels wrong. If you use that shop again, they will remember you. Make use of your experience there to learn about your bike.

THE MAKINGS OF A GOOD MECHANIC

Even if we don't have years of repair experience, we can search out the most clearly written repair manuals to have on hand when the need arises. In the States I've found books by Tom Cuthbertson written in everyday language I understand and with a sense of humour. They're actually fun to read, and the illustrations help a lot. Look for his *Anybody's Bike Book* and *The Bike Bag Book*, (a little book you can take with you on the road). Both are from Ten Speed Press (PO Box 7123, Berkeley, California 94707).

Aside from a good manual, orderly work habits can save you frustration:

- Work in a clean, uncluttered, well lighted area. Tools are easier to keep track of and dropped parts are found more quickly if you aren't working in a mess. Remember the bike mechanic's law: the smaller the screw, the more likely you are to drop it. And the corollary: if you can't find it, the bike shop is sure to be closed. Be neat.

180

- In your eagerness to repair something, don't forget: anything you take apart has to be put back together again. Take time while disassembling to observe how the parts went together. This is learning opportunity Number 1. To reinforce it, as you remove nuts, bolts, washers, or other parts, lay them out in a row on a clean piece of newspaper or in a box lid, in the order in which you removed them. And don't take apart more than you have to.

- Most screws and bolts on a bike unscrew in anti-clockwise direction – just as they do generally in the world of hardware. (There are two exceptions, left pedals and some left-side bottom bracket parts.)

- It's helpful to have some sort of workstand which lets you work with the bike up off the floor, so that wheels can turn freely.

- Keeping your hands clean will be much easier if you apply some hand cream before getting into any dirty work. Also, when you must handle the chain, slip a plastic bag over each hand to keep the mess on the bag, not on your hands. (And the next time you get a pin-hole in your rubber gloves so that they won't do for washing dishes, demote them to the bike workshop.)

- If you do have to lay your bicycle on its side to work on it (or to put it in a car trunk, or even just lay it in the grass), always lay it on its left side if it's a derailleur bike. This way you'll avoid bending the derailleurs out of line – which can happen if you lay the bike down on the chain side. Always protect this side of the bike, and you'll save yourself some hassles.

- Prevent extra repair work by riding with one ear tuned to the sounds of your bike. If you hear a funny noise, stop and check it out right away.

PUTTING A CHAIN BACK ON

You're riding along, you shift gears and suddenly with a strange clunking sound, your bike is at a standstill. You look down and see the chain hanging slack, no longer wrapped neatly around one of your front chainrings.

Don't groan. Here's what to do. Look to see whether your chain has fallen off to the inside (near the frame) or the outside. Now, while continuing to ride, move the front derailleur shift lever so the chain moves away from where it's fallen. If it fell to the inside, for example, shift it to the outside chainring. Like magic, the chain will often reseat itself.

If not, you can still put that chain back on without getting your hands dirty if you use your ingenuity. First, shift your bike into high gear (this gives you more chain to work with because you'll have it on the smallest rear sprocket).

Now, if the chain has become tangled or oddly kinked, you'll have to untangle it. But, quick before touching the chain, think: is there anything you can use to keep your hands clean? Are you carrying a snack in some plastic wrap or a bag you can slip your hand into? To lift the chain, you could use a stick, or a tool you're carrying.

Lay the chain in position on the top of the smallest of the rear sprockets. If necessary, reposition the chain over the teeth of the rear derailleur pulleys so the chain makes a sort of backwards 'S' there. Now pick up the chain near the top of the small front chainwheel and lay it in place around the chainwheel. With derailleur bikes, as you do this push forward on the rear derailleur pulleys to give enough slack.

Rotate the pedals a full revolution to check that the chain is running smoothly.

FIXING THAT FLAT

First remove the wheel. The *front* one's easy. But just in case:

Flip open the quick-release lever at the hub and slide the wheel out of the *dropouts*, those slots at the end of the forks. Don't unscrew the wheel quick-release, or you'll need to adjust it later to close properly. If the brake calipers don't allow enough room for the wheel to pass between them, open the brake quick-release.

If the wheel is nutted, loosen the nuts with your wrench.

To take off the *rear* wheel of a derailleur bicycle, prop up the bike so wheels rotate freely. Put it in its highest gear (chain on smallest rear sprocket) so you have slack in the chain. Open the brake quick-release.

Now loosen the axle nuts or flip open the quick-release lever. Notice the open ends of the dropouts: you'll be sliding the wheel forward out of those slots. Standing behind the bike, take the rim of the wheel in one hand and wiggle it gently while you push forward. At the same time pull back a little on the rear derailleur cage to get the chain out of the way. It's a bit of a juggling act, but you can get the wheel out without removing the chain from the front chainwheel.

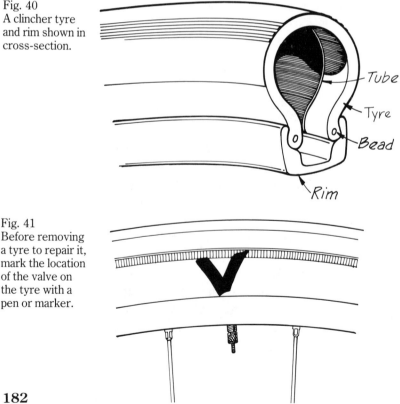

Fig. 40
A clincher tyre and rim shown in cross-section.

Fig. 41
Before removing a tyre to repair it, mark the location of the valve on the tyre with a pen or marker.

Changing a tube. The following method is appropriate for the kinds of tyres most recreational riders use, the 'clincher' or 'wired-on' tyre. It gets its name because the tyre has two steel wires, or *beads* on the side edges. A separate inner tube is inside the tyre, and all of this fits under the edges of the rim.

YOU'LL NEED:
- Two tyre levers
- Spare tube or patch kit

First, take the wheel off the bike, as explained above. (If your tyre isn't flat but you want to practise, deflate it.) Mark the location of the valve on the tyre with a pen or marker.

Then remove the tyre: slip the large, flat end of a tyre lever under the edge of the rim until you can feel you've slid it under the bead. This gives you leverage on the bead. Don't push the lever in any farther than necessary, or you'll pinch the tube. Push the hooked end of the lever down toward the spokes to pry the bead up from inside the rim. Hook that end around a spoke and leave that tool in place. Do the same thing with the second lever, at a spot on the rim 6 to 10 inches away from the first. Remove the first lever and repeat the manoeuvre at another spot the same distance away. Now see if you can free the rest of the bead by running one lever the rest of the way around the rim between the popped-out bead and the rim. If that doesn't do it for you, continue 'leapfrogging' with these levers until you have worked all the way around that side of the rim and the bead is completely out of the rim.

With one side of the tyre free, remove the valve cap and push the valve free of the rim and remove the tube from the tyre. Leave the other half of the tyre on the rim.

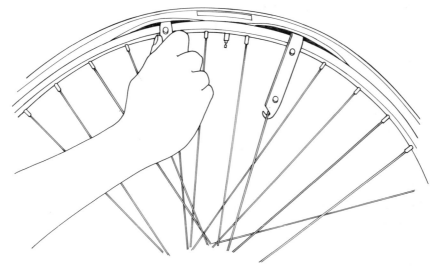

Fig. 42
Remove one side
of the tyre with
tyre levers.

To locate the leak, inflate the tube. Listen for a tattletale hiss, or immerse the tube in water and watch for bubbles. It's possible you might find a pair of holes if, for example, you hit a bump hard and the rim pinched your tube.

Now look inside the tyre in case the thorn, glass, etc. is still in there, waiting to do more damage. That mark you made on the tyre will give you a point of reference to figure about where the puncture was made on the tyre. If you don't see anything that might have made the puncture, feel the inside of the tyre *carefully* with your fingers. There might be a piece of glass or a tack lodged in the tyre. Remove it. Check also to make sure a sharp spoke tail isn't sticking through the rim, needing fixing.

Still looking for a clue to the trouble? Immerse the tyre valve and check it for leaks.

Chances are you'll locate the source of the problem. Now if the hole is very small, like a pin prick, you have the choice of patching the tube with a patch kit (by following the included instructions) or replacing the tube. If the trouble is a leaky valve or a larger hole, replace the tube. Frankly, I replace the tube regardless because spare

183

tubes don't cost much, patches don't always hold, and I don't feel like fussing with them anyway. Don't forget to ask for the proper valve type when buying.

As for the tyre, is it badly cut or worn thin in spots? If not, you can keep on using it. If the cut is more than ¼ inch long, you should *boot* the tyre. That is, put something over the cut on the inside of the tyre to keep the tube from blowing out through the cut. A piece of old tyre about 1½ inches long is often used, or a strip of handlebar tape, or some of that silver duct tape that people often keep about the house.

Pump just enough air into the replacement tube to give it shape. Put it into the tyre, and stick the valve through its hole. To do this, you'll have to pull the bead up free of the rim and then afterwards, ease it back into place.

Now you have one side of the tyre left that is not on the rim. Start at the valve to work the bead under the rim, using your thumbs, not the levers. Work away from the valve in both directions simultaneously. As you go, try to keep the first side of the tyre, plus any part you've already slipped into the rim, in the centre channel of the rim. That will make the last bit easier.

Try if you can to remount those last few inches without using the tyre levers (since the levers could puncture the tube). Toward the end, deflating the tube 'til it's almost flat can help. So will putting a little baby powder or even a dab of saliva on the bead to reduce the friction against the rim. You really have to use a lot of pressure with your thumbs and try to pop only the last couple of inches of tyre over the rim in one effort.

After the tyre's completely mounted, press the valve down into the tyre and then pull it back out. This is to keep the tube from being pinched near the valve.

At last, you can start pumping up the tyre. Take it up to half the recommended pressure and look over the tyre to be sure it's mounted evenly – that nowhere is it too far up under the rim or too far out. If necessary, let a little air out and reseat the tyre. Once everything seems right, inflate to full pressure. Put the wheel back on (close any quick-releases you opened) and congratulate yourself.

Fig. 43
To make the most of your muscle when using a frame pump – and to hold the wheel steady so as to avoid damaging the tyre valve – lean the wheel against a tree, a wall (as shown), or whatever else is handy. Turn the wheel so the valve is at the right height for you to brace your elbow against your knee while you pump with the opposite hand. Here the cyclist holds the pump head firmly in place with her left hand and grips the tyre with her thumb. This position lets her lean into the pumping motion with her upper body weight – helpful because pumping becomes more difficult as air pressure inside the tyre increases.

When buying a frame pump, try it out in the shop first. And ask whether a high-volume pump would be beneficial for the type of bicycle you own.

Replacing a wheel. For the *front* wheel, simply reverse the removal procedure: make sure the quick-release lever is open or big axle nuts are loose. Turn the wheel so the quick-release lever, if you have one, goes on the bike's left side. Slide the wheel hub back into the dropout slots, guiding tyre and rim carefully between the brake calipers. If necessary, open the brake quick-release to allow the wheel to pass.

Centre the wheel between them as you close the quick-release at the hub or tighten the nuts. (The lever should be closed snugly. As you push the lever back toward the front fork, you should feel resistance. If you grasp the front fork while pushing, you'll get some extra leverage. Sometimes a wheel quick-release will refuse to close all the way; turning the quick-release will let you adjust it.) Close brake quick-releases if you opened them. Spin the wheel and make sure it's centred between the brakes and not rubbing either brake shoe. If necessary, loosen and centre the wheel, then retighten.

For the *rear* wheel, again your bike should be in its highest gear. As above, check that the quick-release lever is open or nuts are loose. Slide the wheel between the brake calipers. As you ease the hub into the dropout slots, lay the chain in position on the teeth of the little sprocket on the rear wheel and pull back a little on the gear changer (or on a three-speed, simply pull on the chain itself) in order to have just the right amount of slack in the chain. Make sure the chain wraps down around the derailleur pulleys. Once the axle is securely positioned in the dropout slots and the wheel is centred, tighten up the lever or nuts. Check for centring, as above.

REMEDYING WHEEL WOBBLE

If, despite sharp-eyed vigilance, you ride through a pothole and bend a wheel rim, what can you do for an on-the-road fix-up? If your wheel isn't bent too badly – that is, when you rotate the wheel if it hits the brakes but not the frame – simply loosen the brake with the brake quick-release. You can continue on your way if you are careful in braking, allowing extra braking time because you won't be able to stop suddenly. After your ride you can take your wheel to a shop for truing; this is a delicate procedure, beyond the scope of this chapter. Should your wheel be more damaged than described above, the conservative course of action is to leave the repair to a pro.

REGULAR MAINTENANCE

Three times a world champion, Cindy Whitehead knows that routine upkeep makes riding and racing easier, lengthens the life of a bicycle, and helps avoid equipment failures. She learned that lesson when she broke her seat clamp bolt just after the start of the Sierra 7500. This brutal mountain bike race held in Bishop, California, climbs 7500 feet in the first half of its 50 miles. In 1986 Cindy rode 49 of them standing up without a saddle – an amazing feat of strength and determination.

What happened that day was a result of bad luck, manufacturer's error, and bicycle neglect. Cindy dismounted for the first water crossing. When she jumped back on, the jolt to the saddle sheared off the lightweight alloy bolt which, after a previous failure, a more astute mechanic would have replaced with a sturdier steel one. The saddle gone, she tried to remove the protruding seatpost, but it was rusted in place. 'I'm lax about maintenance but I'm a nut for a clean bike,' she says. 'I'd hosed it off without removing the seatpost afterwards and lubing it. Water got in and rusted it.'

Later in the race she crashed and knocked her handlebars askew. She tried to straighten them, but the stem too was rusted in. Now she was riding lopsided, but she rode hard. And she won the race. Those who saw it will never forget it.

How quickly wear and tear takes its toll depends partly on the amount and the sort of riding you do. In most cases if you follow these guidelines your routine maintenance and repair of minor problems will prevent the occurrence of major ones.

As you'll see, some tasks need doing often while others should be scheduled on a monthly or yearly basis. For these less frequent tasks, keep a record of the date and service performed. Thus, if you should wonder later how long it's been since you installed those tyres or had the wheels trued, you'll have the information at hand.

Before each ride. This quick check covers those parts that can get out of whack from one ride to the next and cause a problem. Some of these points were covered in the 'Safety Checkup'; the number of the relevant portion appears in parentheses.

- Look at the chain, which should appear at least slightly wet with lubricant. (A dry chain makes for noisy, more difficult shifting and uses up some of your energy in pedalling.) Lube (No. 1) if needed. Any time your chain gets a dousing from cycling wet streets, lubricate before your next ride.
- Check that brake quick-releases are closed, and test the brakes. Brake pads should contact the wheel rim only, not the tyre, and brake levers should not travel far enough when squeezed to touch the handlebars. If brakes need adjustment, do so before riding. (No. 4).
- Check tyre pressure with a pressure gauge. Lift the front end of your bicycle and spin the front wheel as you watch for any wheel wobble or rubbing against the brakes, the front fork, or a mudguard stay (No. 3). (Such rubbing increases the work of pedalling and could quickly put a hole in your tyre.) If you do have wheel wobble, look for a bend in the rim or loose bearings in the hub and have it repaired. Repeat checks with back wheel.
- Lift the front of the bike and then let it bounce on the front wheel. Is anything rattling? If so, check for loose parts – a headlight or mudguard perhaps – if you can't find any, then check the headset (No. 9).

Every week or two
- Lube the chain.
- Tighten any nuts and bolts which have loosened. Otherwise, vibration from riding will gradually shake them looser. Test bolts that attach lights, reflectors, mudguards, racks, brakes and brake shoes.

Every month

- Check for frayed brake (No. 4) and gear (No. 7) cables. If even one of the several strands of wire that make up a cable is broken, the cable should be replaced immediately. If there is a kink in the cable housing (which wears the cable and makes braking less responsive), have it replaced. Put a drop of bicycle oil on the bit of cable you see when you squeeze the brake lever and peer inside. Squirt some lubricant into each end of the gear cable casing, but take care not to get any in the moving parts of the shift levers.
- Examine brake pads. If they are worn down past the tread, install new ones.
- Check tyres for wear, bulges, and embedded stones or glass (No. 2). If you have sew-ups (racing tubulars), check to see that rim glue is holding.
- Check for chain-stretch on a derailleur bike. (A stretched chain causes the rear sprockets to wear more quickly.) Since a new chain has links which are precisely 1 inch long, this test is easy: place an accurate ruler alongside a 1-foot length of chain. Line up the end of the ruler with the centre of a rivet; now look at the 12-inch mark on the ruler. On a new, unstretched chain it will be at the centre of a rivet. If the rivet actually measures up at $12\frac{1}{8}$ inches or longer, the chain is stretched and a new one is required.

  Usually when you replace a stretched chain, it's smart to replace the freewheel also, since a worn freewheel can wear out a new chain quickly. But if you keep an eye on chain-stretch with regular check-ups, you can observe when the chain has just stretched $\frac{1}{16}$ of an inch. Replace it then, and your freewheel shouldn't wear and need replacing.

- Check the bearings. If your bike fails any of these tests, take it for the necessary overhaul. First test wheel bearings to make sure they aren't too loose (No. 3).

  Then test to see if the front wheel bearings are too tight: lift the front of the bike off the ground. Does the wheel turn of its own accord, swinging back and forth a few times before gradually coming to a stop? If it stops suddenly or jerkily, the bearings may be dirty, overtight, or require lubricating. (This test is possible because the part with the tyre valve is heaviest. If the wheel doesn't move when you pick up the bike, you may already have the heavy part at the bottom. Try again – give the wheel a partial turn, stop it, then release.)

  On a derailleur bike you can test the rear wheel in a similar way, but first disconnect the chain by removing the wheel and then replacing it, letting the chain dangle underneath.

  Before replacing the chain, test the crank bearings by spinning the cranks to see if they turn freely. To see if they're too loose, turn one crank so it's parallel with a rear chainstay, and place your thumb between the crank and the chainstay. Try to move the crank sideways, watching for any play in it which would indicate looseness. Now replace the rear wheel.

  Check pedal bearings by trying to spin a pedal with your finger: it should spin easily and smoothly unless bearings are too tight. Then grasp the pedal and try to wiggle it; any play in it means bearings are too loose.

187

To test headset bearings, remove the front wheel. Hold your bicycle by the top tube with one hand and tilt the bike slightly to one side, then to the other. Handlebars should move freely left and right without sticking, or headset is too tight.

With an internally geared or coaster brake bike, check the bearings by spinning the rear wheel forward. Too-tight bearings will grab the rear sprocket and cause the chain and cranks to move forward at full speed. (Don't worry if they move a little; that's normal.)

- Test spoke tension. Spokes that are too loose weaken a wheel. To check, with your fingers squeeze together two adjacent spokes on the same side of a wheel. They should feel tight. Continue around that side of the wheel until you've tested the tension of all those spokes, two at a time. All should have about the same tightness. If some are much looser than others, your wheel probably needs professional attention.

Progress to the other side of the wheel, then to the next wheel. Note: on derailleur bicycles normally the right-side spokes of the back wheel are tighter than left-side spokes.

Annually. Your bicycle needs an overhaul, with all moving parts disassembled, cleaned, inspected, replaced as needed, lubricated, put back together, and adjusted. At this time consider replacing brake cable and housing; some manufacturers of brake systems recommend doing this yearly as a precaution. If you do, worn brake pads and handlebar tape also would be replaced to avoid duplicating work later. Have the frame looked over for any damage or misalignment.

Think of the annual overhaul as an investment that will ultimately save money because replacing a few worn parts prevents damage to others. Schedule this task for wintertime when shop mechanics are less busy.

Of course, reading isn't the only way you can learn about bike repair. Experience is a great teacher. Spend time with friends when they're working on their bikes. Watch and ask questions; help if you can. Take advantage of repair clinics given by various cycling organisations, or organise one through your club; allow time for hands-on experience. Or ask at your local shop about a bike maintenance course you could take.

Cycling with the Family

18

'Our kids recognise cycling as something that unites our family,' muses Rita Menet of Appleton, Wisconsin. At 5, 8, and 10 Rita's children are old enough to realise their family activity makes them 'a breed apart from other kids' as Rita puts it. The two oldest do play organised sports, and Rita and her husband try to plan cycling so it doesn't conflict. But the children relish their riding. Last year the oldest completed his first century, winning a trophy as the youngest finisher. 'If it comes down to it, they'll cancel a game to go biking,' Rita says.

Because we enjoy it, naturally we want to share cycling with those close to us. Usually that's the family: husband (and by extension, boyfriend, lover), children if we have them, or sometimes grown sisters, brothers, even parents. Besides, we're often in a bind, wanting more time to spend with the family yet wishing we could fit in more riding. Why not combine the two, as did Suzanne Bailey, 35, of Harrisville, Rhode Island? 'Cycling,' she says, 'was the only exercise I could do with a 3-year-old who would no longer stay in the stroller.'

At its best, cycling draws a family closer together not only while caught up in it, but later in remembering. For example, Laura Castle, 11, of Selma, Indiana, wrote to me:

> Last summer I had many interesting experiences bicycle vacationing with my parents. One night when we were sleeping in our tent, my mother was awakened by the beeping of the computer on her bicycle. When she went out to see what it was, there was a racoon sitting on her bike bag, happily punching the buttons. He must have been fascinated by the sound. Anyway, he and his buddy ate a lot of our food and carried utensils and other things all over the campground. My father got the idea to scare them away with my camera flash, so in the process I got two super pictures of racoons.

Another boon of cycling with our children is the chance to teach them bicycle safety by example. I don't have kids, but I cringe at seeing somebody else's riding after dark without lights or on the handlebars of another kid's bike. If we ride with our children, we see which lessons are really being learned. And as we start them on a sport for life, they'll derive fitness and psychological benefits, just as we do.

But there's more to family cycling than meeting the needs of children. Cycling is a pleasure we can share with any family member willing to be included. Sometimes we have to wait until they ask or we sense the time is right. The rewards are worth it, as Linda Cave, 28, of Sunnyvale, California, relates:

One day my father asked to come riding with me, and I told him yes. At the time he was overweight and smoked – unfiltered Camels, no less. He had done nothing vaguely athletic in thirty years and spent most of his time reading at home. His biggest outing was to drive down to the local Sears and Roebuck.

After several rides with me on my favourite routes, he quit smoking.

Two years later we were on our second bike tour, this time down the coast of New Jersey on our way to Assateague Island, which is home to wild ponies and many shore birds. Our journey included a ferry ride from Cape May, New Jersey, to Lewes, Delaware. We awoke that morning to a clear day and rode fast to catch the first ferry. Once underway, my father and I stood at the bow watching our escort of dolphins play in the boat's wake. After several quiet moments he turned to me and thanked me for showing him what he'd been missing all these years.

PEDALLING WITH YOUR PARTNER

One Sunday afternoon my husband, a friend, and I took a long ride to a lake. On the way back I had a tough time staying with the guys. The sun was scorching, the headwind was fierce, my calories were all depleted, and my husband was irritated. Our friend needed to get home, so he decided to let my husband and me fend for ourselves. This made my husband more irritated with me (if that's possible). Eventually he too left me miles behind.

Since the community where I teach school wasn't far off, I decided to head there rather than home. I figured I could get help if I felt any weaker. Finally I made it to the little corner store across from the high school. But I could barely muster the courage to go inside. I was wearing my triathlon suit, which is very revealing, and I was afraid I'd run into a student or, worse yet, a school board member.

Gailyn Sutton, 31, Longview, Texas

Riding with spouse, boyfriend, or other adult partner is often the first challenge in family cycling. You don't want to fight the battle of the sexes over it but to have a good time.

What if you're the slower or less experienced cyclist? Herewith, some pointers to help you keep up with your cycling spouse or partner.

- Be as generous with yourself in buying a good bike and other equipment as your partner is with himself. Too often a woman skimps because she's half-hearted about the sport to begin with. In buying a cheap, heavy bike she guarantees herself less enjoyment. 'She needs comparable or better equipment,' says cycling husband Mel Kornbluh, of Bridgeton, New Jersey. 'When some of my friends say their wives don't enjoy cycling, I look at their bikes and I can see why. My wife Barbara has a nice, lightweight bike, and one time I encouraged a fellow's wife to try it. Normally she rides a heavy mixte. But she tried this bike and she couldn't stop grinning. She loved it.'

- If you ride together, ask your partner to let you ride in front and set the pace. Always struggling to keep up is demoralising.
- Practise paceline riding (see chapter 14, Tuning Up Your Technique) if you're continually losing ground. In this case, you draft your partner. He gets a more intense workout while you ride faster than normal, sheltered from the wind.

The Rewards

'After biking since only last spring, in August my husband and I signed up for a 62-mile ride. And as we thought it ridiculous to ride 62 miles and then *drive* home from the finish, it was going to be a 70-mile ride . . . nearly double our longest previous distance of 40 miles.

'So the night before I was actually scared. What if we really couldn't make it?

'Leaving the start, I couldn't believe how hard it was to pedal, and panic set in. When logic returned, I realised I had a flat tyre! My husband was so charged up, he didn't hear me call to him and left with the pack. A friend stopped to help and became my cycling partner until my husband finally realised I was missing, 15 miles down the road.

'Even though it rained and we were sopping wet most of the trip, it was really fun. Seven miles from the official finish we "hit the wall" although we were too inexperienced to realise it. We stopped in the shelter of a drive-in and took out little chocolate bars and started giving each other shoulder rubs. The "oohs" and

"ahhs" plus the sugar shot sent us into fits of laughter until tears poured down our faces. A sag wagon driver spotted us and called, "Only 7 more miles, you can do it!" and we knew we could but were laughing too hard to answer.

'The finish line itself was anticlimactic: a few people standing in the rain, waiting for the stragglers. We chatted with them, then hopped on our bikes for the 8 miles home – an awful ride through heavy, downtown traffic.

'Near home it rained again and even now I wonder what the neighbours thought, seeing us ride up and down the block in the rain as if unable to find our driveway. But no way was I getting off that bike until my odometer hit exactly 70.0 miles, not 68.9 or 69.5, but 70.0!

'After stumbling into the house and out of our wet clothes, we fell into a steaming shower and laughed again, enjoying our tremendous sense of accomplishment and the bonding of our love and friendship.' Stephanie A. Johanns, 34, Lincoln, Nebraska

- Be gutsy. Go out and train on your own or with friends. Stick with it. Building fitness takes time, as Anne Smith, 48, of Colorado Springs writes:

My husband and I began cycling in our early forties. He was fairly athletic, but I wasn't. I spent the first year trying to keep up with the group – any group. He spent it trying to keep up with me – waiting or going back to find me!

When I finally got stronger, we moved from Texas to Colorado, and the altitude and hills put me back to square one. After three years and much determination and hard work, I can now ride in a group without my husband and not worry about being left behind or that some friend must look out for me. It's a great feeling and worth all my training.

- If your spouse is so strong that you always feel inferior, build confidence by cycling with others closer to your fitness level. Join a club, or organise a few of your friends. You may ease the tension by riding separately, providing you each have your own companions. But don't pass up all chances to cycle with better riders. You can learn from them.

- A tandem is a great leveller. If the last time you see your partner is leaving the driveway, a tandem may be the solution. Providing you work well as a team, you can combine your strengths. You'll like no longer having to shout conversation into the wind. But do train on your single bike when you don't pair up on the tandem.

- Prepare for instances when you suspect you might be left behind. Is your riding partner the impatient sort who might steam off in a huff and leave you? Might you at some point want to tell him to go on and let you finish alone? Or maybe you simply worry about being a straggler on a club ride.

  These things may never happen, but if you're ready to be self-sufficient, your worry won't be so great. Take snacks with you in case you need an energy boost. Have your own copy of any route maps. Equip yourself with a pump and repair kit and know how to fix a puncture. Carry change for the telephone so, if necessary, you could call a friend or a cab. When you're ready to be independent, if you find yourself on your own, it's just another of cycling's many challenges.

  Don't get me wrong. I'm not saying it's okay for one cyclist to abandon another, especially a new rider, in strange surroundings. Cycling, like many other things, can test a relationship. Assert yourself if your needs as a cyclist aren't being met. If your partner really wants you to be a cycling companion, he should be supportive.

- Are you finding enough time to train? Are household, work, and family responsibilities divided fairly so you, too, can get out? If not, negotiate. As Kate Bauer, 31, of Ewa Beach, Hawaii, puts it, 'Let's see the guys support us for a while. Give us encouragement and *time* to ride. I think that is one of our biggest problems. Let's get men to take us seriously and give us some of the support and time back that we've given them.'

  If you're the cycling enthusiast and your partner is new to the sport, it will be up to you to make it appealing. Without seeming like a mother hen (probably my own shortcoming), try to anticipate the typical novice mistakes and head them off.

  I introduced my husband (then boyfriend) to cycling in much the same way I've encouraged readers of this book to begin. I lent him a bike that fitted and was geared for the hills in our area, and made sure he had a helmet and comfortable shorts. Derailleur shifting was new to him, but I explained the basics and he quickly got the hang of it. He also discovered the bike seat was too hard and we substituted an anatomic saddle (yes, many men find them comfortable, too.)

We were lucky – from his door we could take off on a variety of scenic, rural roads with little traffic. We have some climbs that are corkers, but even so we enjoyed our Sunday and after-work rides there from the start. I'm a firm believer in holding out a carrot, so we planned an autumn bike tour in Italy, our favourite place to travel. Anticipating it gave incentive, and the tour was *magnifico*. We've done more bike-touring since, and some of our favourite fantasising is about where we'll take our *bicis* next.

YOUR PINT-SIZED PEDALLER

If you've decided to make cycling kids' stuff, you can put a child on wheels at virtually any age. In the light of your own intuition about your youngster, consider what two child development experts recommend. In phone interviews they suggested how to help a child make the most of his abilities in an activity like cycling.

As every mother knows, kids aren't the patient plodders adults tend to be. Before about the age of 6½ long-term goals mean nothing to them. Their concerns are immediate and can change within minutes, especially if their task is boring or uncomfortable. Observe your children as they play on their own. 'They stop doing whatever's displeasing or discomforting. They become belligerent about not continuing,' says Vern Seefeldt, PhD, director of the Youth Sports Institute at Michigan State University.

Kids are likely to pace themselves with bursts of energy. They go pell-mell, then tire and dawdle for a while. They recover and want to go top speed again.

Between the ages of 6½ and 7½ comes a tremendous change in a child's ability to concentrate, accompanied by improved motor skills, notes Doctor Seefeldt. A natural competitiveness usually emerges about this point, and kids will push themselves more. Thus gradual conditioning becomes important, since older children, adolescents, and teenagers (like adults) can suffer overuse injuries if they do too much too soon.

'They can get all the various "itises",' says orthopedic surgeon Lyle J. Micheli, MD. These include bursitis, tendinitis, stress fractures, and chondromalacia. The best cure is prevention, with slow, progressive increases in training. The 10 per cent per week limit of increase recommended to you applies to youngsters as well.

If injury should occur to your child's growing bones, cartilage, or joints, it's not a matter to be ignored, warns Doctor Micheli, director of sports medicine at Boston's Children's Hospital and assistant clinical professor at Harvard Medical School. Discomfort and swelling after a long day's pedalling should be checked by a doctor. Says Micheli, kids differ from adults in that children rarely experience 'muscle injury or muscle strain. If you think your child has a muscle injury, it usually means something else is wrong.' Don't ignore it.

Stretching shouldn't be overlooked. Not all kids are naturally flexible, adds Micheli. 'Some kids, particularly more athletic kids, are relatively tight compared to adults.'

Prevent the most serious damage a child can experience – head injury – by providing your kids with approved helmets and insisting they wear them every time

193

they ride. The American Academy of Pediatrics, in their campaign to make bike helmet use the norm for kids, suggests letting children who are old enough choose their own helmets. (In North America, for a brochure including a coupon for 40 per cent savings on a child's helmet, send a stamped, self-addressed business-size envelope to the American Academy of Pediatrics, Bike Helmet Brochure, PO Box 927, 141 NW Point Blvd., Elk Grove Village, IL 60009-0927.)

These helmets are now available in small sizes, so even a baby should be wearing one as soon as she can hold her head up. Some of these weigh as little as a half-pound or less – a good choice for young children whose necks aren't yet very strong. Look for one with the ANSI or Snell seal of approval. I count at least eight American manufacturers whose child helmets meet those standards: Bailen, Bell, Cycle Products, Echo, Etto, Monarch, Pro-tec, and Vetta. The only British manufacturer of children's helmets is Centurion, but some of the American makes are available in the UK, in particular Bell and Vetta. There are also several European makes, notably the Italian Brancale. In a recent study of injuries to passengers in child-seats, head trauma was the most commonly occurring injury in the case of a crash or a bicycle toppling over with a little one on board. Play it safe with a helmet. Of course, you'll set a good example.

One other point: not until puberty do children's bodies sweat as efficiently as adults', so they are more vulnerable to heat stress and need more water than we do. Assist or remind children to drink water often. Carry sterile water in a bottle for your infant – a needed supplement to feedings in hot weather. And remember sunglasses for baby and older children, too, plus sunscreen, as needed.

Finally, be generous with praise. Each little success along the way builds your youngster's confidence and encourages him to keep trying.

Now let's see how parents combine cycling know-how with knowledge of their kids' abilities to nurture their growing bicyclist.

BIKING SAFELY WITH BABY

I know parents who've cycled right across the US with their 2-year-old in a bicycle trailer, happily clutching his hobby-horse as a companion. More likely, your first thoughts are of riding close to home. Regardless, you share a common concern, the safety of your child.

For starters, select the right hardware, bearing in mind the tips below. Buy at a good bike shop, or keep your eyes open for hand-me-down bargains from other cycling families in your club. Another network for equipping children of all ages is the Family Cycling Club, organised by the Kornbluhs in the United States and branching out into the UK through Carl Farmer of London. Contact: Family Cycling Club, Mel and Barbara Kornbluh, RR 8 Box 319E., Gwynwood Drive, Bridgeton, New Jersey 08302, or Carl Farmer, 61 Aberdeen Road, Highbury, London N5 2XB.

Now here are your options:

Trailers. Although expensive (£145 or $250 and up), a trailer is the safest way to cycle with a baby or young child up to several years of age. By securely mounting an infant seat inside, you can provide good head and neck support for even a small baby. A car seat would also work. For toddlers and other young children, a seat insert with restraining harness or the like is essential for comfort and safety.

The trailer can hold not only your small passenger, but also some gear if you choose to go touring. It's versatile; once your child outgrows the trailer, you can use it to haul luggage.

Admittedly these aren't light (about 20 to 30 pounds, empty), and they are wider than a bicycle, so you'd want to avoid congested streets when pulling one. Their low centre of gravity makes them quite stable, however. And better models have couplings designed to keep the trailer upright even if your bike should fall.

Good features to look for are lap and chest harnesses. A bright colour like red or orange is ideal for increasing visibility. (You can add a safety flag on a long pole for even better conspicuousness.) For greatest stability your child's weight should be carried lower than the trailer wheel hubs. Check to see that your little one's fingers can't reach into the spokes; some parents rig plywood mud guards to be sure. A good bike shop can help you choose and should let you test-ride a trailer you're considering.

Preferences vary as to whether the trailer should face a child in the direction she's riding (less likelihood of dogs jumping or nipping at her) or facing back (to see and talk to a parent riding a second bicycle behind).

Baby packs. In the early months some parents choose the sort of carrier which the baby wears like a sunsuit. A panel of fabric gives head support, and Mum or Dad wears the carrier on chest or back. It does not give any protection in case of an accident, however.

Child-seats. At about 1 year when he can sit and hold his head up well, a child is usually old enough for a child-seat – and too big for the above carrier. A rear-mounting child-seat is preferable, as it interferes less with bikehandling than a front-mounted one, and your view will be unobstructed.

Select a child-seat with a waist belt and a chest harness or, if not the latter, then slots for adding one. The seat back should be high enough to support Junior's neck and shoulders, but not so high that his helmet makes him lean forward uncomfortably. Look for a child-seat with integral foot buckets; dangling legs not only tire but there's the danger of frisky feet kicking you black and blue or getting caught in the spokes. To prevent the latter, spoke protectors that mount on your wheel are often included with a child-seat and should be used. Cloth-covered cushions are better than plastic ones because they don't heat up in the sun.

Take your bike with you so a salesperson can help you make sure the seat will fit it properly. For greatest stability, a seat, when mounted, should carry the baby's centre of gravity ahead of your rear axle. You don't want to do a wheelie with her on board! Also make sure the child-seat will not rub on tires or brakes. If you're not certain you can mount the seat correctly, have it installed at the shop.

Speaking of your bike: if you have a true racing bike with a short wheelbase and quick handling, it's not so great for mounting a child-seat. You'd probably shudder at the thought of doing that to your racing machine anyway. But for the record, the other standard bike types (sport touring, touring, mountain bike, hybrid, or city bike) would be more stable. If you're likely to be splashing through wet streets after a rain storm, add mud guards to your bike, or you'll dampen more than your child's enthusiasm.

No matter which equipment you choose, be sure your cycling skills are top-notch. Before putting baby in the trailer or child-seat, practise first with something you love less dearly but that weighs the same, like a bag of potatoes. Strap it in and ride so that you accustom yourself to cornering with the trailer and are mindful of its width. Get used to the effect of extra weight in the child-seat. Because of the load, allow more time to brake when you have your passenger in the child-seat or are towing a trailer.

By the way, never go off and leave baby in the child-seat unless someone else is standing there, holding your bicycle for you. A parked bike can topple over.

PUTTING GROWING KIDS ON WHEELS

There comes a point when a child is too heavy for a child-seat; consider 35 to 40 pounds a maximum, but you may find your bikehandling compromised sooner by the extra poundage. While a trailer remains safe for a longer period of time, the day eventually dawns when your passenger decides she'd rather pedal than just sit.

In cycling this is an awkward age. The child is too small for the smallest (20-inch wheel) derailleur bicycles, necessary for cycling anything but flat terrain. He may have a single bike, but he flakes out before pedalling it very far.

Devoted cycling families find the solution with a child-back tandem or by modifying the rear of a standard tandem. Though one must start with short rides and gradually build up, a youngster can go longer distances on a tandem more quickly. With a parent in the front ('captain's') position, the child can ride through traffic and road conditions that would otherwise be risky. Not only does she share the fun of cycling, but she becomes traffic-wise and starts developing some of the balance needed to solo on a bicycle before even trying it.

As if you haven't guessed already, no tandem of quality will be inexpensive. Unless a lucky contact with other cycling parents nets you a child-back tandem with the correct frame geometry to fit your pint-sized pedaller, you'd need the services of a custom builder. It can be done. A builder can make you a tandem with a rear seat tube as short as 12 inches. But many parents prefer to modify an adult-sized tandem they already have, or buy one and make the modification.

Such conversions are often made with a Junior Pedalling Attachment, or 'kiddy-crank' as it's popularly called. The unit comes assembled, ready to attach to the rear seat tube. It's complete with short cranks, chainwheel, fixed sprocket, boss, and Allen keys. The fixed sprocket means that, as on a standard tandem, when the parent pedals, the child pedals; when Mum or Dad coasts, the child coasts, too.

Adding a kiddycrank is not a do-it-yourself project or something even every bike shop mechanic knows how to do. Contact a specialised shop, such as one of the suppliers listed below, or the Family Cycling Club if you have difficulty finding someone to make this change.

And just as there are child-back tandems, there are triplets for a parent who wants to cycle with two children, or for a couple who relish togetherness and wish to add on for a child. Talk about special equipment! Contact tandem sources listed at the end of this chapter. In the US triplets can be ordered through Mel Pinto Imports, and from Santana of Claremont, California. Prices for triplets of good quality will be steep.

In the UK one sees triplets created through the use of a Swann 'trailer' added to the rear of a tandem. Other brand names for a similar unit are Rann and Hann. The trailer resembles a single bike without a front fork, and it fits on a special mounting on the rear of the tandem.

You're clued in now that tandems and triplets require investing money and effort. If you make connections with other families to recycle equipment, however, you can save money up front and recoup some of your investment on resale.

MAKING IT FUN

If it's important to make cycling fun for yourself and your spouse, it's doubly desirable to make it fun for the kids. Or, as the Kornbluhs put it, 'You have to sort of nurture the whole thing.'

Remember your child's attention span in planning rides. If you don't, she may quickly remind you, as the Kornbluhs' daughter Natalie did at the age of 2. 'When she didn't want to ride any more,' laughs Mel, 'she'd throw her dummy (pacifier) overboard or kick Barbara in the butt.'

With a youngster too little to participate in pedalling, tie a toy within reach. Give an older child in a trailer a bag of toys. Rita Menet's 5-year-old Joy rides listening to music on headphones.

Take more breaks while riding than you normally do. On a warm day a child in a trailer, for example, heats up faster than you because you have a cooling breeze. Even if you provide your passenger with his own water bottle, help him to drink when you stop. On a cool day he'll feel cold sooner (because he's not exercising) and should be dressed more warmly. To boost circulation and burn some energy, always let him run around a little when you take a rest stop. Besides, when it's time to move on, it will be easier to coax him back into the child-seat or trailer by saying you'll stop again soon, where he can play some more.

All kids welcome a change in activity. They 'recuperate' miraculously from tiredness at a rest stop if you pull out a Frisbee or ball to play catch. One mother tells me she never passes up intriguing looking playground equipment when she and the kids are biking by.

Plan an activity for every ride. Pedal to the park or zoo, to a museum or Grandma's, to a lake or your favourite ice cream stand – some place fun for your youngster. This is especially helpful at the stage when the kids are getting heavy back there on the tandem but aren't contributing much to the effort. 'You're doing a lot of work and they're doing a lot of complaining,' says Mel. 'This isn't the time when it's most fun to ride with them. Having a destination helps cut down on complaints.'

Tell children in advance how long the ride will be. Mel and Barbara don't talk in

197

terms of miles. That can sound too long. Mel is more likely to say, 'Well, our first rest stop will come after about as long as it takes you to watch "He-Man" (a favourite cartoon show).'

Cycling with our kids is the best way to pass on the cycling habits we want them to learn (*Dan Burden*).

Riding with other people who have kids is probably the most sure-fire way to keep yours interested. 'If they see John or Jane doing it, they say, "Hey, this is normal for me," says Mel. If they never get to ride with other families, they feel as if they're freaks in a way, he adds. Look for bicycling families through your local YMCA or cycling club.

Through the Family Cycling Club the Kornbluhs, with rollicking success, have organised half a dozen or so weekend tours on which the small fry have outnumbered the adults. A reasonable mileage limit is set for the day (about 35 to 40 miles), and a sag wagon provided to carry luggage, and pooped-out kids when necessary. They're never sidelined in there too long, though: the club's agreed on a 5-mile limit for van rides. That seems to be plenty of time for a child to rekindle his energy and decide he's probably missing out on some fun.

Youngsters play 'musical parents', too, pairing up with an adult other than Pater or Mater. They seem to try harder and do it without griping, for somebody else.

GRADUATING TO THEIR OWN BIKES

Sooner or later youngsters who've been tandeming or trailering will want to ride small bikes of their own. Ease the transition by having them continue on the tandem/trailer for longer excursions, while building stamina on their own bikes with shorter rides. On tour the Family Cycling Club handles it this way: first thing in the morning there's a pre-ride spin of a few miles for tykes on their single bikes; then for the rest of the day they're back on the tandem or in a trailer. At this stage you may find it wise to start with one bike for learning and wait to buy a second, lighter bicycle a little later.

To save your back while teaching a child to balance on his bike, instead of holding on to the seat with your hand when running behind a child and trying to steer the handlebars, take a piece of rope or a leather belt and fasten it to the centre of the back of the saddle. That's a more natural position to run in, and you'll be able to stay with him longer.

As soon as children are riding independently, parents should work with them to reinforce the rules of the road. Head off these three typical kids' errors:

- Failing to look for traffic before entering the street from driveway or pavement
- Not stopping for stop signs or traffic lights at an intersection
- Not looking for oncoming vehicles before moving sideways, or otherwise swerving into traffic

Correcting these failings will reduce by 90 per cent your child's chances of being hit and killed by a car, says Dan Burden, a cycling parent and bicycle coordinator for the state of Florida.

All along children need lots of positive reinforcement for their efforts, and this continues to be the case as they progress to riding their own single bikes. Within their level of ability, your children do try hard to please you and are waiting to hear they're doing just that.

Regarding equipment, although I haven't canvassed the entire market for multi-speed bicycles in children's sizes, you'll find among the sources at the end of this chapter a sampling of brands which offer bicycles with 20- and 24-inch wheels in junior sizes. Some children can find a good fit in a proportional adult bicycle with a 24-inch front wheel.

As children progress to geared bicycles, drop handlebars are more difficult to manage than upright bars. Their children could see better and balance more easily, Barbara and Mel found, when they substituted a mountain bike type handlebar for the drop bars on the kids' first derailleur bicycles. Especially tricky for youngsters at first is learning how to coordinate pedalling with their feet and braking with their hands. A big, empty parking lot is ideal for practice.

Shifting can be mystifying at first also. When riding together, you can help by looking at the terrain from time to time, then looking at your child. Is she pedalling too slowly? Or spinning wildly? Tell her how to shift up or down as needed to find a comfortable cadence.

199

Also at the transition to single bikes, certain commands from a parent need to be followed unquestioningly. When Mel and Barbara's children made the switch, the Kornbluhs felt they couldn't allow as much talking as they'd done back and forth previously.

'On many occasions we'll say, "This is not a time to talk" because we're in a busy area where you need to be aware of everything around you, and talking would distract,' says Mel.

'But then,' adds Barbara, 'we go in other areas where there's not much traffic and we sing songs and tell jokes and ride two abreast.'

Sometimes you can discuss traffic situations with your children as they arise, or later on. Ask their opinion as well as offering your own. Praise their good judgment and improving bikehandling. Encourage your youngsters to be proud of cycling well.

Product Sources:

(Contact the company or distributor to find a retailer near you.)

Helmets in children's sizes:

Bailen Helmets, Bullard Co., 2680 Bridgeway, Sausalito, California 94965, USA

Bell Helmets, Inc., 15301 Shoemaker Avenue, Norwalk, California 90650, USA

Cycle Products Co., Grumbacher Road, York, Pennsylvania 17402, USA

Echo Products, 127 S. 10th Street, Montpelier, Idaho 83254, USA

Etto, Box 7000–456, Redondo Beach, California 90277, USA

Monarch Helmets, Box 3605, Chula Vista, California 92011, USA

Pro-tec, Inc., 11108 Northrup Way, Box 4189, Bellevue, Washington 98009, USA

Vetta, Orleander USA, Inc., 2049 Century Park East, Suite 2115, Los Angeles, California 90067, USA

A sampling of manufacturers of 20- and 24-inch wheeled children's bicycles:

Centurion, Western States Import, 1627 DeHavilland Drive, Newbury Park, California 91320, USA Tel: (805)499-2603

Emmelle Bicycles, Moore Large and Co. Ltd, Crown House, 664/668 Dunstable Road, Luton, Bedfordshire LU4 8SD Tel: (0582) 575155

Fuji, Fuji America, 118 Bauer Drive, Oakland, New Jersey 07436, USA Tel: (201)337-1700

Nishiki, West Coast Cycle, 717 E. Artesia Boulevard, P.O. Box 6224, Carson, California 90749–6224, USA Tel: (800)421-4287

Norco, Norco Products Limited, 7950 Enterprise Street, Burnaby, British Columbia V5A 1V7, Canada Tel: (604)420-6616

Peugeot, Cycles Peugeot (USA) Inc., 555 Gotham Parkway, Carlstadt, New Jersey 07072, USA Tel: (201)460-7000

UK suppliers for tandem modification:
Armalloy Engineering, Ltd, Central Avenue, Corngreaves Industrial Estate,
    Cradley Heath, West Midlands B64 7BY
Jack Taylor Cycles, 105 Church Road, Stockton, Teesside
E.W. Hannington, 34 Marshland Square, Emmer Green, Reading, Berkshire
Richmond Cycles, 36 Hill Street, Richmond, Surrey
Ken G. Rogers, 71 Berkley Avenue, Cranford, Hounslow, Middlesex
Swallow Frames and Cycles, 2 Stannetts, Laindon North Trade Centre,
    Essex SS15 6DJ

US suppliers for tandem modification:
Burley Design Cooperative, 4080 Stewart Rd, Eugene, Oregon 97402 USA
Santana Cycles, Inc., Box 1205, Claremont, California 91711 USA
Tandems East, RR 8, Box 319 E. Gwynwood Drive, Bridgeton, New Jersey 08302
    USA
Tandems Limited, Route 19, Box 248, Birmingham, Alabama 35244 USA
Mel Pinto Imports, PO Box 2198, Falls Church, Virginia 22042 USA
    Tel: (703) 237-4686.

19 *Cycling for Two*

I believe it was athletes like American cyclist Miji Reoch who turned the Western scientific community away from their conservative approach to exercise during pregnancy.

Mary Jane Reoch had been a world-class road-racer and, at 35, was still active, cycling as well as coaching top women riders when she became pregnant with her first child about ten years ago. Miji pedalled from conception to delivery and even raced a criterium during her fifth month. 'I got criticised by a lot of people who thought I was hurting the baby,' she says, 'but my doctors were supportive. I felt I was so attuned to my body as an athlete, I'd know if I was overdoing it.' In fact, she felt so confident about it all that she cycled the 10-mile trip to the delivery room. On the way she spied a boy struggling in too high a gear; she picked up her pace to catch him and explained the advantage of high rpm. Then she excused herself and continued to the hospital, where twelve hours later she gave birth to a healthy, 7-pound, 12-ounce baby girl.

Within memory (mine at least), pregnancy for most women in Western society was a time of inactivity and retreat.

No longer! Today's active woman wants to know how she can keep up with her sport yet protect the health of her unborn child, what limitations she should impose on herself, and what level of fitness she can aspire to. Even inactive women who seem simultaneously to become pregnant and get bitten by the fitness bug, raise questions that have needed new answers.

Until recently, although doctors and researchers acknowledged the benefits of exercise during pregnancy, they assumed that a mother-to-be should try to maintain fitness but not attempt to improve it. Today this vague and (to the athletic woman) rather discouraging advice has been replaced by more specific guidance. Scientists don't have all the answers, but here's what recent findings indicate:

- With certain exceptions, women who've been inactive before pregnancy can nevertheless begin a moderate conditioning programme and improve in fitness. A five-year study at Madison General Hospital in Madison, Wisconsin, proved it with a group of previously inactive women who cycled, rowed, and jogged during the last six months of their pregnancies. The effects of their training (three times a week for thirty minutes) were measurable in lower blood pressure and higher aerobic capacity. And their babies, compared to those of a non-exercising control group, were just as healthy and had comparable birth weights.

Researchers caution that expectant mothers with high blood pressure, diabetes, heart conditions, infections, anaemia, or a history of miscarriage might endanger an unborn child with exercise and should seek their doctors' advice before raising their levels of activity.

Indeed, every pregnant woman would be smart to talk first to her health care provider about plans to exercise, to be sure there are no problems that would affect them. If you're advised against exercising during these months, you have a right to a clear understanding why. So insist on it. If you want a second opinion, don't hesitate to get it. Consult a medical person who's athletic or accustomed to treating athletes. If necessary, get a referral from a women's coach or physician at your local high school or college.

- During a normal, healthy pregnancy the safe ceiling on exertion, some researchers say, is 70 per cent of maximum heart rate. A study reported in 1988 in the *Journal of the American Medical Association* suggested that pregnant women not push their heart rate beyond 150 beats per minute. The American College of Obstetricians and Gynecologists recommends a more conservative limit of 140 bpm.

- The concern is oxygen flow to the foetus. The study mentioned above addressed itself to the temporary decline in foetal heart rate (called *bradycardia*) that sometimes occurs after heavy exertion by the mother. In all but one case, this decline occurred only after exercise that considerably exceeded 150 bpm.

  Learn how to take an exercise pulse (take your pulse for ten seconds, then multiply by six). If you feel unsteady doing it while riding, then stop and take it quickly. After doing this a number of times, you'll get a feel for estimating your level of exertion.

- Don't risk raising core body temperature. One possible cause of birth defects, researchers believe, is *hyperthermia*, a condition in which body core temperature is elevated. Soaking in a hot tub or jacuzzi is risky for a pregnant woman. So is a hard workout in hot, humid weather. Ride early in the day, or indoors on a wind trainer with the air conditioning on. Drink plenty of fluids before and during cycling to avoid dehydration.

- Avoid exercise involving jumping, twisting or sudden turning. Cycling is ideal as long as a woman has good balance.

- How can you expect to feel? As a rule, things seem to require more effort during the first three months than in the second or third. If you start a ride and, even after a warm-up, the effort feels too great, perhaps it is. Don't feel guilty if you make it an easy ride.

  In fact, early in your pregnancy you may not wish to ride at all. If so, take some time off but don't be discouraged. (Maybe a walk or a swim would feel better. Do what seems most comfortable.) In a few weeks or months cycling will probably appeal to you again.

  You can expect some discomfort when you exercise – sore legs and knees, perhaps a sensation of needing to urinate, or contraction cramps.

203

- Should you have any questions about your safety or experience anything unusual, such as vaginal bleeding, raised blood pressure, dizzy spells, or pains in joints, put a halt to your riding and confer with your doctor before continuing.
- Be aware that joints tend to be a little looser during pregnancy as a result of a hormonal secretion called *relaxin*, which relaxes the ligaments to prepare for expansion of the uterus and eventual delivery. Usually the effects are felt during the last three months, although some women notice them in the second. Katherine Brubaker, MD, an obstetrician/gynaecologist and cyclist herself, says joint laxity is usually not troublesome for cyclists, but is more a problem for runners.

  Looseness can be felt in hips, knees, pelvic girdle, lower back, and shoulders. You may notice that your hip 'pops' or doesn't seem to support you. Doctor Brubaker says a woman may feel pain on her saddle, caused by the loosening of a ligament joining two bones in the pubic arch (which actually separate to enable delivery). 'Pelvic rock' exercises can help compensate, along with making sure to sit properly on the sit-bones when cycling. Take the usual precautions for not overtaxing knees.

Keeping Her Appeal . . .

'When I was pregnant with my oldest, I biked quite a bit to get around the Air Force base where we were stationed. Even at eight months when I was feeling a bit awkward, I could still move along just fine on a bike. One evening I was cycling when some guys drove up behind me, and several gave me the well-known wolf whistle. I was bent over on my ten-speed, so it wasn't that obvious I was pregnant. But I went home feeling very good about myself.

'Incidentally, I kept riding up to the day before I delivered. There weren't that many women cycling regularly nineteen years ago, and especially when pregnant, so I was alone out there a lot.'

Rose Davis,
41, Hastings, Minnesota

- The same back exercises suggested earlier in this book are excellent during this time when lower back discomfort seems inevitable.
- It's smart to cycle with a partner or at least to let someone know when and where you are riding. Carry change for the phone in case of emergency.
- Eat a balanced diet, with the appropriate supplements usually recommended to pregnant women, especially iron and calcium.
- Pay attention to subtle changes in your sense of balance which may occur during pregnancy. At some point you may feel safer on a stationary bicycle or trainer than on the road. And, as pregnancy continues, you may find your sense of balance returns. A mountain bike or other bicycle with upright handlebars might prove most comfortable to ride in later months.

- Set reasonable goals for yourself. If you've been highly fit and are used to training hard, don't be compulsive about it during this time. 'Listen to your body,' as the saying goes.
- If you find you're not gaining weight as you should, discuss the situation and your exercise programme with your doctor.
- Seek encouragement for your decision to cycle during your pregnancy. You might share this chapter with the baby's father and whoever else you turn to for support. And once you have the approval and guidance of your health practitioner, ignore fuss-pots who haven't informed themselves on the subject as you have.
- Surely the pregnant cyclist doesn't have to be warned to play it safe. Then again, one of my survey respondents describes an accident she had riding home from the grocery store on her three-speed, eight months pregnant, with a 3-year-old on the back in a babyseat and a sack of groceries in hand. She was descending a hill when a motorist turned in front of her. It caused them to fall, but they were unhurt.

Without labouring the point (no pun intended), a 3-year-old is lighter than the maximum weight – about 40 pounds – that ought to be carried in one of these rear baby carriers, but the extra weight creates instability. Carrying something in one hand hampers bikehandling and usually braking, too. Putting those two things together, along with the 'delicate balance' of eight months' pregnancy, we have an accident waiting to happen. Although the motorist was in error, an unencumbered cyclist might have been able to avoid the crash.

Do take extra care to avoid riding in dangerous conditions.

If the unfortunate occurs and you're injured, experts advise not taking anti-inflammatory agents or other drugs which might affect development of the unborn child. If X-rays are absolutely required, make sure a lead apron is used to shield the uterus.

But let's not allow these words of caution to distract us from the main point: every active woman knows the sense of vitality that fitness brings. What could be more appropriate than maintaining that feeling of well-being as you bring a new life into the world? Certainly that's what Kristen Proffitt believes, as she shows in her diary:

Nine Special Months of Cycling

'Any questions?' the doctor asks. I have a flood of them.

Can you ride centuries and time trials when you're pregnant? Do you have to sit upright or turn up your handlebars when your belly starts to grow? Is it safe to ride the bike at all?

'Well, I've grown fond of exercise in my old age,' I begin. I am 34. 'I like running, hiking, and cycling. I do a lot of cycling. Will I be able to continue all these?'

He says he thinks they'll be good for me. I'm greatly relieved!

Late December: two months

I'm about two months along now. I've kept up my exercise but am battling the 'What's the Use Blues'. It seems there's nothing to look forward to on the bike except getting bigger and maybe so ungainly I won't be able to go at all. Fifteen minutes into every ride I feel a gagging mucus in my throat. I'm afraid I'm going to throw up one of these times but I never do.

January: three months

I've conquered the negative feelings by setting some new goals. Okay, so I won't be time trialing (at least not seriously), and I may be slowing down, but what a wonderful time to keep concentrating on fitness. After all, there are two of us benefiting from this exercise.

There are centuries coming up in April and May, and I'm considering. It's too early to know how I'll feel . . . I'm due 12 July.

The only limit I'm placing on myself is all-out sprints. I believe oxygen debt might not be good for the baby.

On one of the Sunday club rides I'm feeling a bit draggy on the back of our tandem. We excuse ourselves to a fellow riding with us, saying that I'm pregnant.

'You're at your prime!' he congratulates me. With several extra pounds and less than my usual quota of exercise, I do not feel prime.

February: four months

The begining-of-the-ride nausea is all but gone now. I'm developing a distinct ball of baby and it kicks. This baby feels strong.

Although I experience uterine contractions almost always when I am bike riding (or running or hiking), I no longer worry about harming the baby. I am concerned for the baby if we don't get our workouts.

March: five months

I definitely look pregnant now, at least in my tight cycling shirt. I'm not so afraid of a good workout, knowing that the baby seems to be active and growing well although I still draw the line at sprints that leave me completely breathless.

But once in a while on a boring solo ride I cannot resist chasing down another cyclist just to liven things up.

In one particular pursuit I managed to hang on the wheel of a fellow who was young, sleek, and fast – at least compared to me. After several miles he finally slowed to see who was there. I swallowed my gasps, smiled pleasantly, straightened up to reveal my profile and told him it was becoming a bit difficult to keep up in this condition. Actually I felt about ready to die. Not so much from the pregnancy, I think, as for lack of enough good chases like that.

I feel discomforts from time to time, but they're usually minor, intermittent, and seldom a distraction for an entire ride.

My growing abdomen is stretching some new muscles, and sometimes I get a 'stitch' in an unusual place, such as the groin. I also feel uterine contractions and stomach aches, probably a little digestive upset. The baby does rearrange your organs inside.

I begin a programme of abdomen strengthening exercises: leg lifts, situps, to the best of my ability. That feels so good and seems to help, so I add back and arm exercises. I truly feel wonderful, and the best thing is that I am going to make it on the bicycle.

I'm going to ride that century next month. I'm going to ride every day on the Great Western Bike Rally. I'm going to ride the whole nine months!

April: six months
Sometimes I do get discouraged on rides lately. So I give myself a pep talk to combat the dark thoughts when they come.

My husband and I ride the Creston Wildflower Century up in beautiful San Luis Obispo County on our tandem. It's a hilly, tough ride. But we don't do badly at all.

My husband Jim has really stayed by me and encouraged me. It probably isn't easy for him towing around a pregnant wife on the tandem when he could be doing so much better on his own. But he keeps praising my riding. So how can I quit?

May: seven months
On one of my solo rides I have two flat tyres and am delighted to find I can ride the bus to within blocks of home if I remove the front wheel of my bike. I receive some astonished looks, hauling my bike up the steps of the bus in my bulging T-shirt.

I have a definite preference for tandem rides and shorter rides now, although, if anything, I feel better each month rather than worse. I guess I just feel a little safer on the tandem, and more equal.

We ride in the Great Western Bike Rally, three days. On the century, Jim chooses a metric option (62 miles) rather than the full 100. (We had just done a tough 50 the day before.) But he announces this choice only after we've ridden about 30 miles. And I was prepared for the 100!

He says he thinks the full century would take too much out of me, with our rides on the other days. Lest anyone think this an ordeal, mildly competitive riding still seems fun and natural.

When we're home from a ride one day and I'm changing out of my cycling shirt (a nice roomy T-shirt), Jim says, 'You know, you really look great.' No greater love hath any cycling husband than that compliment at this time.

June: eight months
I don't feel particularly ungainly. We haven't even had to turn up the handlebars, and I can still reach the drops.

Jim's knees are inflamed from our constant tandem riding. It's probably a strain with all the starts and stops in traffic near home. So I take to my single, which I can still ride easily. Poor Jim, probably the first husband injured due to exercise when expecting.

20 July: nine months

My other two children came exactly one week late. This one was due July 12, so I expected it yesterday. Last Sunday, the 15th, we rode our hardest on the club ride since we couldn't possibly have to ride again in this condition. It was fun leaving behind some riders who thought we wouldn't be any competition. My only problem now is bending over far enough to reach my toeclips.

22 July: nine months, ten days

Another club ride. We once again give it our all. Who cares if it starts me into labour. We hope it does. My poor, dear husband must have taken me out for at least fifteen 'last' dinners.

I don't care for rides much longer than 30 miles at this point.

At this week's checkup my blood pressure had been quite high. I got a reprieve from an induced labour, but was ordered to have bed rest. (I've been given a different doctor. This one doesn't understand about my exercise.)

The bed rest lasted two hours. My husband asked, 'What are you going to do?'

'I'm going to shorten my rides, take naps, and let my daughter do the dishes,' I answered.

29 July: nine months, seventeen days

It's not possible! Another Sunday club ride.

I've been losing weight (off only 15 pounds I gained). I swear the baby is getting smaller. I can't help worrying now. On almost every ride this week I've felt strong contractions, like the beginning of labour. So it's hard to concentrate.

Jim signs us up for a hilly 45-mile ride because that's the one everyone is going on. I feel nearly weepy for the first time instead of glad. I am too tired, too pregnant. And he's going to want to keep up with the rest of them. And what about my 'bed rest'?

Once we get going, I feel terrific. But he turns us back after only 25 miles. 'I wasn't going to let you ride all of it,' he says.

'It's just as well,' I tell him. 'I feel a lot of contractions.' We've left many strong riders behind.

30 July: nine months, eighteen days

I have my weekly checkup in the morning. My doctor is pleased with the results of my 'bed rest'. She agrees the baby is going to come very soon. By afternoon I'm having real on and off labour, so we don't ride today. Twice we start for a movie, and twice it seems unwise.

We leave for the hospital about midnight.

31 July: nine months, nineteen days

It's an easy labour, a little long but not so hard, not when you're used to these workouts. In fact, I sleep soundly between contractions. At 7.25 am she is born: Penelope Jane, 8 pounds, 11 ounces; the poor baby that was getting smaller! She is a beauty from the beginning, so alert, so vigorous, so strong! We are truly blessed. And we thank the exercise for helping.

So that was my final ride, I think to myself drowsily. Not too unlike a century. The months of preparation, the endurance, the excitement, and the pain. A little over seven hours, not a bad time for the ninth month.

1 May

I felt wonderful after Penelope was born. I started jogging after two weeks and cycling after three; gently at first, but soon working up to full steam.

The best news is the baby. She is robust and playful, full of life and good health. Jim and I feel a special closeness to her, having 'taken' her on so many physical adventures before she was even born. And we feel a renewed closeness to each other, having done so much together, a great deal right on the same bike. And for our other two children, who were right there cheering us on.

It was a time of life I'll never forget. A pregnancy made unique by exercise and the exercise the more exhilarating with the pregnancy.

POST-PARTUM PRECAUTIONS

Getting back on your wheels after the baby's birth is something to ease into. Don't be surprised if you just don't feel up to it, and don't feel guilty.

Yes, we hear about élite athletes who make a comeback after pregnancy and even improve their performance. The latest case in point is Susan Notorangelo, who at 35 rewrote the record books in the 1989 Race Across AMerica (RAAM), that transcontinental megathon for which the race clock ticks twenty-four hours a day until the race is over some eight to ten days later. Notorangelo had won the women's division in 1985 (10.14.25), and bettered her time the following year (10.09.29) while finishing second to Elaine Mariolle's (then-record) 10.02.04. In 1987 Susan took a pass on RAAM and on 4 June gave birth to daughter Rebecca.

Just a little more than two years later, Susan Notorangelo became the only woman finisher in RAAM '89 in a time of 9.09.09. Admittedly the 2,907-mile course was 127 miles shorter, but she shattered Mariolle's previous record by about fifteen hours and her own previous best by about a day. Even more telling, Susan came closer to the men's division winner – at one day, twenty-four minutes behind – than any woman had in five previous RAAMs. Overall, she was seventh among thirteen other (male) finishers. Two other women had dropped out. For Notorangelo it was a quantum leap.

It's important to note that, as in Susan's case, such a return to top-level performance usually takes a couple of years or longer. You, too, can recapture your level of fitness, perhaps exceed it, but give it time. A year before this recent RAAM victory, the ultramarathoner talked to me by phone from her home in Harvard, Illinois. She told me how it felt to try to regain fitness after the pregnancy. For the first six weeks after delivery Susan scarcely mounted her bike.

As Susan Notorangelo proved in the 1989 Race Across AMerica, a woman can come back stronger than ever after pregnancy (*David Epperson*).

'My first ride was a month later, just around a parking lot, and even doing that I worried about ripping out my stitches,' she admitted. 'Actually in those weeks I had difficulty working up the desire to ride.' Her husband Lon (Haldeman, a two-time RAAM winner himself) was out of town for a time. But when he came back they suspended a babyseat (for security and shock-absorption) in their Burley trailer.

'That way I could pull Rebecca. We started out going 10 or 15 miles about three times a week.'

In a few weeks the enjoyment returned, and three months after Rebecca's birth Susan and Lon rode a century on their tandem, pulling Rebecca in the Burley. 'I didn't really feel strong like I do now,' Susan amended. 'I couldn't go out and ride 60 miles in the morning and then feel fresh and eager for a full day's activities – I'd be pretty exhausted. But the pleasure was back.'

At the time of our conversation fifteen months had passed since Susan delivered. She'd just returned from a demanding seventeen-day, trans-America bike tour she and Lon lead, on which she'd ridden about 75 miles every other day. 'I'm just starting to feel good when charging a hill,' she said. 'I'm about 5 pounds away from a nice cycling weight, and I'm getting ready to wear a heart rate monitor again and see how I'm really doing. I have a goal,' she confided hopefully. 'I think I'm going to try to do RAAM in 1989.' Now the results are history.

What's a safe approach for resuming your cycling? The Melpomene Institute for Women's Health Research in Minneapolis, Minnesota, encourages women to talk with their doctor/midwife about plans to resume exercise. Women who have had Caesareans may require special instructions. To women with uncomplicated vaginal deliveries, Melpomene recommends these guidelines, based on their exercise and pregnancy research begun in 1981:

- After an episiotomy you'll probably want to let soreness disappear before vigorous exercise or sitting on a saddle.
- Because you'll be advised against using tampons for about a month, you may wish to wait for bleeding and secretions to stop.
- After bleeding has begun to taper off, if exercise brings on heavier bleeding or bright red blood, this can be a sign you're doing too much and that you need to give yourself more recovery time.
- Continue to allow for joint laxity, as the hormonal levels don't even out until several weeks after delivery.
- During this time, let your body tell you what it needs. If you're up, feeding the baby every two hours during the night, there may be days when you need a nap more than a bike ride. Make your cycling energising, not draining, during these months. (On the other hand, a good spin may help you cope better if you suffer post-partum blues.)
- Drink plenty of fluids throughout the day if you are breast-feeding, and wear a bra which gives good support when cycling.
- Now that you're lifting and carrying your baby, keep up those back exercises.
- Maintain healthy eating habits. Let weight loss take place gradually. Be aware too that if you're breast-feeding, weight-loss will be slower than if you were not. Cycling will help you do it, and in the meantime riding has its own calorie requirements. Don't be discouraged.
- Scheduling your riding will challenge the time-manager in you, especially during the early months. (Susan suggests letting someone else hold and bottle-feed the baby, even if you normally nurse, so you can get away for a bike ride.)
- Make those rides enjoyable. Even though the new baby creates many demands, it's important to provide time for yourself. Your cycling is one way to do it.

20 *Other Feminine Matters*

Prior to cycling I was very ill with three surgeries in the female department. Cycling has eliminated most PMS (premenstrual syndrome), and periods are a breeze now. I used to be in pain most of the month. Now I might have some cramping, but nothing to slow me down.

As I recovered from my last surgery, I found I could no longer do aerobics or any other exercise that involved bouncing. So I dragged out my 15-year-old ten-speed and tried riding it. I went maybe three miles and was exhausted. Every night after that I went a little further and found I could ride without the pain I felt from other exercise. Three months passed, and I worked up to nine miles every night.

Then my friends noticed my weight dropping. So I rode longer and faster each night. My husband bought me a new bike, and from then on I've been hooked. Now I ride twenty to thirty miles every day on the road or use a wind trainer. My weight has dropped 25 pounds and I feel great. No more hard menstrual pains and virtually no PMS.

Bobbie J. Pope, 31, Chino Hills, California

There are no guarantees that every woman will experience the same relief Bobbie describes here. However, as we observed in chapter 4 (To Your Health . . .) one expert in the field, Sally K. Severino, MD, reports that many women do find exercise helpful for PMS. (Several women responding to my survey volunteered that this is so for them although I did not ask a question specifically about it.)

Survey Findings: Cycling and Menstrual Cramps

Q. Do you find a bike ride helps ease menstrual cramps/achiness?

Usually	34.8%
Sometimes	30.3%
Never	15.0%
Don't get cramps	8.8%
Don't know or not applicable	11.1%

I did ask whether a bike ride aids in easing menstrual cramps and achiness. Over a third responding said that it usually helps, while almost another third said that it sometimes does. As I expected, some women added that other kinds of exercise also eliminate or lessen discomfort. One woman in my survey volunteered: 'I find that consistent riding through the month eases cramps better than taking a ride when I have cramps.'

Other studies have shown similar responses, and Carol L. Otis, assistant team physician at UCLA, writes in *Sports Medicine Digest's* (1988) 'Special Report on the Female Athlete': 'Regular exercise often improves the regularity of menses and diminishes menstrual cramps.'

THE RISK OF AMENORRHEA

On the other hand, menstrual irregularity and amenorrhea can occur among athletic women. In fact, these problems are more common among this group than among the general female population, notes Mona Shangold, MD, in 'Gynaecologic Concerns in the Woman Athlete' (*Clinics in Sports Medicine*, Vol. 3, No. 4, October 1984). This doesn't necessarily mean that the dysfunction is caused by athletic activity. And to assume so could be dangerous, as other causes might be at work. Irregular menses and amenorrhea should always be evaluated, says Doctor Shangold.

The most obvious menstrual dysfunction observed in some female athletes – and to date the most studied – is the cessation of menstruation, known as *secondary amenorrhea*. To be precise, a woman who skips three or more periods is considered amenorrheic.

Many of us are unlikely to experience it: I bring it up here as much to put minds at ease as to warn women of the possibility.

This disturbance of the menses is generally thought to result from a combination of factors, although the causes are still not fully understood. It occurs most frequently among élite athletes who train long and hard and often have a comparatively low percentage of body fat. It can happen with recreational athletes who substantially increase their training for a special goal – say, a triathlon. Stress (of competition, trying to meet a training schedule, or as a result of unrelated causes) may be a contributor. In some studies the incidence of amenorrhea has correlated with a vegetarian diet. Or the amenorrhea may be associated with an eating disorder – *bulimia* (vomiting and binge eating), abuse of laxatives, or *anorexia* (self-starvation).

In my survey of women cyclists (in which I simply defined amenorrhea as 'cessation of menstrual periods without being pregnant'), 15.8 per cent of the respondents indicated they had experienced amenorrhea, 'apparently as a result of heavy training' in cycling. A little over half of that group said they had also been involved in at least one other sport at the time. The large majority of survey respondents had not experienced amenorrhea.

Women who do experience this dysfunction should bear in mind:

- Amenorrhea should not be considered a form of birth control. While amenorrhea does indicate that ovulation has stopped or become less frequent, it could resume.

- Early on in the study of this particular women's health concern, the first question was the effect of long-term amenorrhea on a woman's fertility. Often a reduction in the amount and intensity of training, as well as a small weight gain, have resulted in a return of the menses and subsequent pregnancies. However, there are no guarantees, and medical treatment may be necessary before conception is likely, according to Doctor Shangold.

  Women who become amenorrheic may prefer to play it safe at the outset and ease up enough to start menstruating again. It should not be necessary to eliminate exercise to accomplish this. Discuss any dysfunction of this sort with your gynaecologist.

- Today health advisers are also concerned with the effects of long-term amenorrhea on bone density. Recent studies have demonstrated, for example, that amenorrheic female athletes have decreased spinal bone mass compared to both active and sedentary women who are still menstruating. Such losses appear to be related to the decreased production of estrogen in amenorrheic women. Whether or not such loss in bone density is permanent remains a matter of controversy. Ongoing research appears to indicate that some, but not all, of the lost bone density can be regained. Experts encourage amenorrheic women not to wait in seeking appropriate medical advice in order to prevent serious bone loss.

  It's important to remember that exercise, *per se*, does not cause loss of bone density but rather, as we've observed elsewhere, regular exercise strengthens bones. The 'bone thief' is amenorrhea, which can be exercise-related, though it is not always.

  For amenorrheics, according to registered dietician Ellen Coleman, daily calcium intake should be increased to 1,500 mg.

VAGINITIS

One problem which rather caught me by surprise as I read about women's cycling experiences on survey returns is the belief of some women – apparently a small minority – that they have more difficulty with vaginal and bladder infections as a result of cycling. I talked with cyclist/gynaecologist Doctor Katherine Brubaker on the subject.

As she practises in California, she has quite a few cyclists as patients. Some do have this problem. 'There seem to be two kinds of vulvas,' she says, 'those made of leather – and these women can ride twice as many miles as other women, without problems. And then there are women who, as soon as they ride an hour, their tissues break down, they get little fissures, yeast infections, and so on. It doesn't seem to matter how often they wash their shorts . . . It's seasonal and tends to happen in hot weather.'

These kinds of bacteria, as we know, flourish in a warm, moist environment provided, for example, by shorts that don't breathe. A bladder infection might be encouraged by irritation of the urethra, rubbing against the shorts, she notes. This can be complicated by rectal or vaginal bacteria entering the urethra in this situation. And dehydration, Doctor Brubaker adds, contributes to the likelihood of bladder infections.

'If you're a good cyclist, you'll drink and drink and drink,' she says. In addition to plenty of water when riding, cranberry juice and orange juice are excellent to drink at other times because they are acidic, and the harmful bacteria thrive in an alkaline environment.

Doctor Brubaker notes that she has suggested that a woman with recurring infection problems use the appropriate, prescribed antibiotic cream on the shorts lining – a sulfa cream for bladder infections or Canestan or Gyne Lotrimin (generic name, Clotrimazole) for yeast infections. Even this doesn't seem to be insurance against recurrence, she says. And some shorts manufacturers believe doing so will reduce the shorts' breathability. Regardless, after a ride, it makes sense to change out of cycling shorts as quickly as possible.

It's hard to say how widespread a problem this is. 'This is very new,' Katherine Brubaker says, adding that she has just her own experience and hunches to go on. 'I haven't read anything in the literature on it, and women are reluctant even to talk about it.'

The Cycling Gynaecologist

'I'm an ob-gyn, and I like to decorate my exam rooms to decrease the anxiety associated with the yearly exam. I've been cycling a few years now, so in one room I have many bicycle posters. One is a photograph of me at the top of a long climb on the Solvang century at about mile 80. Needless to say, I look pretty wasted. At the bottom of the poster is written, "Are you sure you want your Pap smear (cervical smear) from *this* person?"'

Katherine Brubaker,
36, Irvine, California

MENOPAUSE AND AFTERWARDS

Given a woman's average lifespan of 78 years and the average age of menopause at 50.4 years, a woman today still has one-third of her life to live after menopause. Yet little research has been devoted to the subject of menopause and its effect on us. Even attempts to establish the precise symptoms of menopause arouse controversy. It was just ten years ago that research documented hot 'flushes' as a physiological reality and not just our imagination!

Some new research, however, offers good news to active women during menopause and the years that follow. But first let's be sure we're speaking the same language, as confusion seems to exist even among researchers.

By *menopause* we mean the permanent cessation of menstruation. Symptoms of this change will precede menopause and continue afterward; this transition period is known as *perimenopause*. *Postmenopause* is considered to begin one year after the last menstrual period.

Symptoms which may be experienced include: hot flushes, vaginal shrinking, sleep disturbances, fatigue and weakness, depression, dizziness, numbness, muscle or joint pain, headaches, palpitations, and a sense of the skin crawling in the legs. About 85 per cent of women experience some of these symptoms, says researcher Christine L. Carpenter, MA.

As she points out, estrogen therapy has been widely used in treating these symptoms. Recently some work has been done using exercise as a therapeutic adjunct or alternative – for example, by Janet P. Wallace, PhD, in San Diego. Carpenter worked with her on a follow-up study in which the menopausal subjects found both physical and psychological symptoms eased by an exercise conditioning programme.

There is more work to be done in this area, but in the meantime these findings should be good incentive for us to stick with it.

PREVENTING OSTEOPOROSIS

As noted earlier, loss of bone density is associated with decreased estrogen production at menopause. (For this reason, estrogen replacement therapy may be recommended to help prevent bone-thinning, especially for women who have had early hysterectomies or ovarectomies, notes research scientist Everett L. Smith, PhD. See also chapter 12, Fuelling the Engine, on calcium.) Currently it's estimated that one in every four postmenopausal women has osteoporosis.

But even women who have been inactive prior to menopause can increase bone density with exercise. Doctor Smith and colleagues at the University of Wisconsin's Biogerontology Laboratory demonstrated this in a study of older women (average age, 84). In it an experimental group of twelve women took part in a thirty-minute exercise programme three times a week for three years. They increased their bone mineral content by 2.29 per cent, while a non-exercising control group lost 3.28 per cent during the same thirty-six months.

A number of studies in recent years have shown a positive relationship between exercise and building stronger bones – at every stage of a woman's life.

One important question some research has addressed is what sort of exercise benefits most. Part of the answer is that exercise is specific. That is, bones stressed during exercise tend to increase their bone mineral content and mass, while other bones in the same individual may not change. Studies of runners, for example, have shown that they strengthen the bones in their hips and spines but not in their arms.

Noting that this is a very new field of study, Doctor Smith observed to me in a telephone interview: 'In the beginning we assumed that if you exercised and got cardiovascular benefits, you should also get bone benefits.' The research, however, seems to show otherwise.

It appears that there have been no studies specifically dealing with cycling and its effect on bone mineral content. But Doctor Smith believes we can find some clues in studies of other non-weight-bearing exercise such as swimming and the use of stationary bicycling in the US space programme in an attempt to prevent bone loss. As Doctor Smith says:

> It may be that for the bone to maintain itself, it requires a certain amount of force on the bottom of the foot – which results in a (temporary) bending of the bone. The forces that are applied by a weight-bearing activity like walking are very different from just the muscle pull on the bones in bicycling. So with cycling you may have good muscle tone and help to maintain the bone by good circulation and good nutrition, but that form of exercise may not be of great benefit to maintain the bones of the legs and spine (which are especially at risk of fracture if osteoporosis should develop). I think without some walking or jogging, you won't get the same benefit of exercise for the bone as you would for the cardiovascular system.

Admitting that studies suggest but do not prove the above, Doctor Smith encourages 'women to be involved in a total fitness programme' which would include light weightlifting on a regular basis, 'since most women don't do anything with their upper body'. He recommends that jogging or walking also be included in a fitness programme.

What does this say to women cyclists? Many competitive bicyclists already maintain regular weight training programmes during the off-season or sometimes year-round, with strengthening benefits that improve their riding. Many other women cyclists also do circuit weight training as a change of pace and to round out a fitness programme. Now here is another reason to recommend it. I would suggest that those who haven't tried it do so in a supervised situation using resistance machines such as Nautilus or Universal. These machines can be adjusted to your current strength level so the exercise is not too difficult.

Or perhaps there's a course in a local park where the various exercise stations allow you to use your body weight as the resistance; usually you walk or jog from one station to the next, which would help to fulfil the other part of Doctor Smith's recommendation.

As for weight-bearing exercise, the triathletes among us can rejoice in the benefits of their cross-training. The rest of us can think about mixing in some walking or jogging or racket sports. Or volleyball, aerobic dance (the high-impact variety), basketball, or (I should think) cross-country skiing would be excellent. Cyclocross would be good, as it involves hopping on and off the bike and some running – pretty vigorous stuff. As we wait for further research results, we can apply what is presently known to make the most of our active lives.

21 *Two-Wheel Travel*

Not to romanticise too much, but my first bicycle tour had an incredible impact on me.

A month before my friend was to cycle across the US from Maine to Oregon, he asked if I cared to join him. I laughed at the absurdity. Hours later I accepted on the allure. Why not, I thought. I was bored, cynical of my academic world, and in dire need of change. I was 21. Little did I know, I was also out of shape and ignorant of the mechanics, not to mention the demands, of bicycling that distance. I was ripe for a full share of peaks and pitfalls, aches and ecstasies. What one peak experience do I recall now, nine years later?

Maybe it was the smell of homemade New Hampshire maple syrup pouring over hot pancakes after my first mountain pass the day before. Or perhaps the freshly grilled trout on the first sunny afternoon after two days spent dodging the splash of cars and eating cold peanut butter and honey sandwiches in a downpour. Might it have been the view from the top of Rocky Mountain National Park after two hours of climbing, or moonlit cycling in high desert? Or was it the sight of the Pacific Ocean as we finished our tour?

Rather than a single event, an embracing sense of learning and accomplishment paints my outlook. I was sore at first – 30 miles my first day and I thought I would die. Thirty-five miles the second day was even worse, as I was still sore from the first. I'd never ridden more than 10 miles before. How would I ever get through this? To make matters worse, my running shorts chafed my inner thighs, the soles of my $5 sneakers were soon destroyed by the pedals, and the fingers of my right hand went numb without gloves or handlebar padding to cushion them. All the things I've since read not to do, I did. I cried and cursed my way through (or rather up*) New England, but I never missed the chance to laugh or smell the morning air. Blue skies and no traffic were always warmly welcomed.*

I felt my strength and determination grow steadily. My ability became evident. Even my father admitted I really could *make it home to West Virginia as I rode up with 1,000 miles on my odometer. He stopped offering me bus tickets. I stopped doubting myself and wondering whether I'd have to accept them. I was no longer out of shape, I was learning about bike mechanics, and I was meeting the demands of a long-distance tour. (Luckily, I also discovered touring shoes, gloves, and handlebar padding in West Virginia.)*

And when I saw the Colorado Rockies 3,000 miles later, I fell in love with cycling. We re-routed ourselves to stay there longer . . . and to cross the Continental Divide seven times, spending a glorious month while I enjoyed the climbing for its beauty, its challenge, and its rewards down the other side.

To be honest, my first sight of the Pacific Ocean wasn't the peak of this tour. It was the end. Oregon was cold and wet, the beach was clouded in. We were tired. Six thousand miles had passed by. Beds, showers, and stoves with ovens began to look very appealing. We had $3 between the two of us. We unpacked our bikes and looked for jobs.

Take lots of pictures to savour and share. Your pace on two wheels makes it easy to stop for a photograph (*Dan Burden*).

Beverly Rue, 30, Berkeley, California

Many women have jumped into bicycle touring as Beverly did, inexperienced and ill-prepared, and come through their sudden immersion in the sport as born-again bicycle tourists. One woman describes a similarly challenging tour as 'the most rewarding venture of my life'. A much shorter 300 miles were still formidable to first-timer Nilce Moraes from Doylestown, Pennsylvania, then a student. No one thought she could manage it, but she did. 'I learned so much about myself,' she says. 'About to enter my senior year in college, I experienced more inner growth on that five-day trip than in three years of school.'

Admittedly, the ride-yourself-into-shape approach works best on a longer tour, especially if you keep mileage low at the start. The first days or weeks can be misery if you do too much. Some would-be adventurers – male and female – end up abandoning their trips, swearing never to see a bicycle again. And there are dangers, as inexperience and fatigue increase the potential for accidents.

Strong knees, however, plus a modicum of luck and mounds of determination (not to mention the company of an experienced riding partner) have helped many a novice through. Out of an ambitious itinerary can emerge a well-conditioned and wiser bicycle tourist – a true picaresque heroine.

Or you may prefer a gentler approach. A prudent and increasingly popular option for a first effort is the 'organised tour', prefaced by a few months of training.

Not too long ago most partakers on organised bike tours were either impecunious students doing the youth hostel bit or avid adult members of cycle-touring clubs, with legs well-seasoned for 80-mile days on the typical club trip. To the novice bicyclist or average sedentary traveller the apparent discomforts of two-wheel travel were too daunting, its pleasures a well-kept secret.

But no more. Cycling's growth has spawned a variety of approaches to touring – at least one is sure to be just your style.

Pick a **'luxury' tour,** and accommodations and meals can be as elegant as any you might find on a non-cycling tour. After a day of exploring *à la* bicycle, you trade stories with fellow guests over a glass of wine at that evening's country inn, Mediterranean villa, or old-manor-house-turned-hotel. Your well-earned appetite is satisfied with a meal fit for a duchess.

Plus you have the services of a van to carry luggage (and wilted cyclists if necessary) – though finishing the day in the van doesn't happen too often: distances tend to be moderate enough for neophytes. Guides are usually knowledgeable cyclists who brief you on the basics and provide mechanical backup if you need help with a puncture or other bike repair. A route is suggested for each day (with maps and/or written directions). Typically you're encouraged to set your own pace, travelling alone or with others from the group, as you choose. You can have a fantastic holiday and learn more about cycling at the same time.

Select a **'budget-minded' tour**, and you still enjoy the no-hassle benefit of pre-arranged bookings . . . in humbler but comfortable bed-and-breakfasts or hotels. Maps and/or written directions indicate pleasant cycling routes. As these trips are often self-guided, there may not be assistance with the odd puncture or a sag wagon to carry gear.

Whether you choose a luxury tour or one easier on the pocketbook, you'll discover that bicycle touring is truly one of the best ways to travel. For anyone with a healthy curiosity, the pace is perfect for seeing the landscape and meeting the people of a foreign country or exploring another part of your own.

I spent eight days recently in the Cotswold Hills of England, a region near the Welsh border that preserves the quintessence of English country life in its estates and farms, fairytale towns, and medieval churches endowed by wealthy wool merchants of that era. The sheep remain today, though in lesser numbers and different breeds.

The Cotswolds deserve to be experienced with all your senses, and cycling lets you do it. Here small villages of limestone cottages – centuries old, with roofs of thatch or stone – appear almost to have grown from among the green fields. Dry-stone walls pattern the hillsides. In the drama of changing light, well appreciated from a bicycle, the Cotswold stone glows tawny, even apricot in late-day sun; pales to cream in the dusk; stands a stolid grey on a rainy day.

Unhampered by a car engine's roar, you're surrounded by subtler sounds. A pheasant rustles in roadside weeds and flutters into flight. Sheep (always quietly pastoral in photographs) prove marvellously amusing. As I cycle past a field full of the creatures, they bleat urgently to each other, lambs in soprano, ewes (I suppose) in alto, and the rams in the next field adding bass. A pair of lambs sings out from opposite ends of a field and bounds toward their mother to feed.

On a bike, you breathe in the smells . . . new-cut hay, flowers in a cottage garden, earthy animal aromas, the after-rain freshness.

And when you want to, you stop. *I* do. I photograph wild poppies that turn an oat field to red and green damask. Serendipitously my companions and I happen across a 'benefit' tour which opens private gardens to view in the village of Kencot. (We buy tickets and wheel our bikes from house to house – it's wonderful.)

I find, as I usually do, that a bicycle is disarming. I talk to a gardener hoeing a strawberry patch; later to a woman walking four bouncing, black Scotties. A church sexton expostulates to me about rising real estate prices and other problems of the locals. Amazingly, a seller of antique cameos trusts me to mail her a traveller's cheque for a pin I want to buy.

There's that sense of accomplishment, too, riding from Crudwell to Tetbury to Shipton Moyne to Chippenham and so on, under my own power. I see the points on my map, the route for the day, and my progress is very clear. Life isn't always that way.

Now, with plenty of b&b's, the Cotswolds is an excellent area for a budget tour. As it happened, though, I signed on with Butterfield & Robinson (B&R) and stayed in wonderful country manor hotels. Charmingly restored, they all predate the twentieth century and feel just as English as strawberries and clotted cream. My favorite was the aptly named Lords of the Manor Hotel in a quaint hamlet where a Burberry's fashion ad was being photographed at that quiet intersection as I pulled up on my bicycle. B&R, by the way, is a Canada-based company that pioneered adult luxury bicycle travel in Europe in 1981. Their first tours proved a hit—I can see why—and became the prototype for today's luxury package.

Below you'll find a sampling of luxury tour operators and descriptions of tours, followed by a selection of 'budget' offerings. This will give you a good idea of the sorts of trips available. Write for the brochures; they're great motivation. By the way, for the stronger rider, most companies offer longer, tougher tours or a choice of longer routes on regular tours. To find additional companies, peruse the classifieds in a cycling magazine.

One thing more: don't assume a 'budget' tour any less delightful than a luxury tour. They're less lavish but offer their own pleasures.

A SAMPLING OF LUXURY TOURS

Today a dozen or so North-American based companies offer upscale cycling tours with such niceties as gourmet dining in Michelin-starred restaurants; winetastings galore; visits to famous cultural attractions and natural wonders; experienced guides to hump baggage and point out the best places to shop; a van to carry your luggage and all those purchases; and of course a bicycle to ride.

While Europe remains the most popular destination for luxury cycling, there are more and more such trips in the US and elsewhere. A new sub-category of luxury touring might be called 'island cycling' – in Hawaii, the Caribbean, New Zealand, Japan, and Indonesia. The latest trend combines cycling with other sports and means of transport. You can ski the Alps or raft whitewater in Alaska on a cycling vacation; or sail among the islands of coastal Maine, cycling at ports of call.

In this sampling of luxury tours prices are quoted to give you a notion of cost; rates are from 1990. They are based on double-occupancy lodging and exclude airfare. Asterisked prices mean bicycle rental is extra. Don't try to compare prices too closely, however, as the number of meals included varies from company to company. Usually most dinners and all breakfasts are included.

Backroads Bicycle Touring offers a variety of year-round tours in the US and winter cycling escapes in Hawaii, Bali, Tasmania, New Zealand, and the Baja. Tours range from weekends in California wine country to a nine-day jaunt through south-central Alaska with optional horseback riding and whitewater rafting. Lodgings are in the best available inns and hotels, but some tours – Yellowstone, Grand Canyon, Canadian Rockies – include camping. Sample prices: five-day California wine country inn tour, $998*; ten-day Hawaii inn tour, $1,498*. Backroads Bicycle Touring, 1516 5th Street, Suite Q447, Berkeley, CA 94710-1713 (USA) Tel: Toll-free in US (800) 533–2573; in California (415) 527-1555.

Bicycle touring is the ideal way to travel and meet people – in this case a Balinese man showing off a prize rooster (*Tom Hale, Backroads Bicycle Touring*).

Butterfield & Robinson offers, besides the Cotswolds tour I took, twenty-three cycling trips in France, Italy, Spain, Portugal, southern Ireland, Denmark, and Austria/Hungary. Their most popular are in Alsace, Burgundy, the Loire, Provence, and northern Italy. Sample prices: nine-day Provence tour, $2475; seven-day Cotswolds tour, $2095. Butterfield & Robinson, 70 Bond Street, Toronto, Ontario, Canada M5B 1X3 Tel: Toll-free in US (800) 387-1147; toll-free in Canada (800) 268-8415.

Châteaux Bike Tours has added a Tuscany wine country holiday. Trips in Alsace, Burgundy, the Loire, and Provence feature Michelin-starred restaurants. Sample prices: eight-day Loire tour, $2095; nine-day Tuscany tour, $2090. Châteaux Bike Tours, PO Box 5706, Denver, CO 80207 (USA) Tel: (303) 393–6910 or (toll-free) (800) 678-BIKE.

Europeds offers tours in France, Italy, and Switzerland, including a mountain bike/ skiing adventure in the Swiss Alps. Founder Peter Boynton lived in France for years and leads many trips himself. Europeds trips generally feature more cycling than other tours; and some trips can be linked together. Sample prices: eight-day Dordogne tour, from $1795; seventeen-day Pyrenees: Atlantic to the Mediterranean, $3000. Europeds, 883 Sinex Ave., Pacific Grove, CA 93950 (USA) Tel: (408) 372-1173.

Progressive Travels spices cycling trips with activities like hot air ballooning, hiking, and sailing. Destinations include British Columbia's Victoria and the Gulf Islands and Ireland's western counties. Also Venetia/Lombardy in Italy and France's Burgundy/ Beaujolais, where Progressive's part-owner, Dominique Parisot grew up cycling. Sample prices: nine-day Burgundy/Beaujolais tour, $2150*; six-day British Columbia tour, $1195. Progressive Travels, Terminal Sales Building, 1932 1st Avenue, Suite 1100, Seattle, WA 98101 (USA) Tel: (800) 245-2229 or (206) 443-4225.

Travent International's 5-day "Taste of . . ." tours are proving popular with first-timers and as add-ons for business travelers with limited time; Burgundy and Switzerland are new offerings in those tours. There are longer trips to Holland, Japan, and other destinations, including the expected French tours. A special 7-day Berlitz/cycling tour offers motivation and opportunity to learn or improve in French, with 2 days of intensive study in Paris, followed by 4 days in Burgundy for cycling and additional language instruction. Sample prices: 9-day Japan tour, $2,125; 5-day Normandy tour, $1,125. Travent International, PO Box 305, Waterbury Center, VT 05677-0305 (USA). Tel: Toll-free in the US, (800) 325-3009; in Canada (802) 244-5153.

Vermont Bicycle Touring pioneered inn-to-inn touring in America in 1972. Their fifty-five itineraries, mostly in Vermont, New Hampshire and New York, now include a southern England tour (Cotswolds and Home County) and winter cycling in Hawaii and New Zealand. Most popular is a 5-day exploration of Lake Champlain by sailing schooner and bicycle. Participants sleep, dine (and lounge, if they like) on a 114-foot windjammer. By day they cycle among the farms, orchards, and historic villages of the Champlain Valley in New York and Vermont. Sample prices: twelve-day England tour, $1599*; five-day Sail and Cycle, $699*. Vermont Bicycle Touring, Box 711, Bristol, VT 05443 (USA) Tel: (802) 453-4811.

Bike Quest, US marketing representative of foreign bicycle tour companies, lists dozens of organised tours including luxury cycling in Europe, Australia, Japan, even Bali. Bike Quest operates as a travel agency for cyclists, handling overseas communications and bookings. Tour costs vary widely according to country and company. Bike Quest, PO Box 332, Brookdale, CA 95007-0332 (USA) Tel: (408) 388-2477.

Cycle Tours, representing over seventy bicycle touring companies, will mail you brochures and help you locate the tour you want – without charge – if you complete their questionnaire. Cycle Tours, 7662 Hickman Road, Des Moines, IA 50322 (USA) Tel: Toll-free outside Iowa (800) 322-0012; toll-free inside Iowa (800) 262-8687.

A SAMPLING OF 'BUDGET-MINDED TOURS'

Sometimes it's hard to draw the line between a luxury and a budget tour, as costs are not always cut on the accommodations. Simply going non-profit may make the difference. Regardless, there's no price tag on the discovery and adventure that mark a good tour. To ensure that, choose a tour where maps are provided for everyone so you're free to explore.

On self-guided tours, don't assume you'll be part of a group larger than your own party. Some self-guided tours do transport luggage or are planned as day-trips from a central hotel. On other tours, you'll carry your things in panniers on your bike. (Inquire about storing a suitcase at your departure point so you carry just the essentials.) You still benefit from a pre-selected tour route that should be scenic, lightly trafficked, and provide a host of excuses to stop and investigate.

Lodgings are hotels and/or b&b's; how luxurious they are will vary. Bicycles, including children's bikes, are usually available from the company, and panniers are often provided (ask). An asterisk beside the price means cycle rental is extra. Prices, based on double-occupancy, are for 1990; airfares are not included.

Baumeler Tours hosts both guided and self-guided tours with a wide selection of European destinations. Lodgings are mid-price hotels and country inns. Sample prices: 8-day Tuscany guided tour including all breakfasts and a lunch or dinner daily, $950; self-guided 8-day Provence tour based in one hotel; breakfast and dinner daily included, $370. Baumeler Tours, 10 Grand Avenue, Rockville Center, NY 11570 (USA). Tel: Toll-free (800) 622-7623; in New York, (516) 766-6160.

Bicycle Adventure Club is non-profit. Members plan and lead all tours, to a variety of domestic and foreign destinations. Lodgings are always hotels, more elegant on some trips than others, and meals may or may not be included; there are tours for every taste and wallet. (A popular 21-day New Zealand tour including most meals: $2,208.) A sag wagon is always provided. Participants bring their own bikes. Inquire about membership ($30 per individual or couple per year.) Bicycle Adventure Club, 2369 Loring St., San Diego, CA 92109 (USA). Tel: (619) 273-2602.

Bicycle Holidays custom-designs Vermont tours, planning an itinerary to suit and making reservations with inns and b&b's. Within the Lake Champlain Valley area luggage transport from inn to inn and emergency repair assistance are included. Costs vary with accommodations, but $85-90* per day per person (double-occupancy) is average and includes breakfasts and a few dinners. Bicycle Holidays, RD 3, Box 2394, Middlebury, VT 05753 (USA). Tel: Toll-free (800) CYCLE-VT.

Bikecentennial, a non-profit organization, offers guided 'light tours' through some of America's most spectacular scenery. Accommodations are usually historic inns and lodges, like Old Faithful Inn on the Yellowstone Park tour (7 days/7 nights, $820). Other choices: Glacier National Park, Wisconsin's Door County, and Texas hill country. There's also a 5 day/5 night tour from one central location at mountain bike 'heaven,' Moab, Utah ($610); off-road instruction is provided, so moderately fit begin-

Women-Only Tours

Would you like a chance to meet more women with interests similar to your own? A break from male competition and conversation? A short escape from caring for the family? Offering female-led tours as short as two or three days as well as longer, these American tour organisers may have what you're looking for:

Calypso Excursions, Inc., 12 Federal Street, Newburyport, MA 01950. Tel: (617) 465-7173.

Outdoor Woman's School/Call of the Wild, 2519 Cedar Street, Berkeley, CA 94708. Tel: (415) 849-9292.

SpokeSongs Bicycling Vacations, 130 Fir Street, Suite B, Mahtomedi, MN 55115. Tel: (612) 429-2877.

Womantrek, 1411 E. Olive Way, Box 20643, Seattle, WA 98102. Tel: (206) 325-4772.

Woodswomen, 25 West Diamond Lake Road, Minneapolis, MN 55419. Tel: (612) 822-3809.

ners are welcome. Dinners and breakfasts all included. No sag wagon. Bikecentennial, PO Box 8308, Missoula, MT 59807 (USA). Tel: (406) 721-1776.

Breaking Away Tours are for bike racing fans. Want to go to the Tour de France or the Ironman Triathlon in Hawaii? These tours combine race-viewing with cycling (sometimes portions of the race route). Hotels are two- and three-star; breakfasts only included. A van transports luggage and riders as needed. Expect race-savvy guides and maybe even a meeting with the pros. Sample prices: Tour de France I (8 days), $998; Tour de France II (12 days), $1598. Breaking Away Bicycle Tours, 1142 Manhattan Avenue, Suite 253, Manhattan Beach, CA 90266 (USA). Tel: (213) 545-5118.

POINTS TO CONSIDER AS YOU SELECT AND SIGN UP

Daily mileage. Pick an itinerary that challenges but doesn't exceed your cycling ability. Tour organisers say the biggest mistake folks make is overestimating mileage they can handle. Most people can cycle 45 to 50 miles once, but day after day for a week is more demanding. I find 25 to 30 miles a day plenty for this sort of touring, because to me cycling is only part of the experience. I like to reserve time and energy for sightseeing, taking photos, and striking up chance conversations *en route*. On a bike tour in Northern Italy I once spent an hour and a half drinking coffee in a farmhouse kitchen, talking in broken French and Italian with a woman I happened to meet. It was one of the highlights of that particular trip!

Bike fit. If, like most participants, you opt for a bike provided by the tour operator, make clear on the application form what size and type of bicycle you want. State your bike frame size (seat tube measurement), and don't assume that if the application asks only for your height, you'll get a good fit. If you're used to riding with toeclips, indicate that. By the way, you might consider taking along your own saddle. A comfortable seat makes a big difference, even if the bike itself isn't a perfect fit.

Rain gear. Besides your usual cycling attire, a rain jacket and pants are helpful to have along. Even in the rain, cycling is a lot more fun than riding in the van. If it isn't absolutely pouring, I even welcome a rainy day as a change of pace.

Helmets. A good idea, no matter where you ride, and a few tour companies now require all participants to wear them.

Handlebar bag. The sort that comes with a metal support frame is best; a plastic map case on top keeps cycling map or directions in view.

Touring shoes. For riding and walking, touring shoes are far superior to trainers.

Other attire. On luxury tours, since the van will be carrying your luggage, you don't have to skimp when it comes to evening attire. As these trips generally feature overnight stays in first-class hotels and elegant dining, you'll want at least a couple of dressy outfits.

If carrying your own gear in panniers, you're probably smart enough to realise you want a few basic items of non-cycling attire, like a pair of solid colour slacks you can dress up or down and which can be washed and hung up to dry overnight. I once took a none-too-subtle pair of plaid trousers on a three-week cycle tour and wanted to burn them well before the end.

Breakfast. The standard continental breakfast just isn't substantial enough to see you through a morning of cycling. I stop soon after at a shop for some real food: fruit, a little sandwich, or perhaps some cheese and bread to tide me over 'til lunch.

Communication and culture. Learn something about the language and culture of the territory you'll be cycling through. Read as much as you can – tour organisers often provide a bibliography. If you lack time to take a language course, the knowledge of even a few words, and courage to use them, can make the difference between awkward, helpless silence and a smile that will light up your day.

Bicycling is one of the least insulated forms of tourism, one reason for its growing appeal. On a bike you're not just exposed to terrain and weather, you're also a potential actor in the little dramas of daily life going on all about you. The man hoeing artichokes in a field, the woman picking berries on a steep hillside, the kids walking home from school, all are at least as curious about you as you are about them. The more you're able to extend yourself, the richer your experience will be.

Training Tips for Any Tour

Along with following the basics for conditioning outlined in Building Fitness, you'll be better able to enjoy riding day after day if you:

- Cycle the distance of the tour's longest day at least once or twice. Do it, say, three and two weeks before departure.
- Accustom yourself to riding several days in a row without a rest day. Don't feel you have to do the full distance; just get your muscles used to the idea.

- Resist any temptation to cram in extra training during your last week before the tour. It won't benefit you, and it could keep you from being fresh and rested. Do ride in the last few days before departure, but decrease distances if you'd normally be taking long rides.

MEGA-RIDES

If neither the luxury or the budget-minded tour sounds rollicking enough for you, you might like a mega-ride. That's my term for one of those large, cross-state rides or other long-distance camping parties on wheels. This is definitely the 'more is more' approach . . . more people to pedal with (sometimes thousands) and more miles per day. If you've heard of RAGBRAI (the Register's Annual Great Bike Ride Across Iowa, a grandaddy of this sort of tour) or Bike Events' End to End tour in Britain, you've got the picture.

Each of these rides has its own flavour. On the End to End tour, for example, just as you start up some beastly hill in Scotland, there might be Queen Victoria (or so it appears), smoking a cigar and issuing outlandish orders to her red-coated Coldstream guards while at the same time bestowing knighthoods on passing cyclists; imagine being dubbed Lady Ridewell. Are you delirious? No, it's folks from the Natural Theatre Company who pop up from time to time to help keep the mood properly zany as the 870 miles roll by.

As these rides go, this is a fairly intimate one – a couple of hundred riders. By contrast, RAGBRAI (rhymes with 'horsefly') is a pedal-powered parade with thousands of people, by the time you count unregistered join-ins.

Also by way of contrast, RAGBRAI participants *don't* come for the scenery, unless they happen to like cornfields, mile after mile. They rally for a good time 'with 10,000 of my closest friends', as one woman put it, and to be welcomed into every small Iowa community with corn roasts and pork barbeque, lemonade stands and cake sales to benefit every civic group you could imagine. Square dances and concerts at day's end make for down-home fun and a feeling that Iowans must be the friendliest people in the world.

On a mega-ride when the cycling stops, it's just the beginning of the evening's fun. Two women trade accounts of the day as they retrieve their luggage (*Dan Burden*).

'I've ridden on tours with all the comforts, and they are not as memorable as RAGBRAI!'

Though RAGBRAI, which dates to 1973, was the first, it's inspired a number of other across-state rides, each with its own stalwart supporters, some of whom return year after year to repeat the experience . . . like Deborah Crane, 38, of Tulsa, Oklahoma. Deborah describes a cross-Oklahoma ride called FREEWHEEL.

I just completed my third FREEWHEEL, and it will take a major disaster in my life for me to miss one – I love it! Everyone on a bike is your friend that week, and each year is like a reunion. There must have been twenty people who complimented me on my new bike this year because they actually remembered the other bike I had the year before.

I gain such a sense of accomplishment on this ride. There's so much energy and electricity in the air that you know you can climb that hill. The entire tour is friendly and therapeutic. I don't remember how many hugs I got last week, but I relished every one of them.

Emotions are high in camp the last night. People know it's almost over, and they don't want it to be. No wonder: the people in the little towns have been wonderful, greeting us with banners across Main Street and fantastic hospitality. When we rode into our final town, the mayor was sitting in a yard under a tree, welcoming every rider over a loud speaker. I didn't want the ride to end. I felt so overwhelmed, tears rolled down my cheeks. There were some

2,000 riders in FREEWHEEL, and to that town we were all celebrities.
Besides riding 480 miles last week, I was a star. Now how can you beat that?!

A Sampling of Mega-Rides

These rides are held in the summer. As dates vary slightly from year to year, I've listed only the month in which each is held. Some rides limit the number of participants, so inquire early and enclose a stamped, self-addressed envelope. This is not an exhaustive list. Look for other cross-state rides in cycling magazines' diaries.

Bike Events organises the two-week End to End ride from John O'Groats (northernmost Scotland) to Land's End (England's southwest tip) – a classic journey for British marathon cyclists' record attempts. Held in August, the trip of about 870 miles averages 65 to 70 miles a day. Meals are provided by travelling caterers; luggage is hauled for you. In late July the organisers also run The Great British Bike Ride, from London to the Isle of Skye, with similar entertainments but shorter mileage (50 miles/day); plus shorter rides as well. Sample prices: End to End, £310; The Great British Bike Ride, £285. Bike Events, PO Box 75, Bath BA1 1BX, England.

RAGBRAI follows a different route each July for about 500 miles, ridden in six days. Daily distances are designed to help prepare riders for the traditional 100-mile day. Luggage is trucked each day for you; meals are sold in tents by civic groups at the campgrounds. There's a small registration fee. RAGBRAI, Box 10333, Des Moines, IA 50306 (USA).

FREEWHEEL is a seven-day, approximately 500-mile ride following a formula similar to RAGBRAI's. Held in early June. FREEWHEEL, c/o Bob Haring, TULSA WORLD, Box 1770, Tulsa, OK 74102 (USA).

AFFBRAAM (Annual Fit-Fest Bike Ride Across America) conducts a series of across-state rides which may be done individually or which may be strung together to cross the entire United States in twelve tours (about 5,070 miles total) via a northern route. States crossed include: Washington, Idaho, Montana, North Dakota, Minnesota, Wisconsin, Michigan, Ohio, part of Pennsylvania, New York, Vermont, New Hampshire, and Maine, with occasional forays into Canada. AFFBRAAM, Box 29, Northfield, MN 55057 (USA). Tel: (507) 663-1268.

Bicycle Across the Magnificent Miles of Illinois is 500 miles in seven days in late-July/early August. BAMMI, The Chicago Lung Association, 1440 W. Washington Blvd., Chicago, IL 60607-1878 (USA). Tel: (312) 243-2000.

Bicycle Across Massachusetts is a 200-mile, four-day ride in early July. BAM, c/o Joe Nai, 1141 Amestown Road, West Springfield, MA 01089 (USA). Tel: (413) 733-0370.

22 *Fat Tyre Freedom*

Where the road ends, a special freedom begins. Mountain biking makes me feel like a kid again, flying down gravel roads, discovering the world all brand new, over and over again from my bike! I've found magic, riding in that free, unworried, ready-for-anything kind of way kids have and too many grownups have long forgotten. Sitting upright, I can actually see the scenery. And my fat, knobby tyres hug the terrain, making for a stable, secure ride.

Suzanne Vannell, 48, Troy, Michigan

There's a nasty rumour going around that most mountain bike owners never take them off the tarmac. Somebody whispered to me it might be as high as 90 per cent *never go off-road*. Could it be that those radical ads showing Evil Knievel on knobbies, blasting off a veritable cliff, have convinced sane folks there's no such thing as a gentle mountain bike ride?

You don't have to be intrepid to get into it. I have spent whole summer days rolling lazily along the old Delaware Canal towpath in Pennsylvania near where I live. Cool in the shade of trees overhead, I hadn't a worry about traffic. I was free to look about at the remains of forgotten canal towns and lock keepers' houses from a vantage point the road didn't offer. My skinny-tired bike wouldn't have done as well on the grassy, occasionally rock-studded path, but those fat ballooners were right at home.

If you aren't blessed with canal towpaths where you live, you may instead find dirt roads or old railway beds converted to bike trails, open moorland or gentle footpaths. If terrain is fairly level, you won't need any special skills at all. You can enjoy the outdoors just as if you were walking or hiking, but you can see so much more! Ask at the shop where you bought your bike for good places to try it out.

You may be surprised at what's waiting, perhaps just outside your door. Suzanne Vannell, who says she's not the dare-devil sort, lives in 'a huge apartment complex about 30 miles north of Detroit – an area no one would mistake for off-road heaven'. From her apartment the closest things to wilderness are a golf course and a cemetery. Not long ago she rode along a stand of trees bordering the cemetery and had just entered a short trail that goes past a pond surrounded by cat's-tails.

There I saw a deer, head down, drinking. Slowly I got off the bike and stood still. The deer drank on, then a second deer stepped from the bushes. It caught my scent, ears going up like flags, alerting the first deer too. For a few sweet, electrifying seconds we stared at each other. Then in a flash of white

tails they were gone. I rode to where they had been and looked at their tracks
in the damp sand . . .

TIPS FOR BEGINNERS

Go ahead. Liberate the kid inside. Find out what you and your mountain bike can do –
and what you can discover. Here are some tips for getting started.

- Check your saddle position. For uphills especially, as well as level and easy
  downhill terrain, your saddle height should give you the same leg extension
  you have on your road bike – your leg almost fully extended at the bottom of
  your power stroke.
- Then get the kinks out of your shifting. Make a gear chart if you need to,
  and ride on the road or on the easiest of trails. Accustom yourself to the
  thumbshifters and to shifting up and down smoothly between the three
  chainwheels without looking down.
- Go off-road on some beginner terrain – some gentle, grassy slopes or
  cinder running trails or maybe some bumpy dirt roads – wherever you can
  practise using your gears and get familiar with the feel of the bike under
  you. You want to be able to ride relaxed and have a good time with it, so
  keep the level of difficulty low. If you should find a challenging spot where
  you have to stop and put a foot down for balance (or 'dab', as they say in
  trials riding), try it again, varying your technique a little, and see if you can
  get it. (Try it faster or slower, in a different gear, or with your weight
  positioned differently.) This might be more fun to do with a friend you know
  won't try to rush you. But if you feel self-conscious, just do it on your own.

  Do you find you're having difficulty getting traction? If you've been riding
  the roads until now, your tyres are probably pumped up to the max. If the
  tyre feels hard when you press on it with your thumb, let out 10 or 15
  pounds of air pressure. When you get into soft dirt, mud, loose stones or
  sand – all that great stuff your tyres have been itching to get their treads
  into – you'll find off-road riding is easier with softer tyres. You'll have better
  traction on climbs too, thanks to a broader footprint. And a little give in the
  tyre will take some of the bounce out of a descent. Experiment to see what
  works best. If you're a heavy rider, don't lower the pressure past 30 psi on
  rough terrain, as you don't want to 'bottom out' and flatten a rim. If you
  have the narrower 1.75-inch tyres, 40 psi is safer. Do have a frame pump
  with you so you can pump up before emerging to ride on pavement later.
- Make braking easy. Now that you have a feel for this sort of riding, if your
  mountain bike isn't a recent model consider changing the way the brake
  leavers are mounted – swivelling them down, so that your wrists are
  straight and you're pulling toward yourself. You'll find that lets you make the
  most of the strength in your hands.

231

- After a few of those beginning forays, you'll be eager to see what else you can do. Do you have mountain biking friends you can trust not to be too wild and crazy? You can learn from riding with them, watching their technique and asking questions. Again, begin with easy terrain, build your confidence, and progress gradually to more challenging geography.

- Develop descending technique. At the start of steep descents, make use of the quick-release on your seatpost. More accomplished riders may not bother for a short descent, but the idea of the quick-release is to let you lower the saddle as far as it will go before starting a downhill run. This gives you the opportunity to shift your weight back over the rear tyre so you have a more stable, lower centre of gravity. (Of course, you won't forget to tighten the quick-release.)

Best of Both Worlds

'I got into mountain biking in early 1983, as soon as the first stock bikes were available in a frame size to (almost) fit me. I felt like a kid in a candy store! I wanted to pinch myself and ask, "Is this true? Can I really combine the two things I love to do most – backcountry hiking and bicycling?" The answer is still, "Yeah! And it's great!" Just a week ago three of us rode along a ridgeline on a single track through a field of newly blossomed wildflowers, a view of the Pacific Ocean on our right. There's nothing quite like it!'

Naomi Bloom,
45, Cupertino, California

Also, as you prepare for a downhill run, shift your chain on to the large chainwheel and the next-to-largest rear sprocket; this takes up any slack in the chain that might otherwise let it come off if you hit a bump. Besides, if you don't, that chain slapping on the chainstays will scare off the wildlife for miles around.

Put the pedals in a horizontal position (to avoid catching on any obstacle you go over). Bend knees and elbows to help absorb any bumps, and grasp the handlebars firmly but don't white-knuckle it. If you practise these things on more gradual descents, you'll have it for tougher ones later. On real rough stuff, stay off the seat and crouch back.

- Develop off-road braking habits. On a downhill let the front brake do more of the work than the rear. Why? Too much rear braking locks the wheel, causing skidding. So use the front brake mostly, but don't 'slam' it on, and remember to keep your weight way back over the wheel. As one friend puts it, 'If you burn your bum on the knobs, you're doing it right!' Should you forget, a quick stop could send you, head first, over the bars . . . called a 'face-plant' in mountain bike jargon.

- Sometimes a little speed actually makes descending easier. Yes, you want to be under control, but don't ride the brakes. Squeeze and release, and let some momentum carry you over small bumps that would actually feel larger if you took them more slowly. If you are momentarily airborne, keep your weight back on the bike so that the rear wheel touches down a fraction of a second before the front wheel.

- At the bottom of the hill congratulate yourself – and raise the saddle back to normal position before going on. By the way, many seatposts are marked with numbers so you can easily keep track of your preferred saddle height. But if yours isn't, mark the post yourself. Or you may want to buy a Hite-Rite quick adjust seat locator or SR's 'Quick Post', with an internal spring. These are convenient for anyone and let more experienced types make changes without a dismount.

- Climbing, too, is a whole new adventure. As you approach a hill, try to 'read' it and pick the best gear. Mountain bikes are geared low, partly because riders often stay in the saddle for an ascent. However, steeper climbs will bring you to your feet. When you do stand, keep your weight to the rear by staying in a crouch and hanging your bottom back behind the saddle. If you reach a steep spot and your front wheel has a tendency to lift up, counter that by leaning a little more forward. Trial and error is the teacher in learning a feel for it, so just have fun with it and experiment to see what works for you.

  By the way, downshifting used to be tricky on a climb. Now the new indexed systems make it easy. But if you lack click-shifting and need to gear down on the uphill, pedal hard then let up just as you move the lever.

- What about toeclips? If your bike didn't come with toeclips, think about getting them. They keep your feet on the pedals during a bumpy ride. Believe me, losing your footing is painful if you hit the top tube. If you wear the straps a little loose, you can still slip a foot out when you need to dab.

- Don't forget to have fun. You may wonder if that's possible with all these things to remember, but you'll soon get the hang of it.

  Give it a try and you'll find a new kind of cycling freedom. You may find yourself straying from the path – a sure sign you've gotten the knack . . . and an extra slice of freedom. As Rhoda Morrison, a native New Zealander transplanted to London, says:

  > Most people's mountain bikes never see dirt, but I love it, especially going up and down hills. It's nice to ride up and see a view of open moorland or to go through a thicket and come out on an overlook for a rest. You get *results*: you can feel what you've done. The other day we were high on some open land, and it was perfectly quiet. It's been so long since I just heard absolutely nothing, away from the fumes of London!

- And don't neglect to pass along what you've learned to riders who are even greener than you. They'll be so impressed.

GETTING FRISKY

I'm not against more daring stunts on a mountain bike after you've developed the technique for bombing down difficult terrain.

As in other skill sports, like downhill skiing, technique comes with time and practice. Personally, I'm still working on it. I did get a taste of riding on the wild side last year – on the back of a mountain bike tandem with my former colleague at *Bicycling*, John Kukoda, who is technical editor of *Bicycling Plus Mountain Bike* magazine. We were riding the trails at a state forest in our area, along with John's wife Lesa. She graciously (or craftily?) relinquished her stoker position so I could plunge (forever, it seemed) down a power line cut behind John. As we ricocheted from one rock to the next, the trees on either side were almost a blur. Once my right foot flew out of the toeclip and I was afraid I would follow it. But John slowed so I could settle in again. 'Yeah, you have to really shove 'em in there,' he shouted. Since he was captaining the bike, all I could do was hold on and go with the flow.

Gulp. It really was fun, I decided, after we'd reached the bottom of the hill in one piece. Then Lesa and I switched bikes and I was back on a single, riding the trails at my own pace, enjoying being out in the woods and picking up a few tips. Both he and Lesa helped with the advice I pass along in this chapter.

Since that ride, by the way, I've been making progress on my own mountain bike and have bounced off a bunch of rocks (knock wood) with nary a fall.

GOING IN SNOW

Once you get started, cold weather doesn't have to stop the action. When snow translates a drab winter landscape into sparkling white, Rhoda Morrison, who races for the Fisher MountainBike UK team during the season, thinks 'some of the most fun' is riding her fat tyre bike in the snow, off-road. 'We play around, jump over logs . . .'

Even if you're a new rider, you'll revel in it. Your favourite trails will seem enchanted, and if you've never been an outdoors person in winter, you may take on a whole new attitude about the season. So go on out and play! Stick to familiar or at least predictable terrain where snow won't hide hazards to trip you up.

'You don't have to get "gonzo",' Rhoda says. 'In fact, I hate that word and I hate seeing those mountain bike magazines full of photographs of guys with their front wheel up in the air. I think it puts people off.' You can have fun without the acrobatics.

Worried about getting cold? Remember, you're your own little generator, and because you're moving slower than on a road bike, there's less windchill. To ensure comfort, wear warm boots and mittens and thermal underwear.

As for the roads, when Chris Mawer began riding her new bike in preparation for a mountain bike safari in Kenya, it was winter in Leicestershire, England, where she lived. But she used her MTB on the street, commuting to her job as a university librarian. She found her mountain bike would go in snow: 'I rode my Cannondale home 10 miles in the snow – all the other cyclists were walking their bikes,' she says.

Admittedly, cycling snowy streets can have its risks. Personally I wouldn't do it if there's much traffic, or if visibility is poor, or if there are icy patches on the roads. And I wouldn't blithely urge it on inexperienced riders at all.

But if you're not to be deterred, here are a few tips to increase your snow skill on winter streets:

- Wide, knobby tyres are the ticket for new or hard-packed snow. For good traction on anything more than an inch or 2 of the fluffy stuff, you want the fattest footprint you can get, so let out some air. You can take a 2.125-inch tyre down to about 15 to 20 psi on smooth terrain without bottoming out, since you aren't likely to be doing any wild bouncing around.
- When the road goes up, don't gear all the way down. The greater torque of the bottom gears will make the rear wheel spin unproductively beneath you. A little higher gear will keep you moving. If the wheel does spin, sit back farther.
- Use your X-ray vision. I'm just kidding, of course, but if you ride a route regularly, you know where the manhole covers and gratings are. Avoid them, as they're likely to be icy. If you do hit an icy spot, continue straight across it without trying to turn or stop.
- Even if roads appear clear, be on the alert for ice you can't see, like frozen spray from automobile tyres. If the road is shaded, it may harbour ice even after the sun has melted it elsewhere.
- Wear your helmet and a smile. Try to keep your body relaxed so you won't over-react and over-steer. Let the bike do the work.
  Allow more braking distance on packed snow than you would under normal road conditions.
- If you really get into it, there are tyres available with steel studs for ice.

TAKE IT TOURING

Wherever you can imagine touring on a road bike – and more – that's where mountain bike touring can take you. In Kenya after two days of climbing, Chris and her husband Ray had a thrilling descent from the top of the Kinangop Plateau to the floor of the Rift Valley. It was very cold at the top (9,000 feet el.) but hot at the bottom. 'As we rode on this continual downhill at 40 mph, we could feel the hot air rushing up at us. Close by in the bush we saw hippos, and mongooses, zebra, many antelopes, thousands of birds, even eagles . . .' The trip wasn't easy, but even so, Chris says she'd do it again 'and for a lot longer as well. We were wishing we could have gone up into Tanzania . . .'

Iceland has beckoned rock hoppers like Deb Murrell, of Yorkshire, one of England's top mountain bike racers. She rates her month-long tour of that moon-like country the highlight of her off-road experiences. 'It was quite amazing,' she says. 'The roads are mostly just rocky trails there.' That was just fine with Deb – handling technically demanding terrain is her racing forte.

Tuscany's mule roads sound more like it to me, ascending through sweet-smelling vineyards and past farmhouses to old Italian villages the colour of aged parchment. (I've just been reading about such a trip, so pardon me while I do a bit of daydreaming.) Perhaps you'd prefer the English Lake District, or canyon country in the American Southwest. Or China, Tibet, Baja, Nova Scotia, Vermont, Switzerland . . . Take your pick of the exotic destinations or find your own close to home.

For the first-timer, I'd recommend fat tyre touring with an organised group providing a sag wagon to carry luggage. Or take day trips basing yourself at a mountain bike centre where you can pick up a few pointers if you want them. Carrying loaded panniers or a backpack makes more demands on your bikehandling and energy, so leave that for another time if you can. Some touring companies listed in chapter 21, Two-Wheel Travel, offer off-road adventures, and you can find more in the cycling magazines. Just don't let those frantic photos throw you.

Opposite
Mountain bikes make for a whole new range of possibilities. Here riders tour the Sawtooth Mountains of Idaho (*Tom Hale, Backroads Bicycle Touring*).

Further Resources:

In the UK the organisation, SUSTRANS, can send you information on a growing network of former railway beds that are now bike trails. The organisation's David Thompson tells me they are working on a relatively flat route across the Pennines, one of a number of greenway projects. Postcard maps are available for each of the projects if you write in; enclose a stamped, self-addressed envelope. David also says they're looking for volunteers to work (two weeks minimum) on cycleway construction, so if you want to make friends, be outdoors, build some muscles, and get free room and board, contact the organisation. SUSTRANS Ltd, 35 King Street, Bristol BS1 4DZ.

There's a similar movement underway in the US, spearheaded by the Rails-to-Trails Conservancy. Currently about 2,400 miles of former railway corridors have been transformed into hiking and biking trails in thirty-one states. A guide to many of them, 'Sampler of America's Rail Trails', is yours for $2 (for postage and handling). Write: Rails-to-Trails Conservancy, 1400 16th Street NW, Dept. BI, Washington, DC 20036.

Mountain biking clubs are sprouting up around the UK. Ask at your cycle shop. If you don't turn anything up, *Bicycle Action* magazine runs a club list with names and addresses from time to time, so look for it in the magazine or write and request it. If you want to organise something yourself, send them your name and address. (*Bicycle Action* magazine, 95 Manor Farm Road, Wembley, Middlesex HA0 1BY.)

The American mountain bike racer Jacquie Phelan (known to race fans as Alice B. Toeclips) formed her own club which – in typical wacky Jacquie fashion – she named WOMBATS (Women's Mountain Bike and Tea Society). It's a networking organisation with a newsletter and events in various locations around the States. Write and inquire: WOMBATS, Box 757, Fairfax, California 94930.

23 *Planning Your Own Tour*

My trip to the 1984 Olympics was a dream come true. After a half-day alone, I met (as planned) two women in Santa Cruz (California) who'd cycled from Alaska. We traced the spectacularly scenic coast, staying in hiker/biker campgrounds and meeting many other cyclists on the same 'pilgrimage'. My companions, of course, were instant celebrities wherever we went. In Los Angeles I stayed with a girlfriend, and we attended the cycling road races and track events. It was thrilling to see Olympic history in the making.

Diane Harrison, 32, Berkeley, California

Shaping your own trip around events or activities of special interest is great impetus for planning your own tour. Perhaps you want to go where no organised tour goes, or you'd like to visit friends or relatives. On your own you could stretch your budget farther than on many organised tours and extend your travel time. As an extreme example, I know of one couple who managed 'an absolutely unforgettable' fourteen-month cycling honeymoon, visiting virtually every country in Europe.

Or just the opposite. Maybe on the spur of the moment you make a brief escape, as did Jane King, 32, of Littlehampton, West Sussex:

I cycled for a few days on a heavy, old rented bike along the lower Loire valley. There were tiny, narrow roads along immense blue stretches of river, empty riverside cafés, shops with bread and cheese and little else, fishermen, great suspended nets drying outside ancient farm buildings, stunning châteaux, and friendly cheap hotels. That was magic . . . and no hills!

Perhaps the freedom of travelling only with the companions you've chosen – or alone if you prefer – is the essence of cycle-touring for you.

Regardless, you have the added challenge of selecting your own route. Despite your research, you don't quite know what you'll find. You must plan what to take along and anticipate how to deal with small mishaps that might occur *en route*. And it's these very challenges, the unknown, that are part of the appeal.

'That's what makes travel real – it leaves room for the unexpected to happen,' says Bettina Selby, the well-known writer and cycle-adventurer, who's bicycled alone through Pakistan, Kashmir, Turkey, Syria, Egypt, Sudan, Uganda . . .

When I spoke on the phone to Bettina, she was home for a brief respite from some nasty weather during a summer of extensive touring in her own England (for her new book, *Riding North One Summer*, Chatto and Windus). She described that trip as 'an extensive ramble. I have all the gear, a little tent . . . I just follow my nose. I'm doing much less mileage and more poking around than on previous travels. It's fascinating. And I keep meeting people who want to haul me off and show me their part of the country.' On your own tour, you have the freedom to say yes.

PICKING YOUR ROUTE

You can have as much, or as little, help in selecting a route as you wish. If you've already chosen where you want to go, aside from travel books, you might need nothing more than a sufficiently detailed map. County maps, available at bookstores or county government offices, should show the lightly travelled, back roads. If you need more than one map, as you might, depending on trip length, you can often buy them (in the US) from the state's Department of Transportation, and avoid separate inquiries.

In England I've found the Ordnance Survey 'Landranger Series' maps (scale of 1¼ inch to 1 mile, or 1 : 50,000) excellent. In France I've used Michelin maps, which are less detailed but still very good (scale of 1 cm to 2 km, or 1 : 200,000). In the US topo maps of a slightly smaller scale (1 : 250,000) are available. Maps within this range will serve you well. When possible, choose secondary roads instead of busy highways and avoid tourist routes to popular attractions. Remember to take elevation changes into account in your planning.

If you want a shortcut in planning, or you feel slightly less adventurous, you could try a tour some other cyclist has already road-tested. Or add in some 'detours' of your own to tailor it to suit. Look at bookshops or the library for books of bicycle tours. A local bike club with touring members should have a wealth of mapped tours, suggestions, and enthusiasm to share – good reason for joining.

Membership also has its privileges in the Cyclists' Touring Club (CTC, Cotterell House, 69 Meadrow, Godalming, Surrey GU7 3HS, England.) Routes, maps, and practical advice on the best areas for cycle-touring are available to all members from the headquarters office.

Similar information is available from organisations in the States with national membership:

- One is Bicycle USA (formerly The League of American Wheelmen), Suite 209, 6707 Whitestone Road, Baltimore, MD 21207.
- Bikecentennial offers a catalogue of bicycling books and maps as well as tour routing services. This organisation is particularly well known for developing the Trans-America Bicycle Trail, a cross-country route using public roads; maps and guidebooks are available. Write: Bikecentennial, Box 8308, Missoula, MT 59807.
- A clearing house for bike tour routes, the Touring Exchange will send its index of maps and touring routes if you send them $1. Write: Touring Exchange, Box 265, Port Townsend, WA 98368.

- The Women's Cycling Network also offers route planning assistance to its membership. For information about joining, write WCN, PO Box 73, Harvard, IL 60033.

North of the border, the Canadian Cycling Association can provide some route information from its headquarters, but more complete information will be available from the affiliate provincial districts. Contact the Canadian Cycling Association, 333 River Road, Vanier City (Ottawa), Ontario, Canada K1L 8B9.

Many US states and Canadian provinces, eager to lure cycle tourists, will assist you. Write to the state or provincial Department of Tourism and clearly indicate that you are asking for bicycling route maps and other information. On the lower left of the envelope you might even write 'Bicycle Touring Info Request'.

WHERE TO LAY YOUR WEARY HEAD

You already know there's considerable choice in types of accommodations, so I'll simply mention a few resources that may prove helpful.

Hosteling is not limited to the under-21 set, though it may not be your choice if luxury and privacy are uppermost concerns. These inexpensive lodgings may turn out to be quite romantic, however, as Faith Hahn, 33, of McAllen, Texas, found on her cycle tour through Germany. In her travel diary she describes the hostel in Ochsenfurt as

the smallest, most primitive and most unusual I've been in. It is one of the old towers of the city wall, about 20 feet square and six stories high . . . It really is a seventeenth-century cold, drafty stone tower! The beds are poor but piled high with German woollen blankets that I think I'll need. There are a bathroom and a shower (cold). And there's a fantastic day room at the top, with windows on all four sides and an incredible view of the city. That's where I'm writing and having supper now.

Membership in your country's hosteling organisation should net you a handbook with hostel listings as well as discount privileges in fifty or so member countries. For information contact:

- American Youth Hostels, National Administration Offices, Box 37613, Washington, DC 20013-7613.
- Canadian Hosteling Association, 333 River Road, Vanier City (Ottawa), Ontario, Canada K1L 8B9. Tel: (416) 368-1848.
- (British) Youth Hostels Association, Trevalyan House, 8 St Stevens Hill, St Albans, Herts AL1 2DY. Tel: 0727 55215.

Another alternative that may appeal, particularly to the solo tourist, is hospitality of a more personal sort. The above-mentioned organisation, Bicycle USA, publishes an annual 'Directory', listing hundreds of members' homes nationwide which offer sleeping bag space to fellow members on tour.

On an international scale, the organisation Servas aims to promote understanding among peoples through a host programme. This should not be looked on as just a freebie: generally you'd stay two days in someone's home, and in return for a bed and meals you're expected to talk about your country and share your thoughts on world events. No money changes hands. In this fashion, Anita Slomski wrote in *Bicycling* magazine, 'I cycle(d) 3,000 miles over the backroads of Europe away from the tourist traps to find the real people. Countless times I was rewarded with a richness in human warmth and generosity and the pleasure of some truly unforgettable characters.' Sometimes, she admits, 'telling the same stories every night to a new host and being polite all the time were exhausting. But the rewards were generally worth the effort.'

Reg Tauke takes a breather in the North Yorkshire Moors. The Yorkshire Dales are *the* favourite touring locale for the Taukes, an American couple who have come to the UK for half a dozen different tours of their own planning in the Dales (*John Tauke*).

If such cultural exchange appeals, contact Servas in your country. There are a screening procedure and a reasonable membership fee. Lists of hosts are provided, and you may arrange to visit hosts within your own country as well as abroad.

- The United States Servas Committee Inc., 11 John Street, Room 406, New York, NY 10038. Tel: (212) 267-0252. (This office can also provide information on Servas in Canada.)
- The British Servas Committee, Mr Graham Thomas, 77 Elm Park Mansions, Park Walk, London SW10 0AP. Tel: 071-352 0203.

Beyond these options, of course, is the full spectrum of b & b's, guest houses, pensions, and hotels, to which your own reading can lead you, if not a travel agent.

There is also the camping alternative – and the extra gear you must carry to be able to do it. I've learned that an investment in lightweight, good quality equipment pays off in a lighter, more compact load. It will save your energy and give you more stable bikehandling.

BIKES FOR LOADED TOURING

If you already have a genuine touring bike built for stability under load and a smooth ride, and gearing down in the mid- to low-20s, you're ahead of the game. If you don't, read this before you rush to the bike shop.

Since there are many ways to go touring, it stands to reason there's a range of choices for the bike you might want to transport you. Let's divide the options into three categories:

- You're credit-card touring. You pack your toothbrush, your credit-card, a patch kit, a spare pair of shorts, and a windbreaker in an under-the-saddle bag and off you go. This is perhaps a short trip. Any bike, even a racing bike, could handle that load.
- You're hosteling or hoteling, for a few weeks or a weekend. You'll carry a few changes of clothing, your raingear, perhaps a camera, but no camping or cooking gear, as you'll be eating at restaurants. You may have a sleeping bag if hosteling. You can probably manage with a sport-touring bike, provided it has eyelets for mounting a rear rack. Note suggestions further on for apportioning weight on the bike. Try packing your panniers in advance of the trip and weigh them; you might be surprised how the pounds can add up.
- You're camping, cooking meals, and packing accordingly. You might be carrying 25 pounds, maybe twice that. (Sharon Sommerville, whom you'll meet in this chapter, toured cross-Canada carrying 50 pounds of gear so she'd have all the comforts. However, every 5 pounds you can pare off a burden like that are 5 pounds less to lug uphill and that much less of a load on your rear wheel spokes. Personally, I'd keep the load to 30 pounds or less. I've done it within that limit, carrying a lightweight tent, sleeping bag, and cooking gear.)

If you're in the second or third category, you'll need at least rear panniers and a rack. (See chapter 8, Accessories.) Anyone planning to put more than about 20 pounds in a pair of rear panniers should consider adding a low-rider front rack and small front panniers. This will make for much safer bikehandling. Divide the load so that 35 per cent is in the front panniers, 60 per cent is in the rear panniers, and 5 per cent is in the front handlebar bag.

The more your total load exceeds about 25 pounds, the more you ought to consider the frame geometry of your bike. Will it be stable with your load? 'Question 7' in chapter 6, So You Want to Buy a Bike, will help you decide.

As for gearing, for unloaded touring, gears in the mid- to upper 30s are generally recommended. For carrying up to 30 pounds in your packs, gearing in the low 30s is usually suggested, but many women would appreciate lower. For a heavier load, gearing in the mid- to upper 20s is best.

What about touring on-road with a mountain bike, you say? If you have one and it has stable handling without a load, try adding a rear rack and a moderate load and see how it performs. If it passes the test, then go ahead. Certainly you'll have the gearing for touring!

If you have a knobby-tyred MTB, some street treads will give you less rolling resistance on the road – naturally you'd use them fully inflated. Expect that your pace would be slower with this bike than with a road machine because of the wider tyres and more upright riding position and thus greater wind resistance. If your daily mileage expectations are moderate and if you find sitting up most comfortable, you probably won't mind giving up some speed.

The newest alternative is the 'hybrid' bike, a cross between a road and a mountain bike, which appears to offer the best of both worlds for many tourists.

GETTING LOADED

When packing panniers, try to put an equal amount of weight on each side, placing heavy objects as low in the bags as possible and close to the bike. This keeps the weightiest part of the load closest to the centre of gravity. On the front wheel try to keep weight on or behind the centreline of the steering axis; in plain English, behind the axle instead of in front of it. Bill Boston (who advised us on bicycle handling characteristics) says if your bike handled acceptably without panniers but is now unstable with a load, you probably have the weight too far forward on the front wheel. Before taking off on tour, ride at home with the weight in different positions to see what works best.

Pack so that gear doesn't move around inside your panniers when you take a corner or stop quickly. And don't strap too many things on top of the bags – not only does it make you look like a travelling soup kitchen with a pot tied on here, a frying pan there, a damp towel flapping in the wind, but it can be dangerous. Extra gear can come loose too readily and catch in the spokes.

You may be carrying a sleeping bag and possibly a foam pad on top of your rack, fastened on with straps or elastic 'bungee' cords. If you use the sort with an open hook on the end, make a habit of using it this way: first hook one end to a low portion of your pannier rack and then stretch the free end toward you. Secure your sleeping bag, etc. with it and hook this end high on the rack. Why? Sometimes the hook or cord slips out of your grasp, and you don't want to catch it in the eye. Follow this tip to keep your face out of firing range.

There are now cords with closed plastic hooks that appear to cut down on the hazard – definitely 'new and improved'. But I'd still attach them as described.

Especially as you get accustomed to using your new panniers, check periodically to make sure they're mounted securely on the rack, and that nothing is dangling or bending around into the spokes. (Many bags come with stiffeners to prevent them from bending like this, but if yours didn't, you should improvise a stiffener.) A quick, unanticipated stop because of a wheel jam could send you head over handlebars. For the same reason, if you hear a 'funny sound' while riding, stop and investigate in case something has come loose.

HANDLING A LOADED BIKE

With loaded panniers your bike will have a whole new feel and will handle differently. But you'll get the hang of it, especially if you anticipate the following:

- Acceleration will be slower. When you start from a standstill to cross a busy street, for example, remember you'll need extra time to beat oncoming traffic.
- As a general rule, you'll probably need to keep a firmer grip on the bars than you normally do. You may notice that the bike steers a little to one side, despite your attempts to divide the load equally; be on guard to correct it. Lightening the load in your handlebar bag could improve the situation. Experiment and see what works best for you.
- On a rough road the ride will feel rougher. Full bags add to the bounce up and down or a lateral shimmy. Slow down, if you need to, to keep control.
- Don't forget you're carrying a wide load, even though it's behind where you can't see it. When passing another cyclist, give yourself extra room so you don't do the 'sleeping bag sideswipe'.
- Before a long descent, stop at the top (well off the road). Check brakes and wheels, and look over your tyres for any debris that should be brushed off. Make sure packs and racks are attached securely. This is a good place anyway to stop for a snack or slip into a windbreaker for a cool downhill.
- A loaded bike gathers more speed on downhills and has startlingly different stopping characteristics. When braking, you'll discover that the bike stops, but the bags and your body want to keep on going. Counteract that momentum by shifting your weight quickly but smoothly back on the saddle, levelling the pedals so you can push against them equally; brake from the drops with firm, equal pressure. With or without bike bags, this is a good emergency braking method.

   Allow more time to brake to a stop. Keep downhill speed under control, so you have ample reaction time to avoid a gravel patch or pothole. Remember squeeze-and-release braking to minimise heat buildup. And when you get to one of those delicious, miles-long descents, stop from time to time, off the road. Admire the view (you earned it), and let your rims cool and your hands and arms relax.

- Riding out of the saddle up a hill, you'll find that load on the back wags the entire bike. Don't lean your weight from side to side as you would if unencumbered.
- Sometimes walking is the better part of valour. It's okay! Maybe your gears just aren't low enough or it's one hill too many on a long day. It's smarter to walk up than to wobble all over the road. Gravelly descents should be walked, since they must be taken slowly. Any effort to brake would end up in a skid on this treacherous stuff.

   That's a lot of warnings, I know, but the riding technique gets to be second nature. If you know how to handle the worst, you'll still be there to relish the good things.

SHOULD I SOLO?

Alison Heine is talking about some of the 'good things', when the question of touring alone comes up. Alison, a project officer for the Greater Manchester (England) Cycling Project, tells me her favourite place for bicycle touring is Scotland.

'Roads are unfenced, so you can put your tent anywhere . . . every village has super bakers' shops, and little cafés. There are loads of really cheap b & b's – prices have hardly changed in eighteen years. There's lots of daylight, so you can cycle 'til 9 or 10 pm.'

Alison bought her bike and camping gear when a student and generally camped alone. 'I never felt unsafe,' she says, 'though I'd never have camped on open land, visible from the road, near a city.'

She believes, as I do, that many people exaggerate the proportion of trouble-makers in this world. 'In the Outer Hebrides I met a retired nurse, about 80, who invited me in for an incredible piece of cake,' remembers Alison. 'She made me promise to send her a postcard from home to let her know I arrived safely. She was terribly worried about me. I felt sad that she felt so unsafe on her own little island!'

Many women who have toured alone agree that such kindness is typical, and intentional harm is rare.

One such woman is Sharon Sommerville, of Toronto, who cycled the entire 5,000-mile Trans-Canadian Highway in 1987. Except for a few instances when friends had planned to meet her, she rode alone or with cyclists she encountered *en route*. Sharon doesn't pretend there's no risk in setting off on your own. She prepared for the trip with her personal security in mind.

'But I think if you're prudent and intelligent about touring alone, you're pretty safe,' she says. 'I felt as confident on the road as I do as a single woman in a medium-size apartment building in downtown Toronto. Because when you're on the road, you're really focused on where you are and what you're doing.'

That 'focus', Sharon notes, works in well with the attitude a woman takes in self-defence, as she learned in Wen Do, a form of martial arts designed especially for women. Sharon took an intensive two-day course to prepare for the trip. 'Part of Wen Do is awareness and extracting yourself from potentially dangerous situations. It's also knowing your limitations.' Sharon was prepared with strategies for physical confrontations, but she would do her best to avoid them.

With that in mind she set 'a few cardinal rules': she limited herself to public campsites and always made camp before sunset. And she avoided telling anyone she met along the way where she'd be camping. Sharon did admit to inquiring campsite owners that she was alone, and they often made a point of looking out for her.

She wore her hair boyishly short in a 'brush' cut all summer. Despite a decidedly feminine figure, in a T-shirt, cycling tights, and without makeup, 'no kidding, some people mistook me for a guy'.

Reg feeds the denizens of St Gregory's churchyard in Kirkdale, Yorkshire (*John Tauke*).

She also had a phone-in system with her parents, who had a large map of Canada with her route marked on it. Every three days she'd telephone to say hello and let them know where she was as well as where she expected to be in three days. Her parents knew that if they'd not heard from her by the morning after the third day, they were to call the police to look for her.

That never happened. Along the Trans-Canada, she says, 'there's almost a sense of community, as there's almost always somebody driving by. And who's going to get out of their car and hurt you? That's not likely. What's more likely is that someone would be aware of you on the road and then try to find you at night. During the day when you're riding,' she figured, 'you're as safe as you'd be riding anywhere. And generally people are decent. You get the odd one, and it's the odd one you have to protect yourself against.'

As she'd anticipated, not only were people friendly, but they went out of their way to be helpful, partly because they were fascinated with what she was doing. In fact, one of Sharon's reasons for doing the tour, aside from seeing Canada, was meeting people:

> And it was fabulous for that. I felt such an incredibly high level of stimulation every day. At home, you fall into patterns in relating to the people you know. But when you're on your bicycle all summer and your 'doors' are wide open and your heart is wide open, things come into it. And this is particularly true when you travel alone.

You make that effort to make contact.

Sharon admits she had one experience that appeared to be her worst nightmare come true. She was alone one midafternoon on a truly desolate stretch of the Highway in Alberta.

It was all sage brush and cacti, there was no traffic going by, and I was just trucking along in the heat. Then behind me I heard the sound of motorcycles. Sure enough, two huge Harleys came up and stopped right in front of me on the side of the road. They were classic bikers – long greasy hair, shades, and big beer bellies. It was scary; I felt completely vulnerable.

So what did I do but put on my biggest, brightest smile and cycle by, saying, 'Hi, how ya doing?!'

And they said to me, 'Where in the hell are you going?'

And the obvious answer was, 'Halifax, Nova Scotia.'

They said, 'What?!'

It turned out they could not believe what they were seeing and they had to stop. They were the nicest guys. They called me 'Missy' and said, 'Why don't you get a motor for that thing?'

Of the other benefits of touring alone, Sharon observes: 'It gives you absolute control of your life. I think if you're a daughter, a mother, a sister, a wife, you have certain roles and responsibilities toward other people. Women, I think, are particularly vulnerable to putting their own needs off. One nice thing about going alone on tour is that you can do what you want. You go where you want to go, at your speed. You can potter around or you can ride hard. You do it your way.'

Solo touring will not appeal to every woman (or to every man). The individual who spends little time alone may not be comfortable with it. The cyclist who can't change a tyre, pitch a tent, or use a camp stove has reason to wait until such self-sufficiency is well developed.

And your world view has a great deal to do with whether even a short tour alone would be enjoyable. Women have become aware in recent decades that the protection traditionally given females can be fettering. Yet it's difficult to break the protective bonds. Nor perhaps do we realise to what extent television and newspapers create the sense of a victimising world.

Sharon observes:

If you don't have that attitude about yourself and about the world – that the world is a comfortable place to live in – then you're afraid. If you see the world as a scary place and that the world is out to get you, then you'll be fearful.

Yes, I was a little jittery the first few nights on tour, jumping at every strange little noise. But I'm fairly adventurous. I know I can take care of myself. Experience tells me I can go ahead, push myself a little bit beyond my personal barriers, and I'm going to be okay.

26" wheels

Number of teeth on sprocket →

	24	26	28	30	32	34	36	38	39	40	41	42	43	44	45	46	47	48	49	50	51	52	53	
12	52	56	61	65	69	74	78	82	85	87	89	91	93	95	98	100	102	104	106	108	111	113	115	12
13	48	52	56	60	64	68	72	76	78	80	82	84	86	88	90	92	94	96	98	100	102	104	106	13
14	45	48	52	56	60	63	67	70	72	74	76	78	80	82	84	85	87	89	91	93	95	97	98	14
15	42	45	49	52	55	59	62	66	68	69	71	73	75	76	78	80	81	83	85	87	88	90	92	15
16	39	42	45	49	52	55	58	61	63	65	67	68	70	72	73	75	76	78	80	81	83	85	86	16
17	37	40	43	46	49	52	55	58	60	61	63	64	66	67	69	70	72	73	75	76	78	80	81	17
18	35	38	40	43	46	49	52	55	56	58	59	61	62	64	65	66	68	69	71	72	74	75	77	18
19	33	36	38	41	44	47	49	52	53	55	56	57	59	60	62	63	64	66	67	68	70	71	73	19
20	31	34	36	39	42	44	47	49	51	52	53	55	56	57	59	60	61	62	64	65	66	68	69	20
21	30	32	35	37	40	42	45	47	48	50	51	52	53	54	56	57	58	59	61	62	63	64	66	21
22	28	31	33	35	38	40	43	45	46	47	48	50	51	52	53	54	56	57	58	59	60	61	63	22
23	27	29	32	34	36	38	41	43	44	45	46	47	49	50	51	52	53	54	55	57	58	59	60	23
24	26	28	30	32	35	37	39	41	42	43	44	45	47	48	49	50	51	52	53	54	55	56	57	24
25	25	27	29	31	33	35	37	39	41	42	43	44	45	46	47	48	49	50	51	52	53	54	55	25
26	24	26	28	30	32	34	36	38	39	40	41	42	43	44	45	46	47	48	49	50	51	52	53	26
27	23	25	27	29	31	33	35	37	38	39	39	40	41	42	43	44	45	46	47	48	49	50	51	27
28	22	24	26	28	30	32	33	35	36	37	38	39	40	41	42	43	44	45	46	46	47	48	49	28
30	21	23	24	26	28	29	31	33	34	35	36	36	37	38	39	40	41	42	42	43	44	45	46	30
32	20	21	23	24	26	28	29	31	32	33	33	34	35	35	37	37	38	39	40	41	41	42	43	32
34	18	20	21	23	24	26	28	29	30	31	31	32	33	33	34	35	36	37	37	38	39	40	41	34
	24	26	28	30	32	34	36	38	39	40	41	42	43	44	45	46	47	48	49	50	51	52	53	

Number of teeth on chainwheel

27" wheels

	24	26	28	29	30	31	32	33	34	35	36	37	38	39	40	41	42	43	44	45	46	47	48	49	50	51	52	53	54
11	59	64	69	71	74	76	79	81	83	86	88	91	93	96	98	101	103	106	108	110	113	115	118	120	123	125	128	130	133
12	54	59	63	65	68	70	72	74	77	79	81	83	86	88	90	92	95	97	99	101	104	106	108	110	113	115	117	119	122
13	50	54	58	60	62	64	66	69	71	73	75	77	79	81	83	85	87	89	91	93	96	98	100	102	104	106	108	110	112
14	46	50	54	56	58	60	62	64	66	68	69	71	73	75	77	79	81	83	85	87	89	91	93	95	96	98	100	102	104
15	43	47	50	52	54	56	58	59	61	63	65	67	68	70	72	74	76	77	79	81	83	85	86	88	90	92	94	95	97
16	41	44	47	49	51	52	54	56	57	59	61	62	64	66	68	69	71	73	74	76	78	79	81	83	84	86	88	89	91
17	38	41	44	46	48	49	51	52	54	56	57	59	60	62	64	65	67	68	70	71	73	75	76	78	79	81	83	84	86
18	36	39	42	44	45	47	48	50	51	53	54	56	57	59	60	62	63	65	66	68	69	71	72	74	75	77	78	80	81
19	34	37	40	41	43	44	45	47	48	50	51	53	54	55	57	58	60	61	63	64	65	67	68	70	71	72	74	75	77
20	32	35	38	39	41	42	43	45	46	47	49	50	51	53	54	55	57	58	59	61	62	63	65	66	68	69	70	72	73
21	31	33	36	37	39	40	41	42	44	45	46	48	49	50	51	53	54	55	57	58	59	60	62	63	64	66	67	68	69
22	29	32	34	36	37	38	39	41	42	43	44	45	47	48	49	50	52	53	54	55	56	58	59	60	61	63	64	65	66
23	28	31	33	34	35	36	38	39	40	41	42	43	45	46	47	48	49	50	52	53	54	55	56	58	59	60	61	62	63
24	27	29	32	33	34	35	36	37	38	39	41	42	43	44	45	46	47	48	50	51	52	53	54	55	56	57	59	60	61
25	26	28	30	31	32	33	35	36	37	38	39	40	41	42	43	44	45	46	48	49	50	51	52	53	54	55	56	57	58
26	25	27	29	30	31	32	33	34	35	36	37	38	39	41	42	43	44	45	46	47	48	49	50	51	52	53	54	55	56
27	24	26	28	29	30	31	32	33	34	35	36	37	38	39	40	41	42	43	44	45	46	47	48	49	50	51	52	53	54
28	23	25	27	28	29	30	31	32	33	34	35	36	37	38	39	40	41	41	42	43	44	45	46	47	48	49	50	51	52
29	22	24	26	27	28	29	30	31	32	33	34	34	35	36	37	38	39	40	41	41	42	43	44	45	46	47	48	49	50
30	22	23	25	26	27	28	29	30	31	32	32	33	34	35	36	37	38	39	40	41	41	42	43	44	45	46	47	48	49
31	21	23	24	25	26	27	28	29	30	30	31	32	33	34	35	36	37	37	38	39	40	41	42	43	44	44	45	46	47
32	20	22	24	24	25	26	27	28	29	30	30	31	32	33	34	35	35	36	37	38	39	40	41	41	42	43	44	45	46
33	20	21	23	24	25	25	26	27	28	29	29	30	31	32	33	34	34	35	36	37	38	38	39	40	41	42	43	43	44
34	19	21	22	23	24	25	25	26	27	28	29	29	30	31	32	33	33	34	35	36	37	37	38	39	40	41	41	42	43

248

Selected Bibliography

The Scientific Basis

Beck, John L. and Byron P. Wildermuth, 'The Female Athlete's Knee', *Clinics in Sports Medicine*, Vol. 4, No. 2 (April 1985), pp 345–66

Blair, Steven N., 'Physical Fitness and All-Cause Mortality', *Journal of the American Medical Association*', Vol. 262, No. 17 (3 November, 1989), pp 2395–401

Brehm, Barbara A., 'Hypertension: Does Exercise Have an Effect?', *Fitness Management*, Vol. 1, No. 1 (March–April 1985), pp 11, 56

Britton, A. G., 'Thin Is Out, Fit Is In', *American Health*, Vol. 7, No. 6 (July–August 1988), pp 66–71

Burros, Marian, 'Calcium Tablets Are Not All Created Equal', *New York Times* (27 January, 1988) pp C1, C8

Butler, Ellen, 'The Amenorrheic Athlete', *The Melpomene Report*, June 1985, pp 7–12

Carpenter, Christine L., 'Exercise and Menopause', *Fitness Management* (May–June 1987) pp 20–1

Carpenter, Marshall W., Stanley P. Sady, Bente Hoegsberg, and others, 'Fetal Heart Rate Response to Maternal Exertion', *Journal of the American Medical Association*, Vol. 259, No. 20 (27 May, 1988), pp 3006–9

Coyle, Edward F. and Andrew R. Coggan, 'Glucose Supplementation during Prolonged Cycling', *Sports Mediscope*, Vol. 6, No. 3 (July/August–September/October 1987), p. 4

Cross, Kenneth D. and Gary Fisher, *A Study of Bicycle/Motor Vehicle Accidents: Identification of Problem Types and Countermeasure Approaches*, Vol. 1, US Department of Transportation, 1977

Dawson, Alice, 'Is Pregnancy a Good Time to Get Fit?' *Women's Sports and Fitness*, April 1986, p. 51

Driscoll, Charles E., Edward T. Bope, Sue K. Mihalko, and James C. Puffer, 'Women in Sports: Guidelines for Patient Fitness', *The Female Patient*, Vol. 13, No. 6 (June 1988), pp 41–51

Eichner, Edward, 'Exercise, Lymphokines, Calories, and Cancer', *The Physician and Sportsmedicine*, Vol. 15, No. 6 (June 1987), pp 109–15

'Feeling Fat in a Thin Society', *Glamour* (February 1984) pp 198–201, 251–2

Feldman, W., E. Feldman and J. T. Goodman, 'Culture Versus Biology: Children's Attitudes toward Thinness and Fatness', *Pediatrics*, Vol. 81, No. 2 (February 1988), pp 190–4

Freeman, Zelman, 'Exercise and Sudden Cardiac Death', *The Medical Journal of Australia*, Vol. 142, No. 7 (1 April, 1985), pp 383–4

Frisch, R. E., G. Wyshak, N. L. Albright and others, 'Lower Prevalence of Breast Cancer and Cancers of the Reproductive System among Former College Athletes Compared to Non-Athletes', *British Journal of Cancer*, Vol. 52 (December), pp 885–91

Frisch, R. E., G. Wyshak, T. E. Albright, and others, 'Lower Prevalence of Diabetes in Female Former College Athletes Compared with Nonathletes', *Diabetes*, Vol. 35 (October 1986), pp 1101–05

Godin, G. and R. J. Shephard, 'Psycho-Social Predictors of Exercise Intentions Among Spouses', *Canadian Journal of Applied Sport Sciences*, Vol. 10, No. 1 (March 1985), pp 36–43

Hales, Dianne and Robert Hales, 'Using the Body to Mend the Mind', *American Health*, Vol. 4, No. 5 (June 1985), pp 27–31

Harnack, Catherine and Valerie Lee, 'Maternal Fitness Bibliography', Minneapolis, Melpomene Institute (August 1988)

Kaplan, Jerrold A., *Characteristics of the Regular Adult Bicycle User*, Washington, D.C., Federal Highway Administration, 1977

Kiyonaga, Akira, Kikuo Arakawa, Hiroaki Tanaka, and Munehiro Shindo, 'Blood Pressure and Hormonal Responses to Aerobic Exercise', *Hypertension*, Vol. 7, No. 1 (January–February 1985), pp 125–31

Krakauer, Lewis J., James L. Anderson, Frank George, and others (eds), *The Year Book of Sports Medicine, 1984*, Chicago, Year Book Medical Publishers, Inc., 1984

LaPorte, Ronald E., Stephen Dearwater, Jane A. Cauley, and others, 'Physical Activity or Cardiovascular Fitness: Which Is More Important for Health?', *The Physician and Sportsmedicine*, Vol. 13, No. 3 (March 1986), pp 145–57

Lee, Valerie, Laurie Koltes, Bonnie Schultz, and others, 'A New Look at Nutrition', *The Melpomene Report* (June 1985) pp 19–24

Lutter, Judy Mahle, 'Mixed Messages about Osteoporosis in Female Athletes', *The Physician and Sportsmedicine*, Vol. 11, No. 9 (September 1983), reprint

Lutter, Judy Mahle, Susan Merrick, Lyn Steffen, and others, 'Physical Activity through the Life Span: Long-Term Effects of an Active Lifestyle', *The Melpomene Report* (February 1985) pp 4–8

McKee, Gerald (ed.), 'Special Report: The Female Athlete', *Sports Medicine Digest* (1988)

Mellion, Morris B., 'Exercise Therapy for Anxiety and Depression (Parts 1 and 2)', *Postgraduate Medicine*, Vol. 77, No. 3 (15 February, 1986), pp 59–66 and 91–6

Melpomene Institute for Women's Health Research, 'Guidelines for Exercising while Pregnant: Running and Swimming', (unpublished material), revised 1987

Melpomene, Pregnancy and Exercise Project (unpublished research summaries), Minneapolis, (n.d.)

Melpomene, 'Post-Partum Exercise Considerations', (unpublished guidelines), (n.d.)

Olsen, Eric, 'Exercise, More or Less', *Hippocrates* (January–February 1988) pp 65–72

Orbach, Susie, *Fat Is a Feminist Issue*, New York (Berkley Books) and London (Paddington Press), 1978

Orbach, Susie, *Hunger Strike: The Anorectic's Struggle as a Metaphor for Our Age*, New York and London, W. W. Norton & Company, 1986

Parker, Linda, Personal letter (15 April, 1988)

Polivy, Janet and C. Peter Herman, *Breaking the Diet Habit*, New York, Basic Books, Inc., 1983

Riggs, B. Lawrence and L. Joseph Melton III, 'Involutional Osteoporosis', *The New England Journal of Medicine*, Vol. 314 (26 June, 1986), pp 1676–84

Severino, Sally K., *Premenstrual Syndrome: A Clinician's Guide*, New York, The Guildford Press, Inc., 1989

Shangold, Mona M., 'Gynecologic Concerns in the Woman Athlete', *Clinics in Sports Medicine*, Vol. 3, No. 4 (October 1984), pp 869–78

Siscovik, David S., Ronald E. LaPorte, and Jeffrey M. Newman, 'The Disease–Specific Benefits and Risks of Physical Activity and Exercise', *Public Health Reports*, Vol. 100, No. 2 (March–April 1985), pp 180–8

Sizer, Frances Sienkiewicz and Linda Kelly DeBruyne, 'Nutrition for Sport: Knowledge, News and Nonsense', *Nutrition Clinics*, Vol. 3, No. 3 (June 1988), pp 1–24

Smith, David E., 'Diagnostic, Treatment and Aftercare Approaches to Cocaine Abuse', *Journal of Substance Abuse Treatment*, Vol. 1 (1984), pp 5–9

Smith, Everett L. 'Exercise for Prevention of Osteoporosis: A Review', *The Physician and Sportsmedicine*, Vol. 10, No. 3 (March 1982), pp 72–83

Smith, Everett L. (ed.), 'Osteoporosis: A Symposium', *The Physician and Sportsmedicine*, Vol. 15, No. 11 (November 1987), pp 65–118

Subcommittee on the Tenth Edition of the RDAs, Food and Nutrition Board, Commission on Life Sciences, National Research Council, *Recommended Dietary Allowances*, 10th ed., Washington, D.C. National Academy Press (1989)

US Department of Agriculture and US Department of Health and Human Services, *Nutrition and Your Health: Dietary Guidelines for Americans*, 2nd ed., Washington, D.C., Government Printing Office (1985)

Vannell, Suzanne, Personal letter (5 September, 1988)

Weston, Louise C. and Josephine A. Ruggiero, 'The Popular Approach to Women's Health Issues: A Content Analysis of Women's Magazines in the 1970's', *Women & Health*, Vol. 10, No. 4 (Winter 1985/86), pp 47–62

Further Reading

Allen, John S. *The Complete Book of Bicycle Commuting*, Emmaus, Pennsylvania, Rodale Press (1981) (out of print)

Cuthbertson, Tom, *Anybody's Bike Book*, Berkeley, California, Ten Speed Press (1984)

Cuthbertson, Tom, *The Bike Bag Book*, Berkeley, California, Ten Speed Press (1981)

Forester, John, *Effective Cycling*, Cambridge, Massachusetts; London MIT Press (1986)

Murphy, Dervla, *Full Tilt*, London, John Murray (1965)

Savage, Barbara, *Miles from Nowhere*, Seattle, Washington, Mountaineers Books (1983)

Selby, Bettina, *Riding North One Summer*, London, Chatto and Windus (1990)

Selby, Bettina, *Riding the Desert Trail*, London, Chatto and Windus (1988)

Index

251